The Jewish Way
in Death
and Mourning

The Jewish Way in Death and Mourning

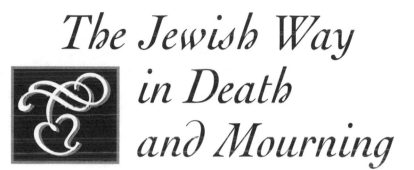

Maurice Lamm

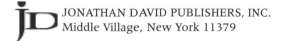

JONATHAN DAVID PUBLISHERS, INC.
Middle Village, New York 11379

THE JEWISH WAY IN DEATH AND MOURNING

Jonathan David Publishers, Inc.
68-22 Eliot Avenue
Middle Village, NY 11379

www.jdbooks.com

10

Library Of Congress Cataloging-in-Publication Data

Lamm, Maurice.
    The Jewish way in Death and mourning/ by Maurice Lamm, — [rev.
ed.].
        p.   cm.
    Includes bibliographical references and index.
    ISBN 0-8246-0423-7 hardcover
    ISBN 0-8246-0422-9 paperback
    1. Jewish mourning customs. I. Title

BM712.L3 1999
294, 4'45—dc21   99-088942
                                                                CIP

Designed by John Reinhardt Book Design

Printed in the United States of America

This Book Is Dedicated To Two Men
Who Have Guided Me In The
Jewish Way of Life

My Maternal Grandfather

RABBI YEHOSHUA BAUMOL, *z'l*
Died September 8, 1948

Author of *Emek Halakhah I* and *II*. As a creative *posek*
(halakhic decisor) and renowned leader, he left a tradition
of scholarship and humaneness. He was profound enough
to be lenient within the law and compassionate enough to
be understanding of human weakness. And he was a
singularly wise grandfather, as you can tell from reading
his ethical will in Appendix Two.

A N D

My Paternal Grandfather

YAAKOV DAVID LAMM, *z'l*
Died March 27, 1939

Who lived proudly and nobly, and whose patriarchal bearing and saintly humility inspired devotion in all who knew
him. He died in dignity as he lived in dignity. His death, the
first in my experience, remains forever etched in my
memory as the climax of a complete life.

Contents

Introduction

In the thirty years since *The Jewish Way in Death and Mourning* was first published, it has reached more people than I ever could have imagined, and most of all, it has attracted myriad readers from different streams and denominations, in and out of Judaism. I hope it will survive long into the future for generations of Jews seeking guidance in the *halakhah* of *avelut*.

Before undertaking this revision, I asked myself whether anything new could really be said on the subject of death in Judaism. I could hear my father's voice from above, saying, "Don't fix it if it's not broken." But I didn't listen to his usually penetrating advice.

I am convinced that over the last thirty years, my outlook has broadened, my passion has mellowed, and the sometimes sharp edges of my comments have softened. But primarily, the subject matter itself has mutated in significant ways. Radical, unanticipated technological advances have triggered changes both in death and in religious law. In the manner of dying, we have gone from catastrophic causes of death to mostly degenerative ones. In halakhic applications to the ethical problems that are attendant upon death, the new medicine literally has empowered new halakhic approaches. There are a number of examples.

Organ donation is the prime example. Three decades ago, it was not to be encouraged; rabbis could not condone possibly hurrying one person's death in order to provide a second person with a slim potential of continued life. Today, the Chief Rabbinate of Israel and many leading American Orthodox rabbis have come to the conclusion that brain stem death is the actual moment of human demise according to *halakhah,* rather than the end of respiration. Now we have a window of opportunity in those moments after the death of the brain, while the heart is still pumping, to harvest organs halakhically for transplanting to other human beings. With new immunosuppresant drugs, doctors can now confidently predict a likelihood of success—donors will be in virtually no danger and recipients will experience fewer organ rejections. We have a clear case today of not taking the life of the donor but conceivably giving life back to the recipient. I have therefore happily rewritten the section on organ donation.

Another area in which technology has had a salutary effect on the *halakhah* is that of autopsies. Today autopsies are hardly necessary or even welcome by physicians and no longer are an indication of a hospital's expertise; they simply do not have the same hold on the medical profession as before. On the other side of the divide, halakhically, autopsies are permitted when knowledge of the cause of death can have immediate consequences for a patient that is "before us," who can realistically be helped. Today, we can make quicker contact with a person in an Ethiopian village than we could thirty years ago with someone in Chicago. All humanity lives in one village—what we learn from an autopsy instantly can be of help to another across the globe. In this age, everyone is "before us."

Likewise, today, not only has science made long strides, but also our sensibilities have sharpened and our awareness has been heightened. We should not simply disregard the sentiments of parents of stillborn children, infant deaths, or even miscarriages, and ignore traditional, characteristically Jewish bereavement practices for them. What about mourning beloved stepparents or stepchildren? Should we not recognize the bereavement needs of converts for their non-Jewish natural parents? Those whose *shivah* is expunged by a major holiday also bemoan the fact that they had no chance to express their sadness. I address all of these matters in a section called "Discretionary Mourning."

Also, the sensibilities of women need to be addressed. I do so in a new section about women saying Kaddish and its

halakhic parameters, assessing the issue and citing its propo-
nents and opponents among leading Orthodox rabbis.

Even a stylistic change has occurred over the last thirty
years, and reflects the sensitivity to feminine literary usage. I
have elected to continue to use *he* and *him*, but I do so as a
term of inclusiveness, for both genders, rather than exclusively for the male gender. I do specify male and female when
the text requires it.

In 1969, I wrote this book in desperate hope that people
would not shrug off Jewish mourning practices. Every month
for three decades I have received one or two letters from
people who say they consider the *halakhah* of mourning to
be a profound help in their crisis, and never as a burdensome
load that their Jewish parents heaped onto their shoulders.
In this revision, I try to expand areas of concern while at the
same time simplifying and making accessible our sometimes
intricate laws. I have provided more analysis, and have wid-
ened areas of human interest to enable people to help themselves and to express those sensitivities in a manner in keeping
with the dictates of Jewish law.

What surely has *not* changed was what I wrote in the introduction to *The Jewish Way in Death and Mourning* thirty years
ago:

> Death is the crisis of life. How a person handles death indi-
> cates a great deal about how he approaches life. As there is a
> *Jewish* way of life, so there is a *Jewish* way of death.
>
> As the Jewish way of life implies a distinctive outlook and
> a unique lifestyle based on very specific views of God and the
> place of man in society and the universe, so does the Jewish
> way of death imply singular attitudes toward God and nature,
> and toward the problem of good and evil. And it proffers a
> distinctive way of demonstrating specific *Jewish* qualities of
> reverence for man and respect for the dead.
>
> For example, the prohibition against cremation (the un-
> naturally speedy disposal of the dead) and also embalming
> (the unnatural preservation of the dead), bespeak a philoso-
> phy of man and his relationship to God and nature. Repug-
> nance to the mutilation of a body expresses a reverence for

man, because man was created in God's image. The ban on necromancy is founded on very precise theological concepts of creature and Creator. Likewise, the commandment to bury the dead without delay draws a very fine, but clear, line between reverence for the dead and worship of the dead. The profound psychological insights implicit in the highly structured Jewish mourning observances speak eloquently of Judaism's concern for the psychological integrity of the human personality.

One truth that I saw in 1969 is still true today: the study of mourning observances is not likely to be undertaken before it becomes absolutely necessary, and when it is necessary, mourners will be in no mood to do so.

But the crisis will come, ready or not. If thinking on the subject is to be deferred, if there is to be no education before the crisis, what chance is there that we shall know how to handle the crisis when it arrives? And if we are not privy to this information, will those who lived as Jews be able to be buried as Jews? Will we not inevitably succumb to the standards established by commercial funeral directors, rather than by authentic spiritual teachers? Will we not tend blindly to embrace every American practice, whether its origin is in the church or in some transitory fraternal organization? What will be left that is Jewish in our Jewish way of death? And if there is no Jewish way of death, what Jewish way of life could there have been?

Three decades later, I am still profoundly grateful to those who assisted me in preparing the first edition of *The Jewish Way in Death and Mourning*: Rabbi David Silver of Harrisburg, Pennsylvania, who helped me as a respected mentor rather than in his position as Chairman of the Beth Din of the Rabbinical Council of America; Dr. Norman Lamm, now President of Yeshiva University, who reviewed my work as a scholar, not as a brother: Rabbi Sidney Applbaum, who served as chairman of the Funeral Standards Committee of the Rabbinical Council of America..

I thank several people in particular for help in revising *The Jewish Way in Death and Mourning*: Rabbi Hershel Schacter, Rosh

Kollel at Yeshiva University, for incisive comments and decisions; my wife, who prodded my pen from planning to publication, then and now; Judy Sandman, for editing my book with respect and stylistic precision; Caryn Starr-Gates, my assistant, for her talented help from editing to computing; Rabbi Alfred Kolatch, my publisher, and Marvin Sekler at Jonathan David, for their persistent but gentle nudges; and members of my congregation, who were a source of unflagging encouragement.

Most of all, I thank God profoundly for giving me the *zekhut*, the merit, to have written this book in the first place, and to have been able to help people in their agony. I have been pleased to learn that reading this book has moved some people toward embracing other traditional practices because they realize the value implicit in them. *Barukh ha-Shem.*

The burial service ends with an ecstatic hope, spoken by Isaiah (25:8): "May God swallow death forever. May He wipe tears from all faces."

MAURICE LAMM
Englewood, New Jersey
Elul 5759, August 1999

Preface

During the course of a lifetime, virtually no one can avoid an encounter with death. Yet it is an experience for which one is rarely prepared. Psychologists explain why, but they do not condone the evasion. Perhaps this excellent volume by a learned and sensitive colleague, Rabbi Maurice Lamm, will help many to think and act maturely when having to deal with this inevitable circumstance of life.

The book differs radically from earlier attempts with the subject, for Rabbi Lamm has written with feeling and insight about every aspect of the problem. He has collated all the relevant laws and customs of Judaism; he has added interpretation; he has related the behavior and practices of our forbears to modern practices and evaluated their relative merit. He has brought to his theme the legal scholarship of the Orthodox rabbi, the competence of one well versed in the behavioral sciences, and the humanity and empathy of a warm human being. Indeed, he is to be congratulated on the wide scope, depth, and thoroughness of his presentation, which will help all people to cope with the circumstances surrounding death. In addition, Rabbi Lamm's approach will give the Jewish reader a greater appreciation of his ancestral heritage.

The Jewish Way in Death and Mourning fills a definite gap that has long existed in the field of Judaica. Rabbi Lamm's superb contribution provides the English reader with the first readable and comprehensive study in an area of vital importance.

DR. EMANUEL RACKMAN
Chancellor, Bar Ilan University, Israel

1   *From the Moment of Death to the Funeral Service*

❦

LIFE IS A DAY that lies between two nights—the night of "not yet," before birth, and the night of "no more," after death. That day may be overcast with pain and frustration, or bright with warmth and contentment. But, inevitably, the night of death must arrive.

Death is a night that lies between two days—the day of life on earth, and the day of eternal life in the world to come. That night may come suddenly, in the blink of an eye, or it may come gradually, with a slowly receding sun.

As the day of life is an interlude, so is the night of death an interlude. As the day inevitably proceeds to dusk, so does the darkness inevitably proceed to dawn. A veil that human understanding cannot pierce separates each portion—the fetal existence, and life, and death, and eternal life.

We, the survivors, who do not accompany the deceased on their journey into the night, are left alone staring into the black void. There is a rage of conflicting emotions that seethes within us: bewilderment and paralysis, agony and numbness, guilt and anger, fear and futility and pain—and also emancipation from care and worry. The golden chain of the family link is broken and swings wildly before our eyes. Our whole being is convulsed. Love and warmth and hope have vanished, and in their place remains only despair. The precious soul that touched our life and enhanced its sense of purpose and meaning is no more. Our only consolation is that he once was. There is a past, but the past is no more; and the future is bleak indeed. The broken, swinging chain hypnotizes us, and we are frozen.

Judaism is a faith that embraces all of life, and death is a part of life. As this faith leads us through moments of joy, so does it guide us through the terrible moments of grief, holding us firm through the complex emotions of mourning and bidding us turn our gaze from the night of darkness to the daylight of life.

At the moment of death painful questions gnaw at our innards—existential and philosophical problems so stubborn they will not go away: Why was this person, of all the people that fill our great world, fated to end his days just now? Why did the end come before the logic of life ordained that it come? Death should be, we feel, a sum under the bottom line—a total of all of life's varied experiences. It should add up to a meaningful conclusion and end naturally. It should not intrude in the midst of the equations of living, starkly disrupting all calculations, confusing all the figures, and belying all the prepared solutions. But, too often, the end is abrupt. Life remains an unknown quality—a large, incalculable problem, bedeviled by death.

At the moment of death, there is severe disorientation. We are perplexed not only by the large questions of life and death, but also by problems of how to feel and how to conduct ourselves properly: How shall we react to the tragedy? What is the proper respect that we should give the dead? How do we achieve a measure of dignity during an interment? Shall we mourn the unfulfilled life of the deceased, torn away before finishing the business of living, or may we feel a loss to ourselves, agonizing over our own personal distress?

And how should we comfort ourselves? Should we appear before family and friends brave, dignified, courageously unruffled? Or may we give vent to our anguish in a stream of tears? Shall the usual amenities of a social occasion obtain at the gathering of the family, or should we concern ourselves with the soul-wound of our own loss and let the world manage for itself?

Thousands of years of our rich tradition provide us with direction during these moments of crisis. The accumulated wisdom of the ages is a source of great consolation.

In the pages that follow, you will find clear guidelines that the Jewish tradition has laid down to lead mourners through the complex maze of uncertainties and ambivalence that attend the tragic moment. The ache of the heart will not suddenly disappear. There will be no miraculous consolation. But Judaism does teach the aching heart how to express its pain in love and respect, and how to achieve the eventual consolation, which will restore us to humanity and keep us from vindictiveness and self-pity.

INITIAL CARE OF THE DECEASED

The principle governing the care of the body immediately following death is the sacredness of man. A human being is equated with a Torah scroll that is impaired and can no longer be used at religious services. While the ancient scroll no longer serves any useful ritual purpose, it is revered for the exalted function it once filled. Man is created in the image of God, and, although the pulse of life is no more, the human form must be respected for having once embodied the spirit of God and for the character and the personality it housed. The manner of respect is governed and detailed by religious tradition rather than by personal sentiment and whim. The following are some of the basic guidelines for the care of the deceased at the time of death:

1. During the last minutes of life, no one in the presence of the deceased may leave, except those whose emotions are uncontrollable or the physically ill. It is a matter of the greatest respect to watch over a person as he passes from this world to the next.

2. After death has been ascertained, the children or friends

or relatives must close the eyes and the mouth of the deceased and draw a sheet over his face.

3. While it has been a custom for many years to rend the clothes and recite the blessing Barukh Dayyan ha-Emet (True Judge) at the time of death, it is now customary to do this at the funeral service. At that time, all the relatives are assembled, and the rabbi supervises the correct manner of rending the clothing and leads in the correct recital of the blessings. The details of the rending may be found in Chapter Two.

4. The position of the body should be oriented so that the feet face the doorway. Other than this, the deceased should not be touched or moved, except for his own honor (such as straightening the body if it is found in an awkward position, or moving it if it has been found in environs not considered sufficiently respectful). Some Orthodox Jews retain the custom of placing the body on the floor approximately twenty minutes after death and pouring water on the floor as a sign to friends and neighbors that a death has occurred.

5. A candle should be placed near the head of the deceased. According to some customs, many candles should be placed all around the person.

6. A beautiful and moving custom calls upon relatives and friends to ask forgiveness of the deceased at this time for any harm or discomfort they might have caused him during his lifetime.

7. The mirrors in the entire house are covered to de-emphasize the beauty and the ornamentation of the flesh at a time when, in the same house, another person's body has begun to decay. Mirrors also are covered to avoid personal vanity during moments of tragedy and to diminish the usual over-concern with one's appearance. Another explanation of this custom is that the image of God, reflected in the mirror, has been diminished by the recent death. This subject is considered in greater detail below.

8. Psalms 23 and 91 are recited. The text and commentary are found in Appendix One.

9. Personal behavior in the room of the deceased should be consonant with the highest degree of respect for his person. There may be no eating, drinking, or smoking in his pres-

ence. Outside the room proper, however, these are permitted. No derogatory remarks about the deceased may be voiced, even though, objectively, they may be true. Discussion in the room should concentrate solely on the deceased and his personal qualities, or on the funeral arrangements. There should be no singing or playing of music or even words of Torah.

10. The rabbi should be called. He will notify the *chevrah kaddisha* (burial society), which will care for the remains. Then the funeral director, who will arrange for the local attending doctor to provide the death certificate and for the removal of the body, should be called.

11. From the moment of death until burial, the deceased may not be left alone. Therefore, the family must arrange for a person called a *shomer* (watcher), whether it be male or female, to be at his side at all times. While it is preferable for the watcher to be a member of the family or a personal friend, this is not always possible. In such cases, a person must be engaged to accompany the body and recite from the Book of Psalms. The rabbi or funeral director will be able to make such arrangements, but the mourner should ascertain clearly whether the *shomer* is reliable, for he or she must remain awake and recite Psalms all through the night. Even though the presence of the *shomer* originally was to keep rodents away from the corpse, today in mortuary freezers, such an occurrence is highly unlikely. The tradition is maintained, nonetheless, out of a desire to be overprotective and serve as the deceased's guardian. Please note that, contrary to public opinion, there are no gender restrictions in the choice of *shomer*, only considerations of integrity, spirituality, and sincerity.

12. If death occurs on the Sabbath, care should be taken not to light the Sabbath candles near the deceased. Only the most minimal arrangements may be made on the Sabbath, and these only out of respect for the dead. The dead may not be removed on the Sabbath by Jew or Gentile. A watcher should be present during the Sabbath.

If death occurs in the hospital, guidelines 4 and 5 may not be practicable, but all other customs should be observed in the hospital room and later at the funeral chapel.

The funeral director is paid to serve the mourners, their religious sentiments, and their personal preferences. He can accommodate them in the observance of all traditional Jewish customs. There is no valid reason for him not to comply with their wishes. If mourners experience any difficulty in this regard, they should discuss this with their rabbi and ask him to intercede. This is what a rabbi does; it is no imposition.

DONATING ORGANS

The ability to transplant organs from one person to another in order to save a life is one of the grand contributions to humanity of the twentieth century's remarkable advances in medical science. In 1954, the first kidney was successfully transplanted; in 1966, the pancreas; in 1967, the liver; in 1968, the heart; in 1983, a single lung; and in 1986 a double lung. As we enter the next century, what had been a bold experiment by superb physicians has become accepted procedure performed in more than two hundred centers around the country.

It also is a tribute to the prodigious vitality of Jewish law that a tradition that was very wary of such donations when I first wrote this book thirty years ago, because of its insistence on the sacredness of human life, is now able to embrace the new progress while rigorously maintaining the letter and spirit of ancient Mosaic law. What is even more extraordinary is that the *halakhah* has done this not sacrificially, giving up Torah principles because it has had to respond to people's natural demand to save a member of the family, but rather out of a sophisticated understanding of Torah and a bold and vigilant application of our ancient law to new medical realities of the twenty-first century. This represents no compromise at all; it is a fully justified and traditional adaptation to new information and new discoveries.

Medically, what has occurred is the breakthrough success of a great majority of all transplants—virtually assuring the living donor that he will suffer no physical damage, and the recipient that it will save his life and enable him to continue living for a number of years. In fact, there has come news of a dramatic accomplishment in genetic engineering that enhances the immune system's ability to accept an alien organ and will radically improve even the present statistics of survival.

Critical data published weekly on the Internet by the United Network for Organ Sharing records that in 1998 almost twenty-one thousand transplants—of kidneys primarily, but also of livers, hearts, kidney-pancreases, and bone marrow—took place. Success is now measured in terms of years of survival and the quality of the ensuing life, rather than simply in surviving the rigors of surgery. Kidney and corneal transplants have been performed for several decades now with very low morbidity and mortality rates. For example, in December 1967, the first heart transplants yielded disastrous results. Today heart transplant surgery has evolved from an experimental procedure to an acceptable therapeutic option. The same is true of kidney and liver transplants. Remarkably, there are people alive today thirty-five years after receiving a kidney transplant, twenty-seven years after a liver transplant, and twenty-two years after a heart transplant. In 1998, 4,855 people who could have lived if they had received a transplant, died waiting because of a lack of donors. In May 1999, the number of patients awaiting transplants totaled 63,365. The greatest challenge in organ transplantation is not in the medical arena at all; it is in solving the critical shortage of donors.

There are two sources for transplants—the first is from a living donor, usually a relative or friend; the second, from a dying person, called a cadaveric transplant. In the case of a living donation, the risk-benefit ratio—a principle of Jewish law—maintains that if the donor is taking only a minor risk to his own life, and the recipient's life can almost definitely be saved, the donor will be doing a great mitzvah by literally giving of himself. Of course, the consent of the donor or next of kin must be given before the transplant. The vast majority of rabbinic responsa permit, though they do not require, a live donor to subject himself to the ever-smaller risk of transplantation in order to save the life of a person dying of organ failure.

Most organ transplants, however, take place when the donor is scientifically declared dead—a cadaveric donation. The problem has always been that biology requires the heart to be pumping so that the organ continues to function. But Jewish law could never sanction removing a heart from a living person. Jewish law requires that the patient be certifiably dead; medicine requires that he be certifiably alive.

This problem could never have been solved had medicine not redefined a fundamental concept, the criteria of death. The difference between life and death is not an intuitively sensed, apparent difference. Medicine, accepting the Harvard criteria of death, determined that death arrives not only with the cessation of a spontaneously beating heart but also with the death of the brain. People who are brain dead are the major source of organs for transplant. Such a person is dead for all intents, but a respirator can keep the heart beating and internal organs alive.

In Jewish law, the halakhic question also revolves around the time of death. The more conventional view holds fast to the beating-heart criterion, even though it is a respirator that breathes artificially for the moribund. This position is held by major thinkers and decisors who have not moved away from the Talmudic and Maimonidean conception that determination of the moment of death can be made "at the nose"—that is, if the patient is breathing he is living; if not, he is dead.

The second view has been championed assiduously by Rabbi Dr. Moshe Tendler, who combines expertise in *halakhah* and biology, holding a chair at Yeshiva University, and Dr. Fred Rosner, Director of Medicine at Mount Sinai Hospital and a superb halakhist. Both are known for their religious devotion, encyclopedic knowledge, and bold intellects.

If you decapitate an animal, the heart will continue to beat, even though the brain is no longer attached to the animal's body. The irreversible death of the brain *stem* is exactly equivalent; a person who suffers such a loss is legally dead in Jewish law, even if the heart continues to beat spontaneously for a while. Indeed, a heart completely removed from the body can continue to beat so long as it is nourished properly. There is not a single case in recorded medical history of a brain-stem dead person who has survived this disease. Brain stem death is the defining factor in distinguishing between life and death.

A word of caution is in order, however. Brain *stem* death should not be confused with "brain death," the cessation of the higher cerebral functions, such as intellect and memory. Those who suffer, for example, from Alzheimer's disease or who are in a permanent vegetative state are alive according to *halakhah*. No organs may be removed from such patients until their hearts stop beating or irreversible brain stem death takes place.

The position that brain stem death determines death is espoused by the Chief Rabbinate of Israel. Rabbi Moshe Feinstein, the greatest decisor of this generation, and Rabbi Shlomo Zalman Auerbach, considered by many to have been the greatest decisor in Israel, supported organ transplants. Indeed, in 1980, Rabbi Feinstein, after he saw the excellent results of organ transplant, himself recommended people for heart, heart-lung, and liver transplants. Also, organ transplants are strongly favored by Dr. Avraham Steinberg, a physician, halakhist, director of the Center of Medical Ethics at Hebrew University, and winner of the prestigious Israel Prize. Numerous American Orthodox rabbis, in fact, have come to the conclusion that, according to the *halakhah*, brain stem death can be considered the actual moment of human demise, in addition to the old, accepted criterion of the end of respiration. Years before, in 1970, Rabbi Joseph Soloveichik, the leading Talmudic scholar in the world, endorsed my own decision to approve transplanting two kidneys from a moribund woman to a teenage girl and an elderly gentleman. The man died soon thereafter; the girl is still alive in 1999.

Continuing progress in the development of immunosuppresant drugs ensures that organ recipients will experience fewer rejections. Because major rabbinic opinion has now concluded that brain stem death determines the true time of death, vital human organs can be salvaged, harvested, and transplanted to those to whom they can bring life. In keeping within these halakhic guidelines, Jewish people may donate livers, lungs, pancreases, colons, corneas, blood, stem cells, even hearts in specific circumstances and in the future perhaps brain cells and other organs. Jews could always receive organ transplants, as all rabbis agree. Now they can give as well as receive. This is no small *kiddush ha-Shem*.

It should be reiterated that there are distinguished rabbis who reject the *pesak,* the halakhic decision, of the rabbis I cited. The concerned reader should consult his own rabbi in all transplant cases. The final rabbinic determination lies with a person's own rabbi. He is familiar with the debate in depth, understands the Talmudic concepts, the opinions of the Codifiers, and those of the recent rabbinic authorities. As the community rabbi, he also has a personal appreciation of the circumstances confronting specific individuals.

A centuries-old quality of the Jewish people is the ability to wring blessing from tragedy. Organ transplant opens a window of opportunity to save a life, and it is given to us by a tragically stricken human being that is thrust into these calamitous moments, when his brain stem has died but his heart is still pumping. During this time, his organs can be harvested halakhically for transplanting to other human beings. Now they, if not he, can live on. Is this not a transmogrified immortality? One life keeps giving far beyond the time of death. Love is stronger than the grave.

TAHARAH: PURIFICATION AND DRESSING OF THE REMAINS

"As he came, so shall he go," says Ecclesiastes (5:16). Just as a newborn child is immediately washed and enters this world clean and pure, so he who departs this world must be cleansed and made pure through the religious ritual called *taharah* (purification).

The *taharah* is performed by the Jewish burial society, the *chevrah kaddisha.* The rabbi or funeral director can make arrangements for this. The members of the *chevrah kaddisha*, who at all times display proper respect for the deceased, will cleanse and prepare his body for burial while reciting the required prayers asking Almighty God for forgiveness for any sins the deceased may have committed, and praying that the All Merciful may guard him and grant him eternal peace.

Membership in the *chevrah kaddisha* has always been considered a great communal honor bestowed only upon those who are truly pious. Non-Jews, under no circumstances, should perform these sacred tasks of preparing the body.

It is tragic that fewer and fewer Jews appreciate the magnificence of serving on the *chevrah kaddisha*, let alone of using its services. *Taharah* is the age-old Jewish manner of showing respect for the dead. The ritual is not merely an "old custom" or a "nice tradition"; nor is it merely a hygienic performance. The *taharah* is an absolute requirement of Jewish law.

In order to clarify the specific procedures of *taharah* that may be helpful to burial societies, there is a special section on the subject, Appendix Three.

Dressing

Jewish tradition recognizes the democracy of death. It therefore demands that all Jews be buried in the same type of garment. Wealthy or poor, all are equal before God, and that which determines their reward is not what they wear, but who they are. Nineteen hundred years ago, Rabbi Gamaliel instituted this practice so that the poor would not be shamed and the wealthy would not vie with each other to display the most costly burial clothes.

The clothes to be worn should be appropriate for one who is shortly to stand in judgment before God Almighty, Master of the universe and Creator of man. Therefore, they should be simple, handmade, perfectly clean, and white. These shrouds symbolize purity, simplicity, and dignity. Shrouds have no pockets. They, therefore, can hold no material wealth. Not a man's possessions but his soul is of importance. The burial society or funeral director has a ready supply of such shrouds.

If time must elapse before a shroud can be obtained, the funeral should be delayed, as shrouds are considered very important.

Shrouds may be made of linen (if it can be afforded), muslin, or cotton. The rule of thumb is that one should not go to greater expense than the cost of linen, but a less expensive cloth may be used.

The deceased should then be wrapped in his tallit—regardless of whether or not it is expensive or how new it is. One of the fringes should be cut. One who was not observant and who was unaccustomed to wearing a tallit may, if he so desires, be buried in a tallit—if this would not make him appear hypocritical. The tallit is not a religious uniform and should be used only when it is appropriate. The family of the deceased should decide the matter in this case.

AUTOPSY

Post-mortem examinations sometimes include autopsies to establish the cause of death and the pathological processes involved. The pathologist strives to acquire reliable information concerning the nature and cause of the disease from which the patient died, and perhaps to investigate the medical procedures used on the patient.

Following is a brief description of the physical procedure—which I have included for the sake of completeness—but it can safely be skipped.

The initial autopsy incision opens the entire body in a "Y" shape. It begins below one shoulder, continues under the breasts, and extends up to the corresponding point under the other shoulder. This incision is then joined by another in the midline extending down toward the pubis, to complete the "Y." The scalp incision begins under one ear, extends across the top of the scalp, and ends behind the other ear. The organs are removed and studied to the extent of each individual autopsy requirement.

Consent from next of kin is required for autopsy. Such consent may be given by the legal custodian of the body who is responsible for the burial, usually the husband or wife. If there is more than one "next of kin" (the interpretation of that phrase is elastic) and controversy arises, the hospital may forgo autopsy or elect the most amenable relative as "the" next of kin.

In 1969, I wrote that it could be fairly surmised that the cause of death is accurately known in most cases, and only rarely is this a medical mystery. In 1999, on the cusp of the twentieth century that has experienced such radical biomedical advances, the cause of death is an established fact, and one should not feel that medical science has been compromised by refusing an autopsy.

Autopsies were most frequently recommended in order to enable medical students and interns to study and practice by dissection of the corpse. Many articles in medical journals have asserted that recent progress in pathophysiological science has made possible the reliable determination of cause of death without an autopsy. It is now held by many authorities, with few exceptions, that autopsies are no longer considered as vital as they once were, and medical schools have sufficient cadavers from those who will their bodies to medical research.

Jewish tradition forcefully rejects autopsies performed for teaching medical students, as this violates a higher principle: the prohibition against mutilating the body of the deceased.

Jewish law is governed by several basic principles. First, man was created in the image of God, and in death man's body still retains the unity of that image. One may not do violence to the human form even when the breath of life has expired. Judaism demands respect for the total man, his body as well as his soul. The worthiness of the whole of man may not be compromised even in death.

Second, the dissection of the body for reasons that are not urgent and directly applicable to specific existing medical cases is considered a matter of shame and gross dishonor. As he was born, so does the deceased deserve to be laid to rest: tenderly and lovingly, not scientifically and dispassionately, as though he was an impersonal object of some experiment. The holiness of the human being demands that we do not tamper with his person.

Third, we have no permission to use his body without his own express desire that it be used, and even then it is very questionable whether the person himself may volunteer to mutilate the image in which he was created. Certainly, where the deceased in his lifetime gave no express permission, even his children have no rights of possession over his body. Thus, we have no moral right, except for the cases to be mentioned, to use the body of the deceased by offering it as an object for study.

Autopsies are indeed valid in certain unusual cases; these are exceptions to the general prohibition. While the possibilities of religiously permitted autopsies are listed below, a rabbi *must* be consulted in *every* instance.

In cases that fall under the jurisdiction of governmental authorities, the decision must be made by the medical examiner. For convenience and clarity, such hospital cases can be divided into two groups. The first group includes cases with impelling legal implications in which an autopsy is usually performed by the medical examiner, and in which permission for autopsy is never requested by the hospital physician.

Examples of such cases are:

- Death by homicide or suspicion of homicide.
- Death by suicide or suspicion of suicide.
- Death due solely to accidental injury.
- Death resulting from abortion.
- Death from poisoning or suspected poisoning, including bacterial food poisoning.

The second group includes cases in which the medical examiner may decide that it is not necessary for him to do an autopsy as part of his post-mortem investigation.

Examples of such cases are:

- Death occurring during or immediately following diagnostic, therapeutic, surgical, or anesthetic procedures, or following untoward reactions to medication.

- Death occurring in an unusual or peculiar manner, or when the patient was unattended by a physician, or following coma or convulsive seizure, the cause of which is not evident.
- Death resulting from chronic alcoholism, without manifestation of trauma.
- Death in which a traumatic injury was only contributory, and in which the trauma did not arise out of negligence, assault, or arson, such as a fracture of the neck resulting from a fall at home and contributing to the death of an elderly person, or accidental burns occurring in the home.

Other circumstances under which autopsies may be religiously permitted in consultation with a rabbi are: cases of hereditary diseases, where autopsy may serve to safeguard the health of survivors; or cases in which another known person is suffering from a similar deadly disease, and an autopsy is considered by qualified medical authority as possibly able to yield information vital to this other person's health.

In cases where the deceased specifically stipulated that an autopsy be performed there has been much rabbinic disagreement. The circumstances must be investigated on an individual basis, and only an informed, highly competent religious authority may decide.

Even in cases where the rabbis have permitted the postmortem, they have always insisted that any part of the body that is removed be buried with the body, and that the part be returned to the *chevrah kaddisha* for this purpose as soon as possible. According to some leading authorities, removal of fluid may be permissible.

Medical dissection must be performed with utmost respect for the deceased and not handled lightly by insensitive personnel.

Because these matters are of great religious concern, questions on post-mortem examinations must be answered by a rabbi who is aware of both the medical requirements and the demands of the tradition. In addition, some forms of autopsy, such as the removal of fluid or blood only, or the insertion of an electric needle, may be considered permissible in most instances. The decision to perform an autopsy should not be made by the physician, no matter how close he is to the family and how reputable a doctor he may be. The prohibition is of a moral-religious nature, and permission should be obtained from an authority on religious law after consultation with medical authorities.

EMBALMING

The procedure of embalming was instituted in ancient times to preserve the remains of the deceased. Preservation was desired for many reasons: for sanitation purposes—the assumption being that the decayed remains were a hazard to health; for sentimental reasons—the family feeling that it wanted to prevent deterioration of the physical body as a comforting illusion that the deceased still lived; and for presentability—to avoid visible signs of decay while the deceased was being viewed by the public prior to the funeral service.

It is worthwhile to analyze the three reasons in order to determine their validity today. First, however, it should be clear that there is no state law in the United States that requires the deceased to be embalmed, except when the body is to be carried by public conveyance for long distances.

Is there a sanitary purpose for embalming? From all available evidence, the unembalmed body presents no health hazard, even though the deceased may have died from a communicable disease. Dr. Jesse Carr, quoted in *The American Way of Death* by Jessica Mitford, indicates that there is no legitimate sanitation reason for embalming the deceased for a funeral service under normal circumstances.

Do reasons of respect and love warrant embalming to preserve the remains as long as possible? Many relatives feel, naturally, that they wish to hold on to their beloved in his human form as long as possible. If this is the major purpose of the embalming, several points should be taken into consideration:

16

1. The body will keep, under normal conditions, for twenty-four hours, unless it has been autopsied. If it is kept refrigerated, as is the standard procedure, it will unquestionably keep until after the funeral service.

2. The body must eventually decompose in the grave. Under optimum conditions, even were the embalming fluids to retard the deterioration of the outer form for a considerable length of time, reliable reports of reinterments indicate that the remains soon become sickening to behold and totally unnatural, as a consequence of the embalming. Indeed, if anything, the rabbis speak of the desire of many to place chemicals on the body to speed its disintegration, because with this comes expiation, Divine forgiveness. Embalming, whose purpose is delay, runs totally counter to Jewish tradition.

3. Sentiment should attach to the person as he lived his life, as he appeared during the years of good health, not to the corpse as it appears while entombed. The deceased himself undoubtedly would want his loved ones to remember him as he was during the peak of his lifetime.

The prohibition of embalming for the purpose of viewing the deceased is considered in a separate chapter later in the book.

There still is great confusion today about the entire process of embalming. The general public understands little about the methods of embalming and little about "restoring," or cosmetology, a term used by the funeral industry for propping, primping, berouging, and dressing the remains to be placed on view. There is little doubt that if the family were aware of the procedures they might be too horrified to request it. A detailed description is available in Jessica Mitford's *The American Way of Death.*

The guiding religious ideal in regard to embalming is that a person upon his demise should be laid to rest naturally. There should be no mutilation of his body, no tampering with his remains, and no handling of the body other than for religious purification. Disturbance of the inner organs, sometimes required during the embalming procedure, is strictly prohibited as a desecration of the image of God. The deceased can in no wise benefit from this procedure. So important is this principle, that Jewish law prohibits the embalming of a person even where he has specifically willed it.

It is not a sign of respect to make lifelike a person whom God has taken from life. The motive for embalming may be the desire to make of the funeral a last gift or a lasting memorial, but surely mourners must realize that this gift and this memorial are only illusory. The art of the embalmer is the art of complete denial. Embalming seeks to create an illusion, and to the extent that it succeeds, it only hinders the mourner from recovering from his grief. It is, on the contrary, an extreme dishonor to disturb the peace in which a person should be permitted to rest eternally.

It is indeed paradoxical that Western man, nourished on the Christian concept of the sinfulness of the body, which is considered the prison of the soul, should, in death, seek to adorn it and make it beautiful. Surely, the emphasis on the body in the funeral service serves to weaken the spiritual primacy and traditional religious emphasis on the soul.

There are, however, several exceptions to the general prohibition of embalming. These are:

1. When a lengthy delay in the funeral service becomes unavoidable.
2. When burial is to take place overseas.
3. When governmental authority demands it.

In these cases, all required because of health regulations, Jewish law permits certain forms of embalming. Rabbinic authority must be consulted to determine the permissibility of embalming and the method to be used. One method frequently used is freezing. This is an excellent, modern, clean method of preserving the body.

The injection of preservative fluid, without the removal of the organs of the body, frequently has been used. If the blood has been released from the veins, it should be collected in a receptacle, which should then be buried with the body. Bloodied clothes, worn by those killed accidentally or by violence, should be buried with the body. The blood is considered part of the human being, and even in death they are not to be separated. As time goes on, and our knowledge of chemistry advances, other methods may be developed that Jewish law will consider legitimate.

The foregoing paragraphs are only general guidelines and do not offer specific dispensation. Specific cases require individual attention and special permission from competent religious authority.

THE CASKET

"For dust thou art, and unto dust shalt thou return" (Genesis 3:19), is the guiding principle in regard to the selection of caskets. The universal practice in ancient times was, and today in Israel and in many parts of Europe is, to bury the deceased on a bed of intertwined reeds, in no casket at all, literally fulfilling the biblical prescription of returning the body to the bosom of the earth. The casket was used in ancient times for purposes of honor, such as for the burial of a priest; to shield mourners from a horrible sight, such as when burying a person who was badly burned or maimed; or to avoid a public health hazard, as in the case of one who died of a contagious disease.

In this country, however, the dead are always buried in caskets. The type of casket purchased should not be determined by cost, and one should not worry excessively about how visitors will consider it.

The following are the basic criteria:

1. The coffin should be made completely of wood. The Bible tells us that Adam and Eve hid among the trees in the Garden of Eden when they heard the Divine judgment for committing the first sin. Said the Talmudic scholar Rabbi Levi: "This was a sign for their descendants that, when they die and are prepared to receive their reward, they should be placed in coffins made of wood."

Another reason for the use of a wood coffin is so that the body and shroud should not decompose too much sooner than the coffin. The body, the cloth, and the wood have comparable rates of deterioration. A metal casket would retard that process. "Unto dust shalt thou return."

2. Caskets made with metal handles and nails theoretically may be used. This satisfies both previously mentioned reasons for the use of wooden caskets. There is a long-standing custom, however, one that is subscribed to by a majority of Jews, that demands that only wooden pegs be used. In funeral chapels these wooden-pegged caskets are called "Orthodox."

3. Casket interiors. Often, the so-called "Orthodox" caskets are purchased with the interior lined, bedded, and pillowed, preparatory to viewing the deceased. Lined interiors are not considered appropriate. They, like the embalming, suit dressing, and viewing that usually follow, violate the basic principles of the Jewish funeral. The interior adds neither "comfort" nor dignity nor respect. It is only an artificial appendage, unless it is designed for "viewing," and viewing the body is an objectionable procedure in Orthodox belief and practice, not to be condoned religiously.

4. Type of wood. It really makes no difference what style or quality of wooden casket has been selected. Whether it is mahogany or pine, polished or plain, is unimportant. Many insist on drilling holes at the bottom of the casket to fulfill the "unto dust" requirement. This is quite proper and should be encouraged.

5. Earth from the Holy Land is frequently buried along with the deceased. This is a touching and meaningful custom. Those who wish to observe it should not be discouraged from doing so. The funeral director easily can arrange for it.

6. The casket does not have to be either costly or inexpensive. The Sages did not consider the expense a barometer of honor to the dead. To some, it may be preferable to contribute monies to charity in memory of the deceased, rather than purchase lavish caskets. The cost is a personal matter, and should fit the budget of the survivors. The essential requirement is that dignity prevail.

7. Ostentatious caskets are not in good taste. President

Franklin Delano Roosevelt left explicit instructions that "the casket be of absolute simplicity, dark wood, that the body be not embalmed, or hermetically-sealed, and that the grave be not lined with brick, cement, or stones." Likewise, while the remains of President John F. Kennedy were conveyed in a bronze coffin before explicit arrangements could be made, his widow wisely decided that the President's spirit and life demanded a simple coffin, and he was removed from the bronze coffin and interred in a wooden casket.

FLOWERS

In ancient days, the Talmud informs us, fragrant flowers and spices were used at the funeral to offset the odor of the decaying body. Today, this is no longer essential, and they should *not* be used at Jewish funerals. In our day, they are used primarily at Christian funerals and are considered to be a non-Jewish ritual custom, which ought to be strongly discouraged. It is much more preferable to honor the deceased by making a contribution to a synagogue or hospital, or to a medical research association for the disease that afflicted the deceased. This method of tribute is more lasting and meaningful. However, if flowers are sent to the chapel, and the sender cannot be discouraged, the following procedure is recommended:

1. If the sender does not mind, the flowers should be kept for display in the house of mourning. Failing this they should be placed at graveside but not displayed during the service.

2. If the sender is so sensitive and the relationship so delicate that he will be offended and these recommendations will cause insult or anger, and no alternative presents itself, it is preferable to accept the flowers graciously and display them as intended, but not in an ostentatious manner. The flowers were for *kavod ha-met*, honoring the dead; but a quarrel at the service will be a *bizzayon ha-met*, a shaming of the dead.

TIMING THE FUNERAL SERVICE

The Bible, in its mature wisdom, required burial to take place as soon as possible following death. It established this requirement by both a positive and a negative command. Positively, it stated, "Thou shalt surely bury him the same day." Negatively, it warned, "His body shall not remain all night" (Deuteronomy 21:23). Jewish law, therefore, demands that we bury the deceased before sunset following the death.

The religious concept underlying this law is that man, made in the image of God, should be accorded the deepest respect. It is considered a matter of great shame and discourtesy to leave the deceased unburied—his soul has returned to God, but his body is left to linger in the land of the living. Even a High Priest, on his way to enter the sanctuary on Yom Kippur, was commanded to render the honor of a personal, quick burial, even on the holiest day of the year, to a *met mitzvah*, an unclaimed corpse. This despite the fact that the *Kohen* (Priest) is normally forbidden to handle the remains. This is the extent to which Judaism goes to honor those who die— even the unknown.

There is, secondarily, a psychological benefit to be derived from following the tradition. It becomes a matter of almost unbearable mental strain for the family to dwell for a long time in "the valley of the shadow of death." No one deserves to be subjected to the despair and anguish of being continually in the physical company of the deceased, no matter how deep his affection. As it is proper for the deceased to be buried without tarrying, so is it advisable for the family not to have to undergo the emotional pain of an unduly long delay.

Interring the dead may occasionally be delayed, but only for the honor of the dead. Thus, the rabbis allowed a delayed burial in the following cases:

1. When the government requires delay, such as for the legal transportation of the body, or for the completion of forms

and papers, or for post-mortem examinations that must be performed prior to burial.

2. If delay is caused by having to wait for the delivery of shrouds or a proper casket.

3. If close relatives have to come from great distances and it is considered an honor to the deceased for these relatives to be present. There should be, however, no unduly long period of waiting such as the common misconception of the permissibility of waiting three days would imply. Also, the delay should be based not on arbitrary guesswork as to when "most" people will attend, but on definite knowledge of the time of the arrival of close relatives such as children or parents.

4. If the eulogizing rabbi is delayed and the presence of this particular rabbi would be an honor to the deceased.

5. If the funeral would be held late on a Friday afternoon. In this case, it may be postponed until Sunday (because the Sabbath intervenes).

6. On major festivals. Jewish law forbids Jews to inter their dead on the first day of the holiday, but permits non-Jews to perform the burial on that day. On the second day of such festivals, it permits even Jews to do the burying, but other than the actual interment, no other violation of the sanctity of the day is permitted. Because conditions in contemporary society are such that funerals on either day of the festival invariably result in needless transgressions of the law, it is preferable to postpone the funeral until after both days of the holiday (in addition, in our age, the body can be preserved reliably for yet another day in a refrigerated morgue). This holds true even for transporting the person for burial in Israel, where the second day of the major holidays was never instituted.

The best time to hold the funeral service is during the morning hours, and this for three reasons:

1. It is proper to perform the mitzvah of burial with dispatch; the earlier the better.

2. For practical reasons, most persons will be able to attend the service and will then be able to return to their own affairs.

3. It will leave time for those mourners living far from the cemetery to begin the mourning period before dark and thus count this day as the first day of *shivah*, the seven days of mourning. (This subject will be treated in greater detail later.)

The timing also depends on the funeral home. They must consider the scheduling of other funerals and also must plan the time so as to avoid arriving at the cemetery during lunch hour, when cemetery employees frequently are not available. The family should consult the rabbi before a time has been established to determine his availability.

ANINUT: BETWEEN DEATH AND INTERMENT

Each immediate relative of the deceased is considered an *onen* from the moment he has learned of the death until the end of the interment, regardless of how much time has elapsed in between.

The *onen* is a person in deep distress, yanked out of normal life, and abruptly catapulted into the midst of inexpressible grief. He is disoriented, his attitudes disarranged, his emotions out of gear. The shock of death paralyzes his consciousness and blocks out all regular patterns of orderly thinking. "The deceased lies *before* him," as the Sages said, and, psychologically, he is reliving the moment of death every instant during this period.

In this state of mind, unfortunately, the mourner must make detailed and final arrangements with the funeral director, burial society, cemetery, and rabbi. He also must notify friends and family. Yet, inwardly, his primary concern is his own loss, the great gap created in his personal life and in the life of his family. Often, at this time, he is burdened with guilt for the moments of unhappiness he might have caused the deceased. The suddenness of his grief, the dismay at the news of death, leave him in a state of disbelief. It seems simply impossible, inconceivable, that someone who was just alive is now dead, cut off, and gone.

Practically, the *onen* must make immediate and significant decisions based on the reality of death. *Psychologically,* however, he has not yet assimilated the death, or perhaps not accepted it. These two elements, coupled with the need to act with respect and reverence in the presence of the deceased, are the fundamental principles of the laws governing the *onen*.

Who Is an Onen?

An *onen* is one who is halakhically required to mourn for the following relatives:

1. Father
2. Mother
3. Brother (married or unmarried; on the father's or mother's side)
4. Sister (married or unmarried; on the father's or mother's side)
5. Son
6. Daughter
7. Spouse

Minor children: A boy under the age of thirteen and a girl under the age of twelve are not properly considered *onenim* (pl.), and they are not bound by the laws of mourning that take place after interment. They are required only to rend their clothes, as will be discussed later.

Suicides: In the case of true suicides, as determined by Jewish law—purposeful, spiteful, and willful—the laws of *onen* or mourning do not apply. The obligation for arrangements and care of the deceased, according to Jewish law, falls technically upon the whole community, and not solely upon the relatives. The relatives have neither the obligation to participate in the arrangements nor the requirement to pay special personal courtesies to the suicide. A suicide—for reasons other than insanity or deep clinical depression—is considered to have destroyed the image of God and to have deprived his family of his presence. By treating the suicide in this manner,

Judaism plainly expresses its abhorrence of such actions, and this usually has served as a deterrent. (In our day, nonetheless, the costs of a suicide burial are most often borne by the family.) The subject of suicides is treated in greater detail below.

A relative is an *onen* only if:

- He busies himself with some aspect of the funeral arrangements.
- Even if he does not so concern himself, that he be in a position to do so should it become necessary. He is not considered an *onen* if there is absolutely no possibility of his participation in the arrangements.

Thus, he or she is not an *onen* if:

- The deceased is not in the possession of his relatives, as when the government has not released the body to the family, or if he was drowned or missing in combat and cannot be found although there may be certain knowledge of his death. It cannot be too frequently emphasized: government agencies often need prodding to release the body because of Jewish law.
- He could not physically be present at the funeral preparations because he is under military obligation, or is confined in a hospital or prison, or is overseas, or is in a city too distant from the funeral. If, however, there is the possibility that he might have arrived in time for the funeral service, he is considered an *onen*, providing no other immediate relatives were present during arrangements.

The *onen* is required to abide by the following rules:

1. He should not eat in the presence of the body.
2. He should not eat meat or drink wine or liquor any place.
3. He should not eat a full-to-bursting meal or attend a party.
4. He must deny himself the luxuries of excessive self-adornment, of bathing for pleasure, shaving, taking a haircut, and having conjugal relations.
5. He may not conduct normal business during this time.

6. In addition to all these, a woman may not go to the mikvah (ritual bath) until after *shivah*. She should light Sabbath candles but not recite the blessing.

7. He may not study Torah, as this is considered a source of profound enjoyment.

8. All observances practiced by the mourner during *shivah* devolve also upon the *onen*, except that he or she is permitted to wear shoes and to leave the house in order to expedite the burial arrangements. Today, however, people can do all their business wearing sneakers, if necessary, and the *onen* should do the same.

9. On the Sabbath most laws that apply to the *onen* are cancelled. He is permitted meat and wine and is obligated to perform all the mandatory Sabbath observances. The *onen* should attend religious services. If there is an alternative, he should not serve as reader or cantor. He should not recite the Kaddish unless he has yahrzeit or is in the midst of the year of mourning for one of his parents. However, he must not participate in matters of private enjoyment, such as conjugal relations and the delight that is reaped from the study of Torah.

10. If the burial must take place on the second day of the holiday (even though, as mentioned above, burials should be strongly discouraged at this time), *aninut* (the state of being an *onen*) goes into effect immediately, even though it is a holiday. In such a case, the *onen* does not recite the Kaddish, or eat meat or drink wine. Some actually hold that he should enact *aninut* on the second day at all times.

11. On Sukkot the *onen* is not obligated to sit in the sukkah. If he desires to do so, he should not recite the blessing for that mitzvah. On the first night of Sukkot, however, seeing that burial cannot take place at night or on the first day, he should recite the Kiddush and perform other observances connected with the holiday.

12. On the first night of Pesach, the *onen* should observe all the mitzvot (pl.) of the Seder night but preferably listen to the Haggadah recitation rather than recite it himself. On Sefirah days, between Pesach and Shavuot, the *onen* should recite the counting of the *omer* but without the blessing, until

immediately after burial. After the funeral, he may count the days *and* recite the blessing.

13. On Purim, the *onen* should listen to the reading of the Megillah but preferably not eat meat and drink wine in fulfillment of the Purim *se'udah*, the religiously prescribed festive meal.

14. On Hanukkah, the male or female *onen* should have the candles lit for him or her and the blessings recited by someone else. If no one else is present, he or she should light the candles, but without reciting the blessings.

15. *Tefillin*: The laying of the *tefillin* (phylacteries) may not be performed on the day of death and on the day of burial. This is not because of the general exemption from positive obligations during the time of *aninut* but rather because *tefillin* are considered objects of beautification and ornamentation, and this is inconsistent with the inner bitterness experienced by the mourner so soon after the loss of his loved one.

The following are some clarifications and ramifications of this law of *tefillin*:

1. Even if burial occurs on the day following death, or two days after, *tefillin* are not donned during this entire period. One resumes the practice on the day after burial. If, for some reason, burial took place at night, the entire following day is considered unsuitable for wearing the *tefillin*.

2. If three or four days elapse between death and burial, then:

- If the mourner is personally involved in making arrangements for the funeral or interment, he does not don *tefillin* on any of these days, including the full day of burial.
- If the mourner is not involved in these matters, he then follows the laws of *aninut*: he does not don *tefillin* on the day of death but resumes wearing them immediately thereafter. On the day of interment, he is prohibited from wearing *tefillin* before the time of burial, but upon returning from the funeral he promptly should don them.

3. If he receives news of the death after interment has taken place, but within thirty days of the time of burial, he may not wear *tefillin* on the day the news arrives. If the news comes at night, he refrains from wearing *tefillin* on the following day.

4. If the interment occurs during a holiday, or during the intermediary days (*chol ha-mo'ed*) of Sukkot or Passover (when the mourning period begins later), there is no prohibition against the wearing of *tefillin* (for those who normally put on *tefillin* during *chol ha-moe'd*).

5. Likewise, a groom who has suffered the death of a relative during the week immediately following the wedding, and whose mourning period begins later, should wear *tefillin* during this week.

VIEWING THE REMAINS

It has become a common practice in America, among all religious faiths, to display the body of the deceased as part of the funeral ritual or service. It is not the way of the Jewish tradition. The custom of viewing the remains is of recent American origin, having no roots in ancient culture or contemporary European usage, with the exception of the "lying-in-state" of kings and emperors.

The lifeless body is removed from the hospital or home and taken to the funeral establishment. There it is embalmed and "restored" by manipulating it, injecting it with chemicals, covering it with cosmetics, dressing it neatly, and supporting it with mechanical devices. It is then displayed in a "reposing room," or in the chapel, before the religious service begins. Clergymen usually insist that the casket be closed during the service itself.

The viewing of the corpse is one of the fundamentals of the economy of the funeral industry. Before the body is offered for presentation to relatives and friends, it must be perfumed, restored to a look of perfect health, dressed in expensive clothing, and placed in a respectable, "comfortable-look-

ing" casket. These requirements of viewing usually constitute the bulk of the funeral costs.

In the Image of God

Traditional Judaism regards burial procedures, for the most
part, as *yekara de-shikhva*, devoted to the respect, honor, and
endearment of the deceased. Mourning laws are primarily
yekara de-khayye, therapy for the living, devoted to the mitigating of intense grief, the slow disentanglement from the
web of guilt, anger, fear, hatred, and rebellion that enshrouds
the mind of the mourner after his relative has been taken
from life.

The Sages wisely noted that one cannot and should not
comfort the mourners while their dead lie before them. Comfort and relief come later, after funeral and burial arrangements have been completed and the dead have been interred.
Until that time, the deceased remains the center of concern.
His honor and his integrity are of primary importance.

Whether, in fact, respect for the deceased is primary, or the
comfort of the mourners is the principal goal, it is difficult to
justify the practice of viewing the remains as a standard feature of the funeral service.

If that sublime concept in Genesis that "God created man
in His own image" is right—and all of our major religions are
based on it—then the whole procedure for preparing the body
and restoring it, which is prerequisite for viewing, is offensive and abominable. If man is fashioned after his Creator,
how can we allow the stapling and nailing, the molding and
the smearing, literally the "man-handling" of that which was
created in the image of God?

It is a horrifying experience to witness the restoring process for those who died after sustained illness, or intense suffering, or as a result of accident, or, for that matter, for all
except those who died in the bloom of health. Can this handling of the deceased be considered a tribute to God's creation and to man's living in the image of God?

Isaiah's description of the righteous dead (Isaiah 57:2): "May
peace come, may they rest in their resting place," is all but

absurd with the development of the restoring process. There is no rest for those who should rest in peace (not even if the ceremony takes place in what is called a "reposing room"). The image that is born, fondled, loved, respected and honored, the dignity that inheres in man as a creation in the image of God, is now desecrated. A person's last right should be the right of utter privacy, the privilege of remaining untampered with after death. It is amazing that this process of disturbing the rest of the deceased is called, "paying our last respects."

Dishonoring the Dead

Judaism postulates that the dignity of man derives from two basic sources. One, mentioned above, is that man is the creation of an all-good God. This endows him with the spark of divinity, and it is the divine image in man that grants him innate value. The other derives not from man's creatureliness, but from his personal social development as a human being living among other human beings. What is important here is man as he exercises the freedom of his will, the person as he develops his own *Anschauung*, how he handles the existential crises that beset him, what he does with the qualities that were inborn in him, his unique individuality. The sum total of his personal experiences and his reactions to them grant him "value" in addition to that innate dignity he derives from being a creation of God.

The Talmud records a dispute between Rabbi Akiva and Ben Azzai as to the most significant phrase in the Bible. They disagree as to which of the two foregoing qualities endows man with greater value. Rabbi Akiva declares that it is man's righteous exercise of the freedom of his will, the love of neighbor, and the social values that are primary. Ben Azzai dwells on the creation of man in God's image as the major source of his dignity.

If we reject manipulating and masking the cadaver in preparation for viewing as a violation of the image of God, we must also reject holding up for display the physical remains of the human being who achieved dignity from the sum of his life

31

experiences, his loves and interests, the *élan vital* that was the hallmark of this man.

Jewish mystics refer to the look of the deceased as *mareh litusha*, "a hammered image." Indeed, the viewer emerges, after the ordeal of the funeral, with a new and sordid dimension added to his memories and feelings. This is not the person he knew in life, nor is it the cadaver gripped by death; it is a make-believe, a figure out of a wax museum, a being neither dead nor alive.

Acknowledging Reality

From the standpoint of psychotherapy, the idea of viewing the corpse as standard funeral procedure because of the therapeutic value inherent in the practice has not been proved clinically and, in fact, appears to contradict the very basic thrust of its method. "Grief therapy"—helping the bereaved to remember a sweet, content, smiling face rather than the vacant, pain-ridden, drawn look of a cadaver—works, it is claimed, to soften the shock of death. It alleviates the sudden cut-off and, momentarily, returns those lost to us. But, if therapy is conceived as a form of self-enlightenment and self-understanding, what valid function can viewing perform? Shall we believe that man requires a neurotic distortion of truth in order to protect himself from the trauma of truth? It seems far more sensible to rely on the faith that man can summon the strength with which to confront the raw, if sometimes bitter, truth without the aid of fabricated distortions. Viewing is as much "grief therapy" as painting a jail with bright colors is "thief therapy."

Not only may viewing be non-therapeutic, it may, in fact, be injurious to the viewer. The first stage of mourning is characterized by anger, despair, and the denial of death. Fixation on any one of these reactions represents, from the psychological point of view, a pathological response. It is entirely conceivable that viewing may lead to a fixation on the denial of death. The refusal to give up the object of love is perpetuated by the illusion of life that the embalmers so mightily strive to create. The religious ritual of the funeral compels one to acknowledge the finality of the physical loss, and thus enables the "working through" of the grief process. To fix one's mind on what should be an ephemeral reaction is possibly to short-circuit the entire effectiveness of the grief process.

Both Judaism and psychotherapy express in their own idioms the view that a masking of reality will not enable the human being to cope with reality. The truth is that the end has come. The deceased shall no longer walk the earth and share happy occasions with his relatives. Man's soul is not so impoverished that he cannot remember the living image of his departed; he is not so neurotic that he cannot be permitted to confront the ultimate truth; nor should he be so self-indulgent that he deliberately disturbs the departed for the sake of his own peace of mind.

Judaism explicitly postulates that the funeral must be a finale. The service, the prayers, and the rituals do not attempt to hide death, much less to deny it. They confirm it and acknowledge it unhesitatingly. It is only the acceptance of the *reality* of death that enables man to overcome the *trauma* of death.

Jewish Practice

The American, quasi-religious ceremony of viewing the remains is made to seem the minimal courtesy a man can pay his beloved; it has become the natural and logical thing for mourners to do to pay their last respects. Viewing the remains is but a reflection of our general American value system. By making a display of the flesh minus the mind, we are, in fact, demonstrating our lifelong emphasis on appearance over value, on externals and possessions over the inner life and growth of the sensitive and sentient human being. As such, viewing is an extension into death of the kind of attitudes that tax life: to use Martin Buber's terms, the attrition of the "thou" in favor of the "it." When we take a human being to whom we once related as a subject, as an equal, as a 'thou," and manipulate him as one would a piece of merchandise, we reduce him to an object, a mere "it." The tendency of those attending funerals is to note that "he looks good" rather than that "he was good," and conversations tend to dwell on the person as a man of means rather than a man of ends. But the person himself, in his own intimation of immortality, hopes and expects not that the shape of his nose and jaw, or the tilt of his chin, will be remembered, but that his deeds, his teachings, his attitudes, his strivings, his good intentions and efforts, and the accomplishments of his children will somehow bring him the immortality he craves.

In Jewish literature and law, the human being is compared with the scroll of the Torah. The death of a person, for example, is equivalent to the burning of a Torah, and, in both cases, the onlooker is required to rend his clothing. As the Torah, used for holy purposes, retains its holiness even when it becomes religiously disqualified, so the human being, having lived for noble purpose, retains dignity even in death. The remains possess the holiness that characterizes the Torah itself. Thus, too, one may not dishonor a corpse, as one may not desecrate the holy Scroll. In traditional Judaism, the dishonoring of the dead includes not only untoward and derogatory remarks or joking and jesting. It also means eating, drinking, and smoking—even studying the Bible in the presence of the deceased—any indulgence in the pleasures and needs of the living in the company of the helpless and non-participating corpse. One may not deal with the dead as though he were living, as if he were merely sleeping. For those who thus ridicule the dead, the Sages apply the phrase from Proverbs 17:5: "Whoso mocketh the poor, blasphemeth his Maker."

When we place on display the remains of the person we loved, we may, in fact, bring ourselves some temporary comfort, but this, surely, does not constitute respect for the dead. What we are doing, essentially, is holding up a lifeless, bloodless, mindless mass of flesh and bones. The "color" of the deceased lay in his wit, character, and personality—or lack of these qualities—not in the embalmer's rouge and lipstick. What should be remembered is the indelible impression upon us of a full-blooded, living person, not the expression on his lips as fashioned by mechanical devices.

What we view is the ghost of a person, not the person. It is sheer mockery to parade before this ghost to say, "Goodbye," or to take one last look by which to remember him. This is not the person, but a death mask, even if prettied up artificially. When we display our dead, we exhibit not their loves and fears and hopes, their characters and their concerns, but their physical shapes in their most prostrate condition. Strangely enough, we readily understand sick people who, wracked with pain and emaciated from suffering, do not wish to be seen in their deteriorated condition. While we appreciate the vanity of the living only too well, we are insensitive to the ghastliness of holding up the helpless ghost, painted and propped, in morbid exhibitionism.

During the cleansing and purification of the deceased in preparation for burial, a very ancient prayer—more than a thousand years old—is recited. The prayer is, as it were, a presentation of the dead before God, asking for His mercy and for forgiveness for the dead. The prayer at graveside is likewise a justification of the God of truth: the Lord who has given and the Lord who has taken. There is no mask of death in the Jewish ritual. The deceased is buried in the earth itself, dust to dust, and the grave is filled in the presence of the relatives and friends. Indeed, it is the closest of friends and the greatest of scholars who are invited to be the first to fill in the grave. The thump of the clod of earth upon the wood of the casket sounds the sure finale to a precious life.

It is a perversion of the true religious import of the funeral to disguise the reality of death. The display of the dead in the most lifelike appearance, the semblance of life through the use of cosmetics, clothing in gowns or tuxedos, propping the head and using pillows, the replica of a happy person asleep, is contrary to the spirit that religion seeks to engender. Man does not, as the happy phrase would have it, merely "go to sleep with his forefathers." Man dies and decays, and his physical existence is no more. His good works live on after him, but his body returns to the earth as it was. His personality, his goodness go on to a greater dimension of existence; the chemical elements decompose and return to their original state.

Viewing the corpse is objectionable, both theologically and psychologically. It shows no respect for the deceased, and provides questionable therapy for the bereaved. On the contrary,

while viewing may seem desirable superficially, deeper consideration will show it to be devoid of real meaning and in
fact, detrimental in terms of both religion and mental health.
Religiously, it expresses disregard for the rights of the dead
and a perversion of the religious significance of life and death.
Psychologically, it may serve to short-circuit the slow therapy
of nature's grief process that begins from the moment of the
awareness of death.

Man, created in the image of God, participating in the dignity of human life, deserves to rest in peace. And the mourner
deserves, at this traumatic moment of intense grief, to be allowed to work through, naturally and at his own pace, an
acknowledgment and an acceptance of his loss.

THE NIGHT BEFORE THE FUNERAL SERVICE

The deceased may not be left alone before burial. As noted
earlier, the watching over of the deceased may be performed
by a relative or by any other Jewish person, preferably an
observant Jew who will recite portions from the Book of
Psalms. The funeral director or the rabbi can arrange this.

The wake is definitely alien to Jewish law and custom, and
its spirit does violence to Jewish sensitivity and tradition. The
custom of visiting the funeral parlor on the night before interment to comfort the mourners and to view the remains is
clearly a Christian religious practice, and not merely an American folkway.

In Judaism, which requires no additional ceremonies to
buttress its own authentic millennial customs, viewing their
remains does not pay respect to the dead. On the contrary, it
is an embarrassment. Also, it is futile to attempt to comfort
the mourners when their dead lie before them in the chapel.
The place for offering condolences is at home, during the seven
special days of mourning called *shivah*.

In addition, a wake is sometimes reduced to the level of a
social gathering. The conversation is often inane, and the

evening has the barest façade of dignity. The family itself must suffer prolonged hours of trivial chatter in the face of terrible grief. That is not the Jewish way.

The wake, therefore, should be strongly discouraged at Jewish funerals under any and all circumstances.

2 The Funeral Service and the Interment

THE JEWISH FUNERAL service is a starkly simple but emotionally meaningful farewell to the deceased. The service does not attempt primarily to comfort the mourners. The Sages wisely noted that it is sheer mockery to comfort the bereaved while their beloved lies dead before their eyes. Moreover, it is psychologically futile to effect reconciliation between the mourner and his fate at this time.

The service is directed, rather, at honoring the departed. The tribute to him takes the form of the recitation of a eulogy; chanting of Psalms and the memorial prayer, El Mal'e Rachamim; following the casket and accompanying the deceased to his final resting place; speaking only well of him; and many other small acts in which each individual pays his own heartfelt respect.

In order to render proper homage to the deceased, tradition serves as a wise and able instructor. The cumulative wisdom of the Jewish people's experience with grief for over three thousand years is distilled in the laws and customs pertaining to this area of life. The following pages offer the most important details of these traditions and some of the wise principles underlying them.

LOCATION OF THE SERVICE

From the days of the Second Temple until modern times, funeral services have taken place either in the home of the deceased or at the cemetery. The Talmud indicates that the service of farewell took place in one of these two places, most often in the home.

The use of the synagogue for such occasions was rare. When the service was held at the local synagogue or religious school it was only so that the entire community might pay honor to an exceptional person. In modern times, the funeral chapel is almost always used. The chapel provides a dignified setting, is able to accommodate many people, and is, therefore, to be encouraged in most instances.

There are occasions, however, when one or another of these four choices—home, synagogue, chapel, or cemetery—is preferable, depending upon the family's decision. It should be noted that the holding of funeral services within the precincts of the synagogue sanctuary is very rare. It is done only for those who, like Rabbi Judah the Prince, are scrupulously observant, great Torah scholars, and noted communal leaders. Respect may be rendered those who are deserving, although they may fall somewhat short of this ideal person, by taking the hearse to the cemetery via the synagogue and pausing in front of the synagogue. The rear door of the hearse is opened, the cantor chants the memorial prayer in honor of the deceased, and then the cortege continues to the cemetery.

If there is no Jewish chapel available, then the community should set aside some room in the local synagogue for such occasions. The vestry or auditorium is the most appropriate place to hold such services. If this facility is not available, then the home should be used. If this too is impossible, the cemetery should be the place for the eulogy and prayers. In inclement weather, when there is no other place for the funeral, a hospital auditorium or a nonsectarian chapel, with all religious symbols removed, may be used.

KERI'AH: RENDING THE CLOTHING

The most striking Jewish expression of grief is the rending of clothing by the mourner prior to the funeral service.

The Bible records many instances of rending the clothes after the news of death. When Jacob saw Joseph's coat of many colors drenched with what he thought to be his son's blood, he rent his clothing. Likewise, David tore his clothes when he heard of the death of King Saul. And Job, who knew grief so well, stood up and rent his mantle.

The rending is also an opportunity for psychological relief. It allows the mourner to give vent to his pent-up anguish by means of a controlled, religiously sanctioned act of destruction. Maimonides, according to the interpretation of B. H. Epstein (*Torah Temimah* on Leviticus 10:6), notes with sharp insight that this tear satisfies the emotional need of the moment, or else it would not be permitted as it is a clear violation of the Biblical command not to cause waste. For this reason, we may assume, the tear for parents must be made with bare hands.

Geoffrey Gorer, in his book *Death, Grief and Mourning*, notes that "although our culture gives no symbolic expression to anger, a considerable number of others have done so." This is seen in such rituals as the "destruction of the dead person's property or possessions or, slightly more indirectly, by the various mutilations which mourners have to inflict upon themselves as a sign of the pain which the dead have caused them. According to some psychoanalysts, this anger is a component of all mourning, and one of the main functions of the mourning process is to work through and dissipate this anger in a symbolic and, to a great extent, unconscious fashion."

Keri'ah also may serve as a substitute for the ancient pagan custom of tearing the flesh and the hair, which symbolizes the loss of one's own flesh and blood in sympathy for the deceased, and which is not permitted in Jewish law (Deuteronomy 14:1-2).

The halakhic requirement to "expose the heart" (that is,

40

that the tear for deceased parents must be over the heart), indicates that the tear in the apparel represents a torn heart. The prophet Joel (2:13) chastises the Jew to rend the heart itself, not only the garment over the heart, indicating that the external tear is a symbol of the broken heart within.

Another, and relatively unknown, reason is advanced in the Jerusalem Talmud (*Mo'ed Katan* 3:5): The "exposing of the heart" is performed because the mourner has lost the precious ability to fulfill the biblical command to honor father and mother. We suffer deeply when we can no longer give love to our beloved. Of course, respect for parents can, and should, be expressed after their death, but, according to many authorities, it is a rabbinic, rather than a Biblical mandate. *Keri'ah*, thus, also symbolizes the rending of the parent-child relationship and confronts the mourner with the stabbing finality of this separation, expressed on his own clothes and on his own person for all to see.

Who Must Rend the Clothing?

Mourners must themselves arrange to personally tear the clothing—at the death of their mother or father—and to have their clothing cut—at the death of the other relatives. Which relatives trigger this *keri'ah* requirement?

1. Seven relatives are obligated to perform this mandate: son, daughter, father, mother, brother, sister, and spouse.
2. They must be adults, males above the age of thirteen and females over twelve. Pre-Bar Mitzvah children who are in fact capable of understanding the situation and appreciating the loss should have other relatives or friends make the tear for them. For youngsters who are too immature to understand the gravity of the situation, one should nonetheless make a slight symbolic cut in the garment. This unites them with the family at the terrible time of tears and tragedy.
3. Divorced mates may cut their clothing, but they are not obligated to do so. They also of course may bemoan the tragedy and accompany the deceased to the cemetery.
4. Sons-in-law or daughters-in-law, if this is their earnest

desire, may rend their clothing out of respect for their spouse's tragedy. However, this should be done only with the assurance that their living parents will not object. If one parent is already deceased, no permission is necessary.

5. Bride and groom should not perform the clothes-tearing ritual during the first seven days following the wedding. This time is one of inviolate joy even in the face of grief.

6. Mentally ill patients, who cannot appreciate the gravity of their loss or may not see the death in its proper perspective, should not tear their clothing. If it is the patient's parent who has died, rending should be performed after sanity has returned. In the case of the death of other relatives, once *keri'ah* has been delayed it is not to be done at all.

7. The physically disabled, or those too weak to make the tear themselves during the *shivah*, should not have their clothing cut subsequently, even if they recover. They felt the pain and anguish at the time of the occurrence of death, and the later rending is purposeless, as the rending must take place during the time of most intense grief.

When Should the Rending Take Place?

The garment should be torn at one of three times:

1. At the moment of hearing of the death, wherever the mourner may be at that time.
2. At the home or the chapel, immediately prior to the funeral service.
3. At the cemetery, prior to or immediately following the interment.

Today, it is usually done at the funeral chapel; this is the preferable procedure. At this time, the rabbi is present and can supervise the rending in accordance with the traditional laws. Also, this is the time that the entire family is gathered together, and the relatives can stand by one another united through this emotionally charged expression of common bereavement.

The following are the laws of rending for special circumstances:

1. On Sabbaths and holidays the mourners certainly should be encouraged to delay the *keri'ah* until the service at the chapel. If, however, they desire to do so as soon as possible, they must wait at least until nightfall.

2. During *chol ha-mo'ed*, the days between the first and last days of Pesach and Sukkot, the *keri'ah* may be performed. Some rabbis may prefer to wait until after the holiday, especially if there are no sons or daughters, and it is, therefore, proper to allow the rabbi to make that decision.

3. If news of the death of one of the seven relatives noted above reached the mourners after interment but *within* thirty days following death, they must rend the clothing upon hearing the news. If the news reached them more than thirty days after the death then:

- For parents there is no time limit. The clothing must be rent no matter how late.
- For other relatives there is no obligation to rend after thirty days.

If the mourners forgot to rend at the proper time, then:

- For parents they should rend as soon as they recall their omission. This may be done even if the time elapsed is very long.
- For other relatives—if it was recalled during *shivah*, the tear should be made then. Afterwards, it should not be made.

However, the blessing that usually accompanies the *keri'ah* should be recited only within the first three days after death, not later. The reason for this is that the blessing may be recited only in the midst of intense grief, and this stage of grief is considered by the law to last until the fourth day, after which time the grief slowly diminishes.

Which Clothing Should Be Rent?

Customarily, the item of clothing to be rent should be one that is worn at room temperature. This precludes the cutting of the overcoat and underclothes.

1. For men, the vest or sweater should be cut, if the mourner usually wears one. If one is not usually worn, the suit or jacket should be rent.

Some Orthodox rabbis, notably the great scholar, Rabbi Eliezer Silver, have permitted and declared valid for the performance of *keri'ah* the rending of a tie that is always worn. The tie, they maintain, satisfies the conditions required for *keri'ah*: it extends from the neck to below the heart, and it is a garment that is almost always worn. It meets the definition of clothing, measuring the width of three fingers square. In light of the fact that most contemporary rabbis do not accept a tie as valid for *keri'ah*, however, it is suggested that a tie be used only if a mourner rejects the other articles of clothing that are recommended for *keri'ah*.

2. Women should cut a dress, blouse, or sweater. The woman mourner must retain her modesty, and, consequently, she herself should tear the clothing at a relatively inconspicuous spot. Also, it is quite proper for a woman to rend another woman's clothing. For reasons of modesty, clothing, such as a T-shirt, should be worn underneath.

It is not necessary or even desirable that new clothes be worn or that black be the chosen color. The mourner may change into used clothing for this occasion.

Should a Pinned Ribbon Be Used?

The rending of the clothes expresses the deepest feelings of sorrow and anguish. It is the symbol of a broken heart and a genuine mark of separation from one who was dearly beloved, with whom one had a blood relationship or ties of matrimony.

The grief we express at such moments taps into the deepest wells of our humanity, and the manner in which we manifest it should be equally authentic. The anguish is exquisite, one might even say sacred, and the way in which we express it should be no less sacred. It is appropriate that this form of release of sorrow should be sanctioned by faith and by centuries of ancient custom, going back to Biblical times.

How shallow, how disappointing, how pitiably trivial, therefore, is the attempt to symbolize these authentic sentiments not by an act of historic and religious significance, but by the little black ribbon or button—invented by enterprising American undertakers! Tradition calls upon us to tear *our* clothing, to put the mark of the broken heart on our *own* clothing—and not to vent our feelings on a meaningless and impersonal strip of cloth pinned on us by a stranger.

Keri'ah is too personally meaningful to substitute for it a petty gimmick, the expression of penury, rather than grief, thereby desecrating our own most genuine human experiences.

Nevertheless, if for some reason the ribbon has been used at the funeral service, the mourner should make a tear in the proper clothing upon his return home.

Where Should the Cut Be Made?

For parents: the tear should be made on the left side—over the heart—and should be plainly visible. It should be made vertically, beginning near the neck, and extend down approximately three inches. The initial cut may be made with a knife (by anyone close by) but then should be torn by hand by the mourner himself. The tear should not be made along a seam, as it must appear to be a purposeful scar in the clothing and not merely an accidental unthreading.

For other relatives: The tear is made on the right side and need not show. Thus, the cut may be inside the lapel of a jacket or the lining of a sweater or dress. Also, it may be done by others, not necessarily by the hand of the mourner himself. Some decisors even say it should be done by others.

How Long Should the Rent Clothing Be Worn?

For parents: The rent should be clearly visible during *shivah*. If a change of clothes is required during that time, the changed clothes, too, should be cut. After *shivah* the rent clothes need not be worn. A daughter, for reasons of dignity and modesty, may baste the clothing that was torn as soon after the funeral as she wishes. The son may baste his clothing only after thirty days. But neither son nor daughter may ever permanently sew these clothes. All rent clothing can be worn or disposed at will. The wound left by the passing of parents may be healed, but the scar never completely disappears.

If a major holiday occurs during *shivah*, the clothes may be basted before sundown. The torn clothing is not worn on the Sabbath during *shivah*.

For other relatives: Mourners for relatives other than father or mother are required to perform the rending of the clothes but need not make the rend visible. Thus, if they change their clothing during the *shivah*, they need not rend the new set of clothes. The clothes may be basted after the *shivah*, and sewn completely after the thirty-day period of mourning. If a major holiday occurs during *shivah*, the mourner may sew the clothes before sundown. "There is a time to rend and a time to mend," says Ecclesiastes (3:7).

Posture During Keri'ah

The law requires that the rending of the clothing be performed while standing. The posture of accepting grief in Jewish life is always erect, symbolizing both strength in the face of crisis and respect for the deceased.

THE FUNERAL SERVICE

The funeral service is a brief and simple service designed primarily as *yekara de-shikhva*—for the honor and dignity of the deceased. The worthy values by which he lived, the good deeds he performed, and the noble aspects of his character are eulogized. The function of the eulogy is not to comfort the bereaved, although by highlighting the good and the beautiful in the life of the departed it affords an implicit consolation for the mourners.

Great psychological benefit can be derived from the funeral service, although this, too, is not its primary purpose. The service enables many friends and relatives to participate in the situation of bereavement and, thus, relieve the terrible loneliness of the mourners. In addition to praising the deceased, all who attend the funeral are confronted with the terrible fact of their own mortality, impelling them to "consider their days," to take stock and live their lives creatively.

The service consists of a selection from Psalms appropriate to the life of the deceased, a panegyric of his finer qualities, which his survivors should seek to implant in their own lives, and El Mal'e Rachamim, a memorial prayer asking that God shelter his soul "on the wings of His Divine presence." Selected psalms and the El Mal'e Rachamim appear in Appendix One.

Psalm 23

The most commonly used Psalm at the funeral service is Psalm 23, which begins "The Lord is my Shepherd." This psalm expresses the most intimate, personal relationship of man with his beloved God. Troubles may abound, agony may strike the soul, but there is this one comforting thought— "The Lord is my Shepherd." As a sheperd seeks to guide and care for his flock, seeks fertile pastures in which his sheep may graze, stays close to his flock and helps them grow and develop; and just as he embraces and raises up the sheep who have been injured; so does God, the Divine Sheperd, watch over His flock. We, the members of the flock, may sometimes, in our despair, doubt the justice of the Sheperd; we may not understand His ways, but we are confident that He is concerned with our welfare.

Eshet Chayil

Frequently, Eshet Chayil, "A Woman of Valor," from Proverbs 31:10–31, is read for a deceased female (see Appendix One). This last chapter of the book of Proverbs attributed to King Solomon, is remarkable for its assessment of woman's value, her traits, and her importance in the Jewish family, in an ancient age, when only a century ago she was chattel in civilized British life.

In this description, the woman is the manager of the household, wise, kind to those who work for her, and indeed, "her value is far above rubies."

"What Is Man?"

Another selection—for a deceased male—recited at many funeral services is "What Is Man?" consisting of verses from a selection of Psalms. What is expressed here is despair over the brevity of man's life. It asks: "What can be the significance of a life that withers so quickly?" But faith informs us that there is a God who guides us. Observe the good person. God will care for the upright in the heart. He will ascend the mountain of the Lord.

The rabbi may choose other psalms or selections from the Book of Proverbs for appropriate occasions and for different personal qualities of the deceased. Special selections often are chosen for a person who died at a young age or under untoward circumstances.

El Mal'e Rachamim

The Memorial Prayer, El Mal'e Rachamim, is a beautiful one having been chanted in the same way for many years. Unlike the Kaddish, this is a prayer on behalf of the dead. While it is not technically to be considered a "lament," custom dictates that it should not be chanted when the Tachanun prayer is not recited in the Synagogue. For this prayer you will have to know the Hebrew name of the deceased and the deceased's father. If these names are not available, the English names should be used.

THE EULOGY

The eulogy is a significant focus of the funeral service. One of the most important obligations of mourners and heirs is to provide for this eulogy. Abraham, the first patriarch of the

Jewish people, eulogized his wife Sarah, and that has been the custom of Jews to this day.

Purpose of the Eulogy

Following the lesson of Abraham, the purpose of the eulogy is twofold. First is *hesped*—the praising of the deceased for his worthy qualities. Second is *bekhi*—expressing the grief and the sense of loss experienced by the mourners and the entire Jewish community.

Very wisely, the Jewish tradition requires the eulogizing of the deceased to be *kara'u'i*, balanced and appropriate. It may not grossly exaggerate, or invent, qualities that the deceased did not in fact possess. Such praise is a mockery and an effrontery to the departed, rather than a tribute to his personal virtues. In addition, the mourners should remember that although the deceased may have been undistinguished in many ways and lacking in certain moral qualities, there is a substratum of goodness and decency in all men, which can be detected if properly sought. Sometimes, the mourners are too close to their departed and see only mediocrity and perhaps meanness. But, sometimes, a more objective view reveals virtues unknown or latent: honesty or frankness or humaneness or respect or tolerance, or simply the ability to raise decent children in a violent and unstable world.

Where Is the Eulogy Delivered?

The eulogy is spoken, almost always, at the chapel or at the home, or, occasionally, at the cemetery prior to burial. For outstanding scholars or community leaders, it may be delivered during *shivah* or on the thirtieth day after the funeral.

Eulogies generally are not delivered if the funeral occurs on a major festival, such as Passover, Shavuot, or Sukkot, or on days immediately following the three major festivals; on other holidays such as Hanukkah, Purim, Rosh Chodesh (the first day of the Hebrew month); on afternoons immediately preceding the above holidays; or on Friday afternoons. The reason for this is that although the funeral is an occasion of grief for the family of the deceased, the joyous spirit of the holiday, which devolves on the entire community, overrides the obligation and desire for lamentation by individuals. However, while *bekhi*, the bewailing, contradicts the spirit of the holiday, *hesped*, spoken in the correct manner, often does not; hence it is, on occasion, permitted to speak a very short eulogy emphasizing only the praise of the deceased and encouraging the relatives to incorporate these qualities into their own lives.

Eulogies should not be made if this was the specific request of the deceased. Because the eulogy is *yekara de-shikhva*, for the honor of the dead rather than for the survivors, an individual may elect to forgo the honor. However, the mourners should not take this decision upon themselves if they merely conjecture that this is what the deceased would have wanted. Most people deserve a eulogy and should not be deprived of it because of speculation, although the conjecture may have been made in good faith.

Preparing for the Eulogy

Frequently rabbis must deliver eulogies for people they have never met. Under conditions peculiar to the modern American Jewish community, this is almost inevitable. In order to make a dignified and honest presentation, the rabbi will have to know certain basic facts of the life of the deceased. Be prepared to tell him all of the departed's good qualities, and do it enthusiastically. Every man is unique. Do not hesitate to put your heart into the description.

Also, the rabbi will want to know whether the deceased has had a good relationship with the family, how he earned his livelihood, what was his educational background, the extent of his observance of Judaism, and his identification with the Jewish people. If there has been a divorce or a particular hatred, or difficulty, or frustration in his life, advise the rabbi of these facts. The discussion with the rabbi should be held by someone close to the deceased but who is not so emotionally exercised that he cannot impart the necessary information.

Rituals of a Fraternal Order

A secular ceremony is out of place during a religious service. However, a nonsectarian burial program of a fraternal order, which is designed solely to honor the deceased and is accomplished only by kind words from friends, may be requested. This ceremony should take place only if it was the sincere and express desire of the deceased, not merely implied by his membership in the order. The family should ascertain that there are no Christological elements in the service, such as the Lord's Prayer. Even though this prayer contains no specific mention of Christianity, its source is the Christian Bible, and it is out of place at a Jewish funeral. Care should be taken that there be no physical contact with the body and that this ceremony takes place before, not after, the religious service. It should be brief and unostentatious.

Members of the Jewish faith should attend to the recessional, performed by wheeling the casket from the chapel to the hearse.

ESCORTING THE DECEASED TO THE CEMETERY

The profound significance of this aspect of the funeral is generally not appreciated. The Sages considered preparing and escorting the deceased to his final resting place an extremely important symbol of respect. They refer to it as *gemillat chesed shel emet*, an act of genuine, selfless kindness. They insisted, as they did in few other instances, that a man should interrupt even the study of Torah to assist in removing the deceased from the home and conveying him to the cemetery. The Sages of the Talmud declared that one who sees a funeral procession and does not accompany the dead—at least briefly—deserves to be banished from the community.

Preparing the Body and Escorting It

Respect for the dead in Judaism means not only spoken honor but also physical assistance that reflects honor for the deceased.

1. When no other Jews are available to care for the deceased, the dead person is considered technically a *met mitzvah*, an "abandoned" corpse, which places the obligation for burial upon the first Jew who finds it. Even the High Priest in ancient times, who otherwise was not permitted to handle a strange corpse, was under full obligation to bury the deserted dead. Thus, when no other Jews are available, one must sacrifice even very important work, or the study of Torah and the performance of other religious duties, and certainly other pleasurable activities, to help prepare the body for burial and also to accompany the deceased to the grave and bury it. It makes no difference whether or not one is related to or acquainted with the departed.

2. When other Jews are available for preparing the body but one is not sure whether there will be a minyan for the average deceased, or a respectable representation for the scholar and community leader, there is no requirement to cease working or studying during the period of preparation. However, there *is* an obligation to escort the departed to the cemetery even if one must sacrifice time from work.

3. When Jews are available to prepare and accompany the body, and if one is not doing required and important work or study, one should escort the deceased to the cemetery—at least symbolically, by walking some six or eight feet behind the hearse in order to indicate respect for the deceased and sympathy for the mourners. It does not matter whether or not one knew the departed. There is an obligation of respect for all Jews.

4. When Jews are available for preparing and escorting the body, and one is involved in urgent business or studying Torah, it is sufficient to stand in respect as the procession passes.

5. When pressed for time, the priorities for attendance, in order of their importance are:

- Attend the service and then, briefly, follow the hearse.
- Be present at the cemetery during actual burial.
- Visit during the *shivah* mourning period.

Formal visitation in a chapel before the service is not a Jewish custom, as indicated previously, and should not be practiced. Gathering in a room at the chapel is perfectly acceptable.

6. For a child less than thirty days of age, attendants for the funeral procession are not required. A minimum of three people in attendance at the cemetery is sufficient.

May a Divorced Mate Attend Funeral Services?

There is no Jewish legal requirement that a divorced person attend a former mate's funeral service, but it is certainly not prohibited. For one contemplating divorce, obligations for mourning depend on whether there was agreement to proceed with the divorce. If only one mate contemplated divorce, and no legal action had been taken, there is an obligation to mourn. If both agreed to the divorce, even though no action was taken, there is no requirement to mourn according to Jewish law.

Should Bride and Groom Attend Funeral Services?

A bride and groom, during the first seven days after the wedding, are not required to attend any funerals at all, even for parents, if they are honeymooning away from home. If, however, they returned home or they are at work within the seven days, they should attend the funerals of any one of the seven close relatives but not go to the cemetery.

Should Mourners Attend Funeral Services?

Mourners, within the first three days after the interment, should not attend funerals except if it is for one of the seven closest relatives—father, mother, brother, sister, son, daughter or mate—or for one who has no Jewish attendants escorting him. Mourners should not, however, escort the dead to the cemetery.

After the third day, the mourner may attend the funeral for other members of the family (not just the seven relatives). He should accompany the hearse for six or eight feet and then return home; he should not go to the cemetery.

Accompanying the Non-Jewish Deceased

One may accompany a Gentile to the cemetery. If a person's absence would be noted and considered disrespectful, one should also attend the ceremony at the interment. While one should not, by any means, be discourteous in these matters, one may not participate in the Mass or other religious service held at the chapel. No intelligent Gentile would quarrel with, or even question, a friend's religious scruples. We are living in an age of understanding and tolerance, and people of diverse creeds should not sacrifice their religious conscience for fear of being misunderstood.

BURIAL IN THE EARTH

Jewish law is unequivocal, uncompromising: the dead must be buried in the earth. The soul rises to God, but the physical shelter, the chemical elements that clothed the soul—man's body—sink into the vast reservoir of nature. God's words to Adam are, "For dust thou art and unto dust shalt thou return" (Genesis 3:19). Later, the Bible crystallizes God's words into positive law, *ki kavor tikberennu*, "Thou shalt surely bury him" (Deuteronomy 21:23).

In our society there exist contradictory tendencies that reflect man's confusion in treating the dead. Shall he hasten the dispatch of the deceased or preserve the body and delay the inevitable decay? Some choose to embalm the deceased, deposit them in metal cases, encase the caskets in concrete vaults, or store them in mausoleums. They strive to preserve the remains, although they know quite well that eventually the forces of decomposition will triumph. Others wish to avoid even the normal, steady decay of nature, and choose to cremate the remains (see below) and reduce the deceased to ash—without pomp or ceremony. The ash is stored in an urn and shelved, left in the basement of the chapel, strewn over the ocean by plane, or buried in a small box.

The Torah absolutely and unqualifiedly insists on the natural decomposition of the remains. The wood of the casket, the cloth of the shrouds, the unembalmed body decompose in nature's own steady way. No artificiality—and no slowing or hurrying of this process—is permitted. The world goes on at its own pace. Those who die follow the flow of nature and the world.

CREMATION

Cremation is never permitted. The deceased must be interred, bodily, in the earth. It is forbidden—in any and every circumstance—to reduce the dead to ash in a crematorium. It is an offensive act, for it does violence to the spirit and letter of Jewish law, which never, in the long past, sanctioned the ancient pagan practice of burning on the pyre. The Jewish abhorrence of cremation was noted by Tacitus, the ancient historian, who remarked (about what appeared to be a distinguishing characteristic) that Jews buried, rather than burned, their dead.

1. Even if the deceased willed cremation, his wishes must be ignored in order to observe the will of our Father in Heaven. Biblical law takes precedence over the instructions of the deceased, when they conflict.

2. Cremated ashes are not buried in a Jewish cemetery. There is no burial of ashes, and no communal responsibility to care for the burned remains. The only exception is when the government decrees that the ashes be buried in the ground.

In other strange and unusual circumstances, a rabbi must be consulted. Rabbi Yechiel Weinberg, author of *Sridei Esh* and a great scholar of the mid-twentieth century, did rule, in certain special instances, that ashes could be buried—at a minimum of eight feet from the nearest grave. For such exceptional cases a portion of the Jewish cemetery should be dedicated and marked off.

Jewish law requires no mourning practices for the cremated. *Shivah* is not observed and Kaddish is not recited for them. Those who are willfully cremated are considered by tradition to have abandoned Jewish law and to have surrendered their rights to posthumous honor.

It need not be said that those who are murdered and burned to ash by enemies committing violent crimes; or those who die *al kiddush ha-Shem,* for the sanctity of God's name, such as those souls cremated in the Holocaust; or those who are burned to death in a fire or other accident must receive sensitive and respectful burial, no matter the condition of their remains. I have officiated at the interment of the ashes of a Jewish chaplain, killed in a Vietnam plane crash, who was buried by a Hasidic burial society in Jerusalem.

MAUSOLEUMS AND CONCRETE VAULTS

The specific Biblical mandate of interment refers to burial in the earth. This means that:

1. A mausoleum is permissible only if the deceased is buried *in the earth itself,* not above it, and the mausoleum is built around the plot of earth. This was frequently done for scholars, communal leaders, those who have contributed heavily to charity, and people of renown.

2. However, to have the deceased buried above the ground, not surrounded by earth, within the mausoleum, is unquestionably prohibited. The Bible repeats its injunction: *kavor tikberennu,* "thou shalt surely bury," to emphasize that it is not a legal burial if the casket is left above the earth.

3. If the deceased willed burial in a mausoleum, one should not follow his will in such a case, even though in most instances his will is ironclad and is obligatory upon the mourners.

4. In certain parts of the country the earth is unstable and shifting, and government authorities require caskets to

be enclosed in concrete vaults. In such cases, vaults are acceptable. In other instances, where the motive is solely to preserve the remains, it is preferable not to use the vault. Clearly, the concrete vault is not in the spirit of the tradition and should be avoided if possible. However, theoretically it is permitted.

BURIAL OF LIMBS

The blood and limbs of an individual are considered by Jewish law to be part of the human being. As such, they require burial. If the deceased was found with severed limbs, or with bloodstained clothes, both the limbs and clothes must be buried with him.

If limbs were amputated during one's lifetime, they require burial in the person's future gravesite. If he does not own a plot as yet, or if he is squeamish in this regard, they should be buried in a separate plot, preferably near the graves of members of his family. The limbs are cleansed and placed in the earth. No observance of mourning is necessary.

THE BURIAL SERVICE

An attitude of somberness, regret, and hesitation prevails during the procession of the casket from the hearse to the grave, and then into the earth. This moment should be viewed as a sacred occasion, which requires our personal participation in the final honoring of the deceased. Both of these aspects, the personal duty to give honor and the hesitation to perform that which is necessary, govern the program and style of the processional.

Pallbearers

Pallbearers from among family or friends should carry the casket and deposit it in the grave. This custom dates back to the Bible when Jacob's children carried him to his last resting place. In ancient times the body was carried on the shoulders. Regardless of whether carried on shoulders or by hand, or wheeled on a special cemetery device, this should be considered a signal honor and a symbol of personal tribute for those who participate.

There are several customs in selecting pallbearers, any one of which is acceptable in Jewish law. One is that the primary carriers should be the children and brothers of the deceased. Some say that friends or other relatives should do this, but not the immediate family. Most hold that women and children should not carry such a heavy burden, and that is most often correct. It would indeed seem more advisable for others to carry the casket rather than the immediate family, for fear of their being overcome with grief. If there is no such fear, children or brothers may participate if they so desire. In any case, if there are no others, the immediate family must perform this task.

Those who handle the casket must be of the Jewish faith. It is after all a sacred religious honor. In instances of very close Gentile friends, or when there are not enough Jewish pallbearers, everyone can help. It is a violation of the Jewish spirit to consign the deceased to anonymous gravediggers, especially when their faith is not known and their personal behavior and moral standards are not known to the family. Handling the casket is not merely a physical activity that requires brawn, but a personal one, which demands love and respect.

Personal enemies may help carry the casket; their efforts should not be considered hypocrisy but a form of regret. Surely the family should be consulted, but they should be encouraged to use sympathetic judgment and compassionate concern.

In light of the requirement of pallbearers, it is necessary to tell the funeral director or the driver of the family car *not* to follow their customary practice of holding the family limousines far behind the hearse so that the casket can be removed and carried to the grave by cemetery gravediggers. Some cemetery officials encourage this because of the possible insurance hazard in case of accident while family members are carrying the casket. Proper cemetery insurance coverage, however, commonly takes into consideration the traditions of the Jewish people on a Jewish cemetery.

The Processional

The spirit of the processional is governed not only by the desirability of personal participation and accompaniment of the deceased, but also by hesitation and unwillingness to remove the presence of the dead. For this reason the procession pauses briefly several times before it reaches the gravesite, except on festive days when the spirit of communal joy serves to modify the expression of grief at funerals.

There are several customs regarding the number of pauses made in order to indicate our unwillingness to end the service, and when and for whom they should *not* be made. One custom establishes seven stops, another three stops, and another maintains that the procession should stop every six or eight feet. Seven pauses are customary in most communities.

The Midrash cites a strange, but insightful, reason for halting seven times. Death confronts men with the need to reassess their own existence and ponder the "big" questions of life: What is the use of all our strivings? Does life have a deeper meaning? Does man, after all, come to naught? These are the great issues that disturb Ecclesiastes as he seeks to understand the true meaning of life. "Vanity of vanities," said Ecclesiastes, "vanity of vanities, all is vanity" (1:2). Vanity, in this context, signifies the vapor (*hevel*) that appears when one exhales on a cold day. It has no substance and disappears into "thin air."

Is life only vapor? The Sages noted that "vanity" in this oft-quoted verse is said three times in the singular and twice in the plural, which adds up to seven times. Each of these "vanities" is symbolized by a pause, as one carries the casket to the grave. With each stop, the fact of ultimate death teaches us to avoid the life of vanity, to be creative and kind, to repent of evil, to walk in the path of goodness.

All those in the funeral party should follow the casket, not walk before it. Usually, only the rabbi precedes the procession—to indicate where and when to pause.

During the procession, the very beautiful and moving Psalm 91 is recited (see Appendix One). This psalm has been ascribed by Bible commentators to Moses, or a poet under his influence. It is said to have been recited at the building of the Tabernacle in the desert. Others ascribe it to a dialogue held between David and Solomon, or recited by them, at the dedication of Jerusalem and the Temple. It is referred to as the "Song of the Spirit," guarding man against the evil that surrounds him. It is an expression of confidence that God will watch over His people, and that tragedy will not once again befall them, because they trust in the Lord.

> For He will give His angels charge over thee,
> To keep thee in all thy ways.

It concludes with a prayer for the living:

> With long life will I satisfy him,
> And make him to behold My salvation.

Tzidduk Ha'din

The Tzidduk ha-Din, or Justification of the Divine Decree, is a magnificent and moving prayer recited at the gravesite immediately before, or immediately after, the body is interred (depending on local Jewish custom), when the reality of the grave confronts the mourners (see Appendix One).

The prayer has three major themes:

1. God ordained this dreadful end, and His decree is justified. God gives to each his due, in accordance with reasons He alone knows. Although we may not understand His ways, we know that there can be no imperfection in Almighty God.

2. We pray that God be merciful to the survivors. Although He has taken the life of this dear person, may He, in His great mercy, spare the lives of the remainder of His flock and stay the hand of death. Even at this most personal moment of grief, the Jew must concern himself with unselfish thoughts and pray for all of humanity.

3. God's decree must be accepted. To the very end we remember that as God in His kindness gave us this dear person and brought him into life, He is the same just God when He beckons that soul to return to Him. "The Lord has given and the Lord has taken." We thank the Lord for the years that were given to us. "Blessed be the name of the Lord."

This prayer is not recited for children who expire before they are thirty days old. It also is not recited if the burial occurs at night; if the funeral is held on one of the major festivals such as Pesach, Shavuot, Sukkot, or Shemini Atzeret; on other holidays such as Hanukkah, Purim, Rosh Chodesh; on all afternoons preceding the holidays and the Sabbath; or on the days immediately following the three major festivals. This would conflict with the spirit of joy that should obtain at these times.

INTERMENT

❧

The sacred principle of the Jewish burial law that establishes that the deceased be buried in the earth requires lowering the casket to the bottom of the grave. Leaving the casket at ground level during the service, in the company of the entourage, and then, without completing the interment, to turn one's back on the unburied casket and return home, is a distinct affront to the dead. If the service is graveside, the eulogy customarily is made before lowering the casket.

The minimum dimensions of the grave must provide, at least, that the opening be as wide and as long as the casket, and at least ten *tefachim*, or forty inches deep.

The use of a mechanical device to lower the casket into the

grave is not contrary to Jewish law. It is, however, a slow process, and surely not as quick as lowering by hand. Its use, therefore, is a matter of family preference. A Jewish friend or relative should release the lever to begin the operation of the mechanism.

The grave must be filled at this time. At the very minimum, the casket must be fully covered with earth to take on the form of the grave. After that, the laborers may assist in filling the grave if the others cannot perform this deed.

Some follow the practice of covering the open grave with a green, plastic, grass mat, but do not fill it with earth. This is *not* the traditional Jewish way. Indeed, it is a signal honor and duty to help in shoveling the earth to cover the casket. This duty is usually reserved for the learned in attendance, for the community leaders who are present, and for the closest relatives and dearest friends. It is the personal "good-bye" of beloved neighbors.

That this duty is a heartbreaking one is all too evident. But this spells the finality of death, and it must be faced and accepted as such. Psychologically, the heart-rending thud of earth on the casket is enormously beneficial. In proclaiming finality, it helps the mourner to overcome the illusion that his relative still lives; it answers his denial that death has indeed claimed its victim; it quiets his lingering doubt that this may be only a bad dream. The earth-filling process dispels such illusions and starts the mourner on the way to recovery and reconciliation. To attempt to spare him this unpleasantness merely retards the psychological healing process.

Is there a specific method of filling? The earth originally dug out should be replaced. Custom has it that the shovel should not pass from hand to hand, but each person should replace it in the earth. This is a silent, symbolic gesture expressing the prayer that the tragedy of death be not "contagious," and that the remainder of family and friends may live long and peaceful lives. The law does not stipulate how many shovelfuls should be used. Some customarily use the back of the shovel to indicate a difference from its use for other purposes.

Please remember: do not refer to "earth" as "dirt." We do not shovel dirt onto our beloved. We place him into the warm embrace of mother earth, from whence, the Torah says, we were all created.

BURIAL KADDISH

The Burial Kaddish (see Appendix One) is different from the other forms of Kaddish recited in the synagogue. (The Mourner's Kaddish is considered in detail in a later chapter of this book.) It takes the form of a prayer, and not a formal doxology. It is, therefore, not circumscribed by all of the regulations regarding the Kaddish of the synagogue service. This is why it may be recited directly following burial, whereas the synagogue Kaddish is recited only after a portion from the Psalms or Torah is read.

The Burial Kaddish is a prayer affirming that God, in His good time, will create the world anew, and that the deceased will be raised up to everlasting life. With the advent of the new world, the Temple, the Beit ha-Mikdash, will be reestablished, and the true worship of the One God will replace the idols of the masses. The Burial Kaddish bespeaks the hope that there is a future for the deceased, and it gives new faith to the mourners, even as its recitation at the moment of interment evokes new tears.

The Burial Kaddish is recited after the grave is filled with earth. In cases of emergency, such as excessive grief at the time of great tragedy, of if the hour is late and the Sabbath or a holy day is approaching, it is permissible to say the Kaddish after the casket is fully covered with a layer of earth, without waiting for the grave to be completely filled.

The Burial Kaddish is omitted on festivals and during "joyous celebrations" (which are defined later) when Tachanun is not recited in the synagogue. At such times, Psalm 16 is recited and the traditional Mourner's Kaddish is said. The Mourner's Kaddish replaces the special Burial Kaddish if no mourners are present. Some rabbis recite it at every graveside service. Kaddish is not recited at all when the grave cannot be filled in the presence of a minyan.

Recessional from the Gravesite

The purpose of the recessional is to redirect our sympathies and concerns from the deceased to the mourners. It marks the transition from *aninut* to *avelut*, the new state of mourning that now commences. The theme changes from honoring of the dead to comforting the survivors. To act out this transition, those present form two lines facing one another. As the mourners solemnly pass between them away from the site of their bereavement, those present recite words of comfort: *Ha-Makom yenachem etchem betokh she'ar avelei Tziyyon vi-Yerushalayim,* "May the Lord comfort you among the other mourners of Zion and Jerusalem." If no mourners are present, the parallel lines are dispensed with, as words of comfort are obviously out of place. A beautiful Israeli custom has the mourners place a stone on the covered grave and ask forgiveness for any injustice they may have committed against the deceased.

Washing Hands

After the funeral, those in attendance wash their hands. This is symbolic of the ancient custom of purification, performed after contact with the dead. It emphasizes the Jew's constant concern with life, its value and dignity, rather than overzealous attention to, and worship of, the dead. The washing is done upon leaving the cemetery or before entering the home. It is performed with a cup of water poured alternately on both hands. As we do with the shovel at the filling of the grave, the cup is not passed from hand to hand.

PLOT AND GRAVE

It is an ancient Jewish custom to purchase a gravesite during one's lifetime and to own it outright prior to burial. The Bible states explicitly that Abraham bought a grave for Sarah. Likewise, Joseph was buried in the family plot that his father Jacob had acquired in the city of Shechem.

Purchasing a Plot

The purchase of a cemetery plot may be made through a burial society of a fraternal or religious organization, through one's synagogue, or directly from the cemetery owners. It must be located among other Jewish graves, or on grounds bought by a Jewish organization for use as a Jewish cemetery. This has been the custom through the centuries. On first settling in a new country or a new city, the community purchased land for a synagogue, a school, and also a cemetery.

The following are criteria for determining whether a particular cemetery is a proper burial place for Jews:

1. The purchase contract should stipulate that the area of the plot is designed exclusively for Jews.

2. Burial rights must be permanent. The cemetery corporation should not be permitted to exercise any authority with regard to the removal of the remains from any grave.

3. All facilities for Jew and non-Jew must be absolutely separate—with separate entrance gates and with each section fenced completely.

The Family Plot

A very frequently asked question is where exactly among the family plots, should the deceased be buried.

1. The basic grave formation in most cemeteries is arranged according to families. There has been a custom in later centuries, observed by many memorial societies, of burying men and women in separate sections. Neither custom is obligatory. One should make inquiry regarding this procedure before one joins the organization, in order to avoid problems at a moment of crisis, when it is too late to make any change.

In many cemeteries it is standard procedure—and a religiously appropriate custom—not to bury a woman next to any man other than her husband. This is of concern especially when contemplating erection of a double monument.

Therefore, the graves alternate—husband, wife, wife, husband, husband, wife, etc.

2. If man and wife were separated in marriage, or even divorced and not remarried, they may nevertheless be buried alongside one another. If one of the partners, however, stipulated that he or she be buried separately, the request must be followed.

3. One who has never been married should be buried alongside his or her parents. If it does not violate cemetery regulations, a mother may be buried next to her unmarried son.

4. Married Children. It is customary, though by no means mandatory, that the wife is buried with the husband's family. When no graves are available, they should be buried elsewhere in the same cemetery. If they live far from the parental grave, or if there are other personal advantages to selecting another cemetery, they may establish their own family plot.

5. If, by being buried in a family plot, the departed will be buried alongside a lifelong enemy, he should be buried elsewhere in the family plot. If this enemy died more than a year before, this is not necessary, and should be left to the discretion of relatives and friends.

6. Second marriages. If a preference for burial location was expressly made, it must be honored. If this preference was not made expressly, but was implied, in that he or she clearly and undoubtedly lived better with one mate than the other, then he or she should be buried with the more beloved mate.

If no preference is known, then:

- If there are children from the marriage of only one of the mates, whichever it is, he or she is to be buried at that mate's family plot or at the discretion of those children.
- If there are children from both mates, or no children from either mate, some customs suggest burial with the first mate.

7. Intermarriages. If the Jewish partner remained Jewish he or she is entitled to full burial in a Jewish cemetery.

The unconverted Gentile partner, however, may not be buried in the Jewish cemetery. Even if the Gentile male partner had been circumcised, but for purposes other than conversion, he is considered non-Jewish, and may not be buried in a Jewish cemetery.

Children of a Jewish mother may be buried in the Jewish cemetery, including sons who have not been circumcised.

Children of a Gentile mother, who themselves have not been converted, may not be buried in a Jewish cemetery, even if they were educated in a Jewish school. This includes sons who have been circumcised but without intent to convert.

Religious converts are buried as full Jews, in the plot of the Jewish mate, or in a newly established family plot. This situation is not considered an intermarriage.

8. Suicides. Traditionally, those who commit the stark offense against God and man of taking their own lives willfully, and in full sanity, are buried separately near the cemetery gate, or at least eight feet from other Jewish dead. Chapter 6 discusses the subject of suicides fully.

9. Observant and ethical Jews should not be buried alongside confirmed sinners, such as those who publicly and purposefully blaspheme God. Wherever it is possible, this principle should be adhered to, and other arrangements should be made.

10. Burial in Israel. The burial of Jewish deceased in the Holy Land, especially those who ardently loved the land, were religiously observant, or contributed to the support of Israel, is considered an act of pious devotion, even though visitations to the grave may be rare or not at all possible.

The Bible records that Joseph made the special request to be buried not in the land where he reigned as vice-regent, but in the land of his forefathers, the Holy Land. The rabbis consider burial in Israel equal to being buried directly under the altar of the Temple. Reinterment is permissible for such purposes. For making the proper arrangements, the mourners should consult the rabbi, the funeral director, or a rabbinic organization.

11. Burial land bought in a cemetery, even though it was officially designated for a specific person, may be resold.

DISINTERMENT

The removal and opening of a buried casket is generally prohibited in Jewish law. The abhorrent sight of the decomposing flesh is considered to bring disgrace to the deceased. It is revolting and depressing for the living to see the end of man as a mere rotting skeleton. The basis of the law is twofold: first, that disinterment is an indignity to the deceased and a disturbance of his peace; second, that it conveys precisely the wrong message to the survivor. The law is very strong in its condemnation of those who needlessly open graves after burial. Disinterment may never be undertaken without first consulting an authority in Jewish law, not funeral directors or cemetery managers. Most cemeteries or societies require written approval of a rabbi.

The following are cases that might warrant such consultation:

1. If important valuables have fallen into the earth that was used to fill in the grave.

2. If a large sum of money was placed in the casket, or if the deceased was wearing very expensive jewelry that somehow was not removed before burial, especially if the survivors are indigent, or creditors will have to sustain great losses because of lack of funds.

3. If the remains were not prepared according to religious law, disinterment may be possible if this was realized *shortly* after burial.

4. If the body was not identified accurately before burial, thus preventing the wife's remarriage for fear that her husband yet lives.

If there is only slight suspicion that any of these circumstances have occurred *after* the casket has been placed in the grave but *before* the grave has been filled, it is permissible to open it without further consultation.

REINTERMENT

☙

The deceased may not be moved from one grave to another, even if the second gravesite is a more respectable one. By holding up the lifeless corpse, once the glory of creation, now it its unsightly, decomposed state, we show disrespect to God, who made Man in his image. The rabbis of the Talmud, therefore, frown upon reinterment. The medieval sages add to this by noting that after death man stands in judgment before God, and reinterment disturbs that state of judgment. Also, they add, the removal of the remains to another site is a "mocking of the dead," and a slight to the other dead who have passed on and are now reposing in the same cemetery.

Reinterment may be permitted, however, after consultation with a rabbi, in the following instances:

1. The removal of the remains from an individual plot to a family plot where other immediate members of the family are already buried. This may be done even if the deceased did not know of this plot.

2. The deceased was not buried in his own gravesite. For example, if he mistakenly was placed in someone else's grave or placed in a grave that was not rightfully his; if part of the grave is on public land; or if he was placed in a grave with the owner's permission, but it was never fully paid for.

3. If he is interred in a non-Jewish cemetery, even though he owned the plot himself.

4. If the present gravesite is not guarded against destruction by vandals.

5. If the cemetery may be damaged by water or other natural phenomena.

6. If the government appropriates the property for highways or other communal needs.

7. If the deceased is to be reinterred in Israel.

8. If the grave was considered temporary and this was expressly stipulated when the deceased was interred.

9. If it was discovered that the deceased expressly desired

to be buried elsewhere, even though there was no stipulation that he be moved after burial.

10. War dead buried in national cemeteries may be reinterred in Jewish cemeteries at home.

The above listed exemptions are only guidelines. A decision regarding reinterment was considered to be of such a serious nature that it was not made even by a duly ordained rabbi without first consulting other rabbis. There are many specific questions to be considered, such as the time that has elapsed since death, the state of the remains, the state of the casket. These, and a multitude of other details, require competent, rabbinic authority to decide.

The vacated grave, following reinterment, may be given to the indigent dead or to a relative, without remuneration, although the value of the monument after the engraving has been obliterated is questionable, if it has any value at all by present-day standards. The gravesite may not be sold, nor any material benefit derived from it. The monument may be moved along with the body.

Ritual of Reinterment

The exhumed remains, no matter what the state of decomposition, must be guarded and respected just as on the day of death. The remains are not to be handled.

These are the prescribed mourning laws for the day of reinterment:

1. Mourners must rend their clothing. See above for the details of this law.

2. Full mourning, as during *shivah*, is observed for only one day, the day on which reinterment takes place, from morning only until nightfall, even if the reinterment was not completed by nightfall. No further mourning needs to be observed after this time. Relatives who know of the reinterment and the date on which it is to occur must observe these mourning laws on that one day. If they are made aware of the rein-

terment after that date they are not required to observe any of the mourning laws.

3. A child should not participate physically in the reinterment of his parents.

4. All foods, including meat and wine, may be eaten on that day.

5. There should be no words of grief; only praise for the deceased.

6. The interment should not take place on the holidays, of course, and also on the intermediate days of Pesach or Sukkot.

7. The reinterment should be started in the morning or early afternoon. If it begins too close to nightfall there will be no time for the mourning observances.

8. Three handbreadths of earth, approximately twelve inches, from the original gravesite must be reinterred with the body, if the body was originally buried without an enclosing casket.

CEMETERY ETIQUETTE

The subject of proper conduct at the cemetery is generally neglected. The consequence of this neglect is, frequently, gross impropriety and a superabundance of superstition. There are two basic principles that can serve as a guide to correct Jewish etiquette at a cemetery. These are *kalut rosh* (levity) and *lo'eg larash* (making a mockery).

Kalut Rosh

The holiness of the cemetery is directly equivalent to the holiness of the sanctuary. Our actions within its confines must be consonant with this high degree of holiness. Also, because the graves in the cemetery are places from which we may derive no benefit at all, we are restricted from lounging in the area. *Kalut rosh* is a spirit of levity and undignified behavior. Under the category of the prohibition of *kalut rosh*, the following points should be observed, not only at the gravesite, but also within the boundaries of the entire cemetery.

1. Eating and drinking should not be indulged in at the cemetery. This holds true for unveilings as well. The frequent, but unfortunate, frivolity that marks such occasions should certainly be discouraged. It is a violation of every code of honor.

2. Dress should be proper to the occasion and the place. One should not dress to impress relatives who attend. When one visits the cemetery or the grave of a deceased, it is certainly not the time for scant or frivolous-looking dress, athletic attire, or work clothes.

3. One may not step on, or sit on, the gravestone, which directly covers a grave. One may, however, sit on seats near the graves or on roadside railings and gates.

4. Flowers that, perchance, have bloomed on the grave itself may not be picked for use at home. Naturally, trimming all growths on the gravestone is commendable.

Lo'eg Larash

Indulging in pleasurable activities, even if they are religious observances in which the deceased or any of the other occupants of the cemetery once enjoyed participating but now cannot, represents a slighting of the dead. Thus:

1. One should not study Torah, recite the Psalms, or conduct formal, daily services within approximately six feet of a grave.

2. One should not carry *tefillin* or a Torah with him into the cemetery.

MEMORIAL GIFTS

Those who wish to honor the dead or their survivors should do so in a worthy manner. It is not in keeping with the traditional spirit for a memorial gift to be flowers. It is more significant and more useful to contribute a sacred article for synagogue or school use. This might include Bibles, prayer books, scholarly works, Torahs, or Torah ornaments. The synagogue or school usually will acknowledge these immediately so that the mourners will be notified of the gift during *shivah*.

While making a contribution is not mandatory, a donation to charity at the time of the funeral is an ancient Jewish custom. The custom has three roots in our tradition:

1. The Biblical verse, "Charity saves one from death" (Proverbs 10:2), is meant to be taken not only literally, but in the spiritual sense, that one who is evil is not considered to be truly alive. Charity saves from spiritual death. The association of charity and death here is a direct one.

2. Charity symbolizes the unity of all Israel. A contribution of time and effort and substance for the good of the community is a cherished expression of togetherness. At the funeral it symbolizes the anguish felt in common by all Jews for the family of the deceased.

3. The mystical Jewish tradition, embodied in *Pirkei de-Rabbi Eliezer*, says that because of charity the dead will be resurrected in the world to come.

It is in the spirit of dignity, and in keeping with Jewish tradition, to make such contributions as memorials to the dead, rather than to bring outright gifts to the mourners. Naturally, if the deceased felt close to a specific charity, such as a medical research program, it might be wise to contribute to that fund. The memorial gift may be selected by the giver or left to the discretion of the mourners.

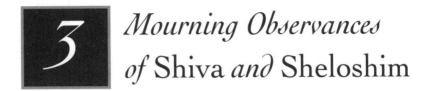

3 *Mourning Observances of* Shiva *and* Sheloshim

JUDAISM, WITH ITS LONG history of dealing with the soul of man, its intimate knowledge of man's strengths and foibles, his grandeur and his weakness, has wisely devised graduated periods during which the mourner may express his grief and release with planned regularity the built-up tensions caused by bereavement. The Jewish religion provides an exquisitely structured approach to mourning.

The insight of the Bible, together with the accumulated religious experience of centuries, has taught the Jew how best to manage his grief. It was only with the rise of modern psychology, with its scientific tools and controlled experimentation, that the value of this grief structure has come to be recognized.

Joshua Loth Liebman, in his book *Peace of Mind*, maintains: "The discoveries of psychiatry—of how essential it is to express, rather than to repress grief, to talk about one's loss with friends and companions, to move step by step from inactivity to activity again—remind us that the ancient teachers of Judaism often had intuitive wisdom about human nature and its needs which our more sophisticated and liberal age has forgotten. Traditional Judaism, as a matter of fact, had the wisdom to devise almost all of the procedures for health-minded grief which the contemporary psychologist counsels, although Judaism naturally did not possess the tools for scientific experiment and systematic study." The Jewish tradition has thus designed a gradual release from grief, and has instituted five successive periods of mourning, each with its own laws governing the expression of grief and the process of return to the normal affairs of society. It fits so closely the normal cycle of bereavement that some have maintained that the laws of mourning are descriptive rather than prescriptive.

THE FIVE STAGES OF MOURNING

The first period is that between death and burial (*aninut*), during which time despair is most intense. At this time, not only the social amenities, but also major positive religious requirements were cancelled in recognition of the mourner's troubled mind.

The second stage consists of the first three days following burial, days devoted to weeping and lamentation. During this time, the mourner does not even respond to greetings and remains in his home (except under certain special circumstances). It is a time when even visiting the mourner is usually discouraged—it is simply too early to comfort the mourners when the wound is so fresh.

Third is the period of *shivah*, the seven days following burial. (This longer period includes the first three days.) During this time, the mourner emerges from the stage of intense grief to a new state of mind, in which he is prepared to talk about his loss and to accept comfort from friends and neighbors. The world now enlarges for the mourner. While he remains within the house, expressing his grief through the observances of *avelut*—wearing the rent garment, sitting on the low stool, wearing slippers, refraining from grooming and shaving, reciting the Kaddish—his acquaintances come to his home to express sympathy in his distress. The inner freezing that came with the death of his relative now begins to thaw. The isolation from the world of people and the retreat inward now relaxes somewhat, and normalcy begins to return.

Fourth is the stage of *sheloshim*, the thirty days following burial (which includes the *shivah*). The mourner is encouraged to leave the house after *shivah* and to rejoin society slowly, always recognizing that enough time has not yet elapsed to assume full, normal social relations. The torn clothing may still be worn for deceased parents, and haircutting for male mourners is still generally prohibited.

The fifth and last stage is the twelve-month period (which includes the *sheloshim*) during which things return to normal and business once again becomes routine, but the mourner's inner feelings are still wounded by the rupture of his relationship with a parent. The pursuit of entertainment and amusement is curtailed. At the close of this last stage, the bereaved is not expected to continue his mourning, except for brief moments when Yizkor or yahrzeit is observed. In fact, our tradition chides a person for mourning more than the prescribed period.

In this magnificently conceived graduated process of mourning, an ancient faith raises up the mourner from the abyss of despair to the undulating hills and valleys of normal daily life.

THE MOURNER AND THE MOURNED

All good-hearted people mourn those who have died. They are sad, regretful, and feel bereaved. But *halakhah* prescribes specific norms and observances only for those relatives stipulated in the Torah and Talmud.

Who Is a Mourner?

Jewish law formally considers the bereaved to be those who have lost any one of the seven close relatives listed in Leviticus (21:1–3): father; mother; wife or husband; son; daughter;

brother or sister (or half-brother and half-sister, married or unmarried). The Bible originally listed these relationships in terms of the ritual impurity of the *Kohen* or Priest: the Priest who ordinarily was to have no contact with the dead, was, however, instructed even to defile himself in order to bury these relatives. The oral tradition considered that the laws of mourning apply to these same relations as well. (The idea of priestly defilement is discussed in a special chapter below.)

Bride and Groom

There are a number of special rules that apply to the newly married:

1. During the first seven full days following the wedding, bride and groom are not at all obligated to observe the laws of mourning, even for a parent. They should attend the funeral service but not go to the cemetery, following the decision of the great fourteenth-century decisor, the Maharil. Immediately following the seven days of the formal wedding celebration they should begin observing *shivah* and *sheloshim*.

2. Now, the law distinguishes between a case where the death occurred *before* the beginning of the seven days of rejoicing and one where the death occurred in the midst of this week. In the former case, the bride or groom begins the complete period of *shivah* and *sheloshim* immediately after the week of rejoicing is over. In the latter case, he or she rejoins the rest of the family, which is observing *shivah*, and finishes the *shivah* observance together with them. At the marriage of a widow and widower, the couple has a formal rejoicing period of three days after marriage, rather than seven.

3. If a holiday, which normally nullifies the entire mourning period of *shivah*, occurs during the week of rejoicing that is coextensive with *shivah*, the bride or groom must, nonetheless, fulfill the *shivah* after the holiday. Thus, if the wedding occurred on Saturday night and the death of a parent occurred on Sunday, the holiday, which falls during that week, nullifies the *shivah* period only for those who have started to observe the mourning period. But the bride or groom, be-

cause she or he is not obligated, and did not begin to mourn formally, must observe the complete *shivah* after the conclusion of the holiday.

4. Bride and groom do not rend their clothing until after the week of rejoicing. They do, however, recite the blessing Barukh Dayyan ha-Emet (True Judge) with the other mourners at the funeral service as this is an expression of immediate and spontaneous grief, and cannot be meaningfully delayed.

5. During their honeymoon week, bride and groom technically are not considered mourners. By law, therefore, they are not required to be visited and consoled in the manner of others observing *shivah*.

6. Bride and groom need not accompany a deceased parent to the cemetery, but, by all means, should follow the hearse from the home or funeral parlor for several blocks, so as to give honor to the parent.

7. The groom is obligated to don *tefillin* even on the day after death, which is not obligatory upon other mourners, because he is legally, though not emotionally, considered to be in a state of rejoicing rather than mourning.

8. In the event of the death of a parent of the bride or groom *prior* to the marriage ceremony, or after the ceremony but prior to the *consummation* of the marriage, a qualified rabbinic authority should be consulted.

All the foregoing cases concern a bride and groom during their formal seven-day honeymoon period, if they have set aside these days exclusively for each other. If, however, they have returned to work or school prior to the death, even though it is during the week of rejoicing, they must mourn in the usual manner.

Divorced Mate

A divorced mate need not observe any of the mourning laws and need not attend the funeral. If one of the mates contemplated divorce but took no legal action, he or she is fully obligated to mourn. If both agreed in principle to the divorce, and definitely determined to proceed with it, although no legal action was officially started, there is no requirement to mourn.

Converts to Judaism

A convert to Judaism has no obligation to mourn his non-Jewish parents in the prescribed Jewish manner. While it is expected that the convert will show utmost respect for his parents, he is, nonetheless, considered detached from them religiously. The grief that the convert expresses, although technically not required by Jewish law, should possess a markedly Jewish character. Please see "Discretionary Mourners" in Chapter Six for more information.

Adopted Relatives

There are few more angelic acts than to adopt a child, taking on the pains and bearing the costs of raising him for a lifetime. The task of child rearing involves so much agony, worry, devotion, and physical energy, that people who adopt must rank among the true philanthropists of any age. One such adoption, that of the Biblical Esther by Mordecai, literally saved the Jews from extinction and stimulated them to receive the Torah all over again, as at Mt. Sinai—an adoption that replicated the results of God's revelation!

Yet there is no strictly halakhic requirement to mourn for adoptive parents and stepparents, adopted brothers and sisters, or adoptive children and stepchildren, because there is not a natural familial bond that triggers *avelut*. Here, as we noted in other sections on nonmandatory mourning, the *halakhah* could not make an obligation to observe mourning practices based on sentiment. Further, who can determine universal sentiment in such complex human relations as adoption? Jewish law makes its determination in characteristically legal fashion and deals with facts of relationship rather than feelings of relationship. That is how Judaism survived—through law, not feelings.

But sentiment is of primary importance to all human beings. How shall we address that? In the case of adoptions, while there is no legal obligation to mourn, there should indeed be "sympathetic mourning," namely, abstaining from public rejoicing and such, in order to demonstrate a full measure of sorrow. The discretionary mourner should follow the suggestions for elective mourning procedures in the section on discretionary mourning in Chapter Six.

Minors

Minors have no obligation to observe the laws of mourning. Thus, a boy under the age of thirteen and a girl under the age of twelve need not "sit" *shivah* or follow the other observances. However, their clothes should be rent for them, and they should be encouraged—in congruity with their intelligence, sensitivities, sensibilities, and maturity—to restrict their daily activities. This procedure should be followed especially in the case of more mature children, although they still are minors.

SHIVAH

A time must be set aside for the expression of grief for the loss of a close relative. This is indicated in the Torah, which mentions *shivah* frequently in the early historical narratives. For example, the *Kohen Gadol*, the High Priest, Aaron, is stunned by the sudden death of his two sons at the apex of their careers. When Moses asks why the sacrificial offering was not eaten on the day of their deaths, Aaron replies: "There have befallen me such things as these, and had I eaten the offering, would it have been pleasing in the eyes of the Lord?" (Leviticus 10:19). Aaron's explanation is that the time of mourning is not an occasion for feasting before the Lord; it is, specifically, for the expression of grief.

So too, Amos refers to a special time for mourning. He prophesies the disastrous consequences of injustice and immorality, and declares: "And I will turn your feasts into mourning, and all your songs into lamentations; and I will bring sackcloth upon all loins, and baldness upon every head; and I will make it as the mourning for an only son; and the end thereof as a bitter day" (Amos 8:10). The day of grieving is *yom mar*, a "bitter day."

The Sages noted that it was the practice in ancient times, even prior to the revelation at Mount Sinai, to mourn heavily, not only for one day but for one week—*shivah*. Thus, Joseph was an *avel* (mourner) for seven days following the passing of his father, the patriarch Jacob.

After the revelation, Moses established the seven days of mourning by special decree, declaring, as formal doctrine, that which had been practiced only as custom. He enacted, the Sages asserted, the seven days of mourning as he enacted the Biblical seven days of rejoicing after a wedding. The connection between the two opposites is hinted at in the verse from Amos: "And I will turn your feasts into mourning." Just as feasts were observed for seven days, so mourning was to last for one week.

Thus, from the earliest moments of recorded Jewish history, the Jewish people have observed *shivah* for deceased relatives as "days of bitterness." The occasional disregard of *shivah* in some quarters of the Jewish community, or the casual decision in other quarters to observe an arbitrary number of days of mourning to suit one's own needs or to coincide with a weekend, amount, in fact, to a noxious disregard of generations of sacred observance.

WHEN DOES *SHIVAH* BEGIN?

Avelut, the process of mourning, begins immediately after the deceased is interred and the casket is completely covered with earth. The mourners walk between parallel lines of friends and relatives and are formally comforted by them. They then proceed directly to the home where *shivah* is to be observed. There, the observances commence as soon as the mourners demonstrate formal acceptance of mourning by removing their shoes and sitting on a low bench or stool.

Mourners who do not accompany the deceased to the cemetery begin their *avelut* at the approximate time of burial or, at the very latest, when the other mourners have returned from the cemetery.

There are exceptional circumstances in regard to the beginning of *shivah*.

Burial at Twilight

Twilight is neither day nor night, or perhaps it is both day and night. The law, however, must be clear.

1. When burial occurs late in the day, provided it takes place before nightfall (i.e., even during the approximately twenty minutes between sunset and dark, the legal duration of *bein ha-shemashot*, or twilight), mourning should begin at the cemetery, a short distance from the grave itself. The mourners remove their shoes and then seat themselves on a stone or railing. Thus, while it may already be night when they arrive at the home where *shivah* will be observed, the law considers that mourning was formally begun during daylight at the cemetery. That day is, therefore, counted as the first of the seven days of *shivah*. The mourners, however, should be informed that mourning technically began at the cemetery. (This is possible only if the mourner has not yet prayed the evening Ma'ariv service. If he has already prayed the service, *shivah* begins the next day.)

2. So, too, if one is notified of the burial of a relative at twilight, while on the road or in another public place, one should make formal mental note of the fact that mourning has begun. One is then permitted to count that day as the first of *shivah*, even though the mourner is not able to remove his shoes and sit on the low bench—the formal, outward, recognition of *shivah*.

Burial Close to Sabbath or Holidays

The conjunction of the sadness of mourning and the delight of the Sabbath requires elucidation:

1. If the mourners have made mental acknowledgement of *avelut* before the beginning of Sabbath services, or in the case of a woman before the kindling of Sabbath candles, even though he or she has observed the mourning for only a brief time, mourning is considered to have commenced on the day before the Sabbath or holiday. The Sabbath would, thus, be considered the second day. If the second day falls on a major holiday, which cancels the *shivah* altogether, there are no further observances of mourning as customarily practiced on the first seven days.

2. If notification of the burial came after the Sabbath had begun (after Kabbalat Shabbat), but before the evening service (Ma'ariv; and for a woman mourner after candle lighting, but before nightfall), the day of burial is counted as the first day of mourning. Even if only a gesture of formal observance was performed prior to the nightfall of the Sabbath, we may count Friday as the beginning of mourning. Prior to a major holiday, there also must be some actual observance of mourning, no matter how short its duration, in order for the holiday to cancel the rest of *shivah*.

3. If knowledge of the burial came after Ma'ariv, or after dark, even though the burial occurred during daylight, the first day of mourning begins as of that night, and not as of the previous day.

Burial on Sabbaths and Holidays

While we should not perform a burial on these holy days, specific critical occasions may arise that demand it. How do we mourn in these cases?

1. If burial occurred on the Sabbath (in case of some emergency—the burial being performed by non-Jews, or by Jews by decree of the government), mourning technically begins on the Sabbath, although there are no outward observances on that day.

2. If burial took place on a holiday, whether on the first or last days, or the intermediate days of *chol ha-mo'ed*, mourning begins on the night following the entire holiday.

3. If the burial took place on the first day of a two-day holiday, such as Shavuot, and the second day falls on the Sabbath, the counting of *shivah* begins on the Sabbath, although the formal practice of mourning is not observed outwardly at that time. We should be clear that there is to be no burial on the Sabbath.

4. If burial occurred on the first day of Rosh Hashanah, counting begins on the second day of the holiday.

Out-of-Town Burials

Those who accompany the casket to the cemetery begin the *avelut* immediately after burial, rather than after the extended period of time required to return to one's home. Those who remain at home should begin mourning when the mourner discontinues traveling with the body, or when the body and those traveling with it are out of sight, such as at an airport.

Temporary Burial

Virtually all burials are permanent acts, but sometimes, because of indecision or practical considerations, a burial is temporary. How does this affect mourning laws?

1. If the intention is to remove the body to a permanent plot at some time during the first seven days, mourning is delayed until the permanent burial.

2. If reinterment is not scheduled until after seven days, mourning begins immediately. If circumstances change, and the body is then transferred during the *shivah* period, the counting of *shivah* begins anew with the permanent burial.

3. If there was no intention of removal at all, and unforeseen circumstances compel a reinterment during *shivah*, mourning need not begin anew.

Labor Strike

In the case of a labor strike, government injunction, or other major obstacles that prevent immediate burial in one's own plot, the following procedure should be observed:

1. The family should provide its own laborers, or should enlist the help of family and friends, if the union will permit this.

2. It is preferable, especially if it is expected that settlement will come only after an extended time, to effect an immediate, temporary burial in a Jewish cemetery not affected by a strike, and later to remove the remains to one's own plot.

3. If this is not feasible, or if settlement of the strike is imminent, the body will be stored by the cemetery, and the mourners should proceed with all initial mourning practices. They should rend their clothes and recite the blessing, recite the Kaddish and end the period of *aninut*, but not observe the *shivah* and all observances associated with it. They should insist on being called to the interment when it does take place and only then should they begin *shivah*.

4. If delaying *shivah* is impractical, or for some reason cannot be effected, *avelut* and *shivah* begin as soon as the casket is received by the cemetery authorities.

5. In all such matters a rabbi should be consulted.

Notification of Out-of-Town Relatives

One who learned by telephone, telegram, E-mail, or fax of the death of a relative, but who lives at too great a distance to attend the funeral, should begin *avelut* at the time of burial, if he knows it exactly. If not, he should begin *shivah* at once. (Delayed news of death and burial is treated in Chapter Six below.)

Minors Who Come of Age during Shivah

Boys who reach the age of thirteen years and one day and girls the age of twelve years and one day are obligated to observe all of the laws of the Torah as adults. If minors come of age during the mourning period for parents, they need not start the entire *shivah* from the beginning, but are required to observe only the remainder of the mourning period. However, youngsters immediately prior to Bar or Bat Mitzvah should be taught to observe the mourning laws but without the full strictness of adult observance. If the child attains his majority after the conclusion of the *shivah*, he need not observe any of the laws of the seven- or the thirty-day period.

We fear excessively the effects of such experiences upon our youngsters. Psychologists, however, in counseling normally behaved children, generally consider it preferable for the child to face the unpleasant fact rather than to have it masked and to repress it. In our age, we can assume the child will come to know about it quickly.

Those Who Neglected to Mourn

Those who did not observe any of the mourning laws at all, out of mindlessness, or ignorance, or spite, or for some other reason, must begin the *shivah* observance upon the realization of this neglect, so long as it is still within thirty days from the time of burial. If the mourner observes some part of the mourning, even for only a short time, he is considered to have erred in not performing all of the laws, or to have demonstrated a lack of respect in his nonobservance. But the *shivah* is considered fulfilled, and he is not required to begin the entire process of mourning anew.

If, because of mental illness or some physical illness, he was not apprised of the death, he should begin mourning when his doctors consider him capable of doing so, provided the thirtieth day after burial has not passed. If the sick person was aware of the death and was stable enough, mentally, to accept the fact of mourning, he is considered to have fulfilled the *shivah* requirement, although he may have been completely unable to perform the actual observances. In such a case he need not begin mourning at a later time.

Missing Persons Assumed Dead

This situation is one of the most agonizing and perplexing in the whole category of human suffering. Reason assures the bereaved that there is no possibility of the missing person being alive. The spirit repudiates this as pure invention, as imagining, as cold, heartless, hopeless. But life insistently demands a resolution.

1. If the remains of the deceased are lost but are expected to be found soon, such as those of a person who was drowned in a lake or in another landlocked body of water, or those of a person who was killed by an animal in a known general location, or those of a person who was murdered, mourning should begin when the body is discovered, or when, after exhaustive search, all hope of finding the body is abandoned. So long as there is reasonable expectation that the body will be found, mourning should not be observed.

2. If there is no expectation of finding the body, as in the case of one who was drowned in the ocean, lost in mountainous terrain, or judged to have been killed in an unknown location; or if an exhaustive search has yielded no results, and there are absolutely no witnesses to the death, then:

- If a wife survives, there should be no demonstrative ritual mourning, because of the distinct concern that others may consider her a widow, eligible for remarriage. In fact, this eligibility is by no means certain in the eyes of the law, since there were no witnesses to the death of her husband. This involves the law of *agunah*, a woman bound to a marriage that does not exist and that prevents her from remarrying. Rabbis of every age have tried to resolve this disability, and have largely succeeded in cases of war, etc., when it is at all possible. If there is one witness, or one who heard of the death from a witness, that should be told the rabbi. In any case, rabbinic guidance must definitely be sought.
- If no wife survives, or the deceased is a bachelor, or divorcé, mourning is begun when the judgment of death is made. However, this is quite an unusual occurrence, and the determination of death is a difficult and complex rabbinic decision. The mourner must appreciate that this is a complicated issue for which there is no general rule, and he must seek expert advice.

THE DURATION OF *SHIVAH* AND *SHELOSHIM*

⚘

While no general law can be of benefit equally to all, these graduated programs of mourning come close to being appropriate to virtually everyone.

The Shivah *Period*

The seven days of mourning begin immediately after interment and end on the morning of the seventh day immediately after the Shacharit (morning) service. Those present extend condolences, and the mourner rises from his week of mourning. If no public Shacharit service is held in the mourner's home, *shivah* ends after the mourner has recited the prayers, or after the community's services, provided that it is after sunrise.

In computing the seven days, Jewish tradition follows the principle of considering a fraction of a day as a complete day. Thus, the day of burial is considered as the first day, even though interment may have been concluded only a few moments before nightfall. So, too, the seventh day is considered a full day even though mourning was observed for only a short time after sunrise. Two fractional days of mourning are therefore counted as two whole days of *shivah*.

To illustrate, if interment occurred on Wednesday afternoon, Wednesday is the first day, Thursday the second, Friday the third, Saturday the fourth, Sunday the fifth, Monday the sixth, and Tuesday morning the seventh and final day. A simplified method is to consider the *shivah* as concluding one week from the morning *before* the day of burial.

The Sheloshim *Period*

The following principles are used in computing the thirty-day period:

1. The counting of *shivah* and *sheloshim* starts from date of burial, not the date of death.

2. Partial days are considered full days (the same as with *shivah*).

3. *Sheloshim* ends after morning services on the thirtieth day after burial.

THE SABBATH DURING *SHIVAH* AND *SHELOSHIM*

The Sabbath day does not terminate *shivah* as a major holiday does, for while *public* mourning observances are suspended, *private* mourning practices are observed. The Sabbath is, therefore, counted as part of the seven days. Because public mourning observances are suspended and the bereaved are permitted to put on shoes and leave the house for services, it is necessary to establish the exact duration of the Sabbath respite. Also, the torn clothing is not worn on the Sabbath during *shivah*.

The bereaved should not arise from *shivah* on Friday until as close to the Sabbath as possible, allowing themselves the time necessary for Sabbath preparations, such as cooking or dressing. This should not take more than approximately an hour and a quarter. In an emergency, approximately two and a half hours are allowed for such preparations. Contrary to popular opinion, *avelut* does not cease at noon on Friday.

The bereaved should return to their mourning on Saturday night immediately after the evening services.

It is customary in some communities not to begin *shivah* after the Sabbath. If, for example, a person died on Passover, and Passover concludes on a Friday, Sunday would be the first day of *shivah*, not the Sabbath. One would need to determine his community's custom by consulting his rabbi.

MAJOR HOLIDAY PRACTICES

A collision of emotions, a clashing of rejoicing and despairing in the hearts of the devoted is tangible when the holiday occurs.

1. The spirit of joy that is mandatory on major holidays is not consistent with the sorrow of bereavement. In Jewish law, therefore, the holiday completely cancels the *shivah*.

Thus, if mourning was begun even moments before dark, so long as the *avel* had conscious awareness of the situation and performed any one of the mourning practices, even personal ones, even for a moment, the onset of the holiday nullifies the remainder of the *shivah*, and we count the brief *shivah* observance as the equivalent of seven full days.

If, however, death occurred during the holiday, or even before the holiday, but without the consciousness of the mourner, *shivah* begins after the holiday is concluded, and *sheloshim* starts immediately after burial.

2. Also, if *shivah* had been completed even as late as on the morning before the holiday, the remainder of the *sheloshim* is cancelled and all its observances suspended. Thus, a man may shave and take a haircut immediately prior to the holiday, in honor of the festival, the *sheloshim* having been fulfilled. (See page 140)

3. If the holiday occurred in the midst of *shivah*, not only is *shivah* considered completed, but also the days of the holiday are counted toward the *sheloshim*, and the counting of thirty days need not be delayed until after the holiday.

The following is a summary of the somewhat complicated holiday regulations. Please take into consideration that in Israel there is only one day at the beginning and end of the three major festivals, and the second days are normal weekdays.

If mourning began before:

Passover

1. The partial mourning before the holiday equals seven days.
2. Eight days of the holiday, added to the seven, totals fifteen days.
3. Required for *sheloshim*: fifteen additional days.

Shavuot

1. Mourning period prior to holiday equals seven days.
2. The first day of Shavuot is considered the equivalent of another seven days, which equals fourteen days.
3. The second day of the holiday marks the fifteenth day.
4. Required for *sheloshim*: fifteen additional days.

Sukkot

1. Mourning period prior to holiday equals seven days.
2. Seven days of holiday, added to the seven, totals fourteen days.
3. The holiday of Shemini Atzeret, which falls on the eighth day of Sukkot, is like Shavuot in regard to *sheloshim*, and is regarded as another seven-day period. This makes twenty-one days.
4. The day of Simchat Torah, which follows Shemini Azeret, marks the twenty-second day.
5. Required for *sheloshim*: eight additional days.

Chol ha-Mo'ed

If somebody died during a festival (for example, if death occurred during the Passover Seder), and burial takes place on *chol ha-mo'ed* (Passover or Sukkot), we count as follows:

1. *Shivah* observance begins at the completion of the holiday (in the case of Sukkot, after Simchat Torah).
2. The last day of the festival (Passover, Shavuot, Sukkot, and Rosh Hashanah) is counted as the first day of *shivah*. (There is some question, if the Sabbath follows the festival, of whether it is appropriate to begin *avelut* on the Sabbath.)
3. The days of the holidays are, nevertheless, counted as part of the *sheloshim*. Hence the unusual circumstance of having the *sheloshim* begin *before* the *shivah*.
4. Shemini Atzeret is counted as only a single day.

Rosh Hashanah and Yom Kippur

Although there is no specific Biblical halakhic mandate to "rejoice" on these holy days, they are considered the same as the major festivals in these three respects:

1. They cancel the remainder of the *shivah*, if mourning was begun prior to the holiday;
2. They delay the beginning of mourning, if interment occurred during their observance;
3. They cancel the remainder of the *sheloshim*, if the *shivah* was completed before the onset of the holiday.

Thus, for Rosh Hashanah, mourning prior to the holiday equals seven days, and Yom Kippur completes the *sheloshim*. For Yom Kippur, mourning before the holy day equals seven days, and Sukkot completes the *sheloshim*.

PURIM

Purim does not cancel *shivah*. There is a de-emphasis of public mourning as on the Sabbath (some hold there is no mourning at all), but private mourning must still be observed. Thus, sitting on the low stool and the removal of regular shoes are not required on Purim. Similarly, Purim observances, such as the festival meal (the meat and wine, but without the rejoicing) and the sending of gifts—*mishlo'ach manot*—are obligatory upon the mourner as upon all Jews. While the mourner is halakhically required to send gifts to others, it is not permitted to send gifts to him. In such a case it is better to address the *mishlo'ach manot* to a spouse, child, parent, or friend.

The mourner should attend the Megillah reading at the synagogue, and if he is the only person capable of reading it publicly, he is obliged to do so. Wherever possible, though, the mourner during *shivah* should not read publicly or lead services on Purim. Shushan Purim, celebrated the day following Purim, should be observed as Purim proper only when the mourner has always observed it as a festive day.

HANUKKAH

🐾

Hanukkah, too, does not cancel *shivah*. Indeed, while important religious authorities held that there is no mourning on Purim, and surely no public mourning, Hanukkah provided no such relief, and all mourning observances must be kept. Hanukkah festival observances, such as the kindling of candles, is obligatory; and the mourner, but not the *onen*, should recite all three blessings including Shehecheyanu, the prayer to God for sustaining us in life "unto this time." However, he should not kindle the menorah on behalf of the congregation and in so doing publicly proclaim these words, since the joy it naturally evokes is not in harmony with this period of distress in his life.

The mourner does not recite the Hallel prayer in the house of *shivah* because these are psalms of joy. He should, however, absent himself briefly so that the other worshippers may recite it as required. In the synagogue proper, the mourner should recite the Hallel.

WHERE IS *SHIVAH* OBSERVED?

🐾

Shivah can be observed wherever it is most comfortable for the mourners. Ideally, though, *shivah* should be observed by all the bereaved relatives in the house of the deceased. Where a man has lived, there does his spirit continue to dwell. It is, after all, in that home that one is surrounded by the tangible remains of a person's lifework, and it is only right that evidence of his life should be evident during *shivah*. In addition, it is considered of exceptional tribute to the deceased to have the family united as it was.

It is permitted, therefore, to travel even long distances after the funeral in order to observe *shivah* in the house of the deceased. But, in such an instance, the acceptance of mourning should be demonstrated formally at the cemetery, in the cemetery office, or on the grounds, by sitting on a low stool or fence or rock, and removing the shoes for a short while.

Of course, circumstances are not always ideal, Therefore, if there is a need to sleep in one's own home, the mourner may commute, but should do so when the streets are quiet after dark. He should then return to the house of the *shivah* early in the morning, before people generally rise.

So, too, if a person wants to sit *shivah* at home, with his spouse and children, he may do so, even if he must travel some distance from the cemetery. However, if he is to travel, he should first formally accept his mourning at the cemetery, as noted above.

UPON RETURNING FROM THE CEMETERY

Before leaving home for the funeral service, arrangements should be made for three rites that are obligatory on the mourner immediately on returning home:

- Washing hands before entering the house;
- Meal of condolence;
- Preparing the house for the *shivah* observance.

WASHING HANDS

It is an ancient Jewish custom to cleanse oneself after touching the deceased or a casket, or even being under the same roof as the deceased. This is done, symbolically, by washing hands before entering one's home. A container of water should be prepared for this purpose outside the entrance.

The custom of hand washing is traced to many different

origins. One is that it is a symbolic cleansing from the impurity associated with death. This impurity, which is a spiritual-legal conceit and is not a matter of physical or hygienic cleanliness, underscores Judaism's constant emphasis on life and the value of living.

Another reason is that it stems from the practice ordained by the Bible when a person was found dead and the cause of his death was unknown. The elders of the city washed their hands and proclaimed, on behalf of the residents of the city, that none of the citizens had directly or indirectly caused this person's death.

A third reason commentaries offer is that washing is testimony that these individuals participated in the interment service and did not shrink from performing the burial honors due the dead.

Whatever the origin, the custom of washing the hands is universally observed among traditional Jews. The cup of water is not transferred directly from one person to another. This is a symbolic expression of our hope that such a tragedy should not transfer from person to person, but should end where it, unfortunately, began.

THE MEAL OF CONDOLENCE

The neighbors of the bereaved traditionally provide the meal of condolence, the first full meal that the mourners eat on returning from the service or the interment. So important was this basic courtesy that some Sages maintain that it was Biblically ordained. Indeed, the rabbis of the Jerusalem Talmud admonished neighbors who left the bereaved to prepare their own meal. They even pronounced a curse upon such people for displaying callousness and indifference to the plight of their fellow men.

This beautiful custom, which may at first blush appear strange to some American Jews, possesses several profound psychological insights. One astute medieval rabbi, long before the Freudian era, observed that the mourner harbors a strong death wish when he returns from the cemetery to his home and its familiar surroundings. His home is now bereft of warmth and life. He has abandoned someone he loves. Life doesn't seem worth living anymore. His hidden wish is to join his beloved. In this frame of mind he would tend to deprive himself of food, in order to achieve this symbolic death. Indeed, we frequently hear: "Who can eat when my husband lies dead in the cold, friendless earth?"

Another aspect of the meal of condolence is that it is the second formal expression of consolation. The first, as mentioned earlier, is the parallel rows of well-wishing people, walls of friends, through which the bereaved walk as they depart from the gravesite. This is a silent tribute, to the accompaniment of a condolence wish, but it is eloquent testimony that people share the pangs of their neighbor's anguish. This second expression of consolation takes us one step closer to the mourner in his state of misery. We move unnoticed from the role of spectator to participant, from sentiment to service. We bring the mourner the sustenance of life, figuratively and literally, the "bread" of his existence. That is why this meal of condolence is mandatory upon the neighbors, not the mourners.

This expression of consolation should also be a silent one. The meal should not be an occasion for socializing or for idle chatter—no power lunch this—which is discouraged during the *shivah* period of mourning and, in any case, is in poor taste.

The third formal consolation, the *shivah* visitation, is the time that is ripe for the beginning of the mourner's verbalization of his feeling of loss. Here, too, the rabbis urge visitors to sit in silence until the bereaved himself desires to speak. Even then, the rabbis advise visitors to speak only on the subject of the deceased, difficult as that may seem. (This theme will be treated below.)

There are a number of considerations regarding the menu of the meal of condolence.

1. Minimally, the meal should include bread or rolls—the staff of life. It also should include hardboiled eggs, which are symbolic of the cyclical or continuous nature of life. Some

explain that the egg is one of the only foods that harden the longer it is cooked; the lesson: a person must learn to steel himself when death occurs. The meal of condolence also may include cooked vegetables or lentils, and a beverage such as coffee or tea. Some customs have it that wine should be served. Obviously such an occasion for drinking will not induce light-heartedness or an excess of conviviality.

2. The meal of condolence must be the very first meal eaten upon returning from the funeral to the house of *shivah*. This mandate refers only to the first meal and not to the second meal of the day, nor, if the mourners choose to fast, to the meal taken after dark or the next day. Of course, if neighbors were unwittingly delayed, or if they were ignorant of the custom, the meal should be graciously accepted.

If interment took place at night, the appropriate time for the first meal is considered to be all night, or any time during the next day.

3. Ideally, the meal should be prepared by the neighbors. If they do not, the son or daughter, or other relatives of the mourner should perform this mitzvah. If that is not possible, the mourners prepare it for one another. If no one is available to perform this mitzvah, the mourner should prepare his own meal. No mourner is expected to fast.

If the meal of condolence is not ready when the mourners have returned from the funeral, they may partake of light refreshments on their own, such as coffee and cake, providing they do not eat bread or cooked food or sit down at the table as at a formal meal.

4. The meal of condolence is not served at a time when there is no formal, public observance of mourning, such as on the Sabbath or on the major festivals (Passover, Shavuot, and Sukkot), or on late afternoons preceding these days. However, the meal should be served on the days of Rosh Chodesh, Hanukkah, Purim, and *chol ha-mo'ed*.

The meal also is not served for those mourning the loss of infants who have not survived thirty days, or after the death of intentional suicides. (See Chapter Six.) Also, if news of the death of a close relative came more than thirty days late, the meal is not served.

5. If a second death occurs during *shivah*, a second meal of condolence should be served.

PREPARING THE HOUSE FOR *SHIVAH*

🍂

It is not only the mourners, their thoughts, feelings, and observances, that are important to the *halakhah*; their home environment also should be in keeping with the mood of *avelut*.

Candles in the House of Mourning

The house of mourning should be prepared with a special candle, usually provided by the funeral director, that will burn for seven days. The *shivah* candle in memory of the deceased is kindled upon returning from the cemetery and kept burning for the entire seven-day *shivah* period.

To the Jew, the candle signifies a special event, some notable occasion in life. There is candlelight on Sabbath, on major holidays, customarily at the bris (circumcision), the *pidyon ha-ben* (the ceremonial redemption of the first-born son), under the wedding canopy, and often at occasions of *simcha shel mitzvah*—meals celebrating the successful conclusion of a commandment.

During *shivah*, candlelight is the quintessential spiritual symbol of the human being. The wick and the flame symbolize the body and soul, and the bond between them. The flame is the soul that strives ever upward and brings light into darkness. Jewish mysticism has suggested profound and insightful analogies of the flame to the soul of the deceased in its elaborate comments on the *shivah* candle, yahrzeit lamp, and Yizkor candle.

1. Because of the deep significance of the flame, the *shivah* candle should not be an electric fixture, ideally, but one of wick and flame, either of olive oil or paraffin. If these are unavailable, an electric light may be used. If there is any dan-

ger of fire, the electric light, of course, should be used.

2. Where the candle should be kindled is a matter of opinion. It is most proper to observe *shivah* in the home of the deceased, where he lived and died, regardless of where the death occurred. If it is not feasible to observe the *shivah* at the residence of the deceased, the *shivah* candle should be kindled wherever the mourners are sitting *shivah*.

3. The candle should be kindled immediately upon returning from the cemetery, or upon hearing of the death within the seven days. It is left burning for the duration of the *shivah*, even throughout the Sabbath, at which time demonstrative mourning is not observed. Also, on *chol ha-mo'ed* of Sukkot and Passover the candle is lit immediately, even though *shivah* begins after the holiday is over. In such a case, a candle should remain kindled through the holiday and until the end of the *shivah*. It is preferable on those days, however, to place the candles in a room other than the dining room so as to make the symbol of grief less prominent on the holiday, which is a joyous occasion for the entire Jewish people.

4. One candle is sufficient for the household. There should be one candle lit in each home in which *shivah* is observed.

Covering Mirrors in the House of Shivah

It is a time-honored Jewish tradition to cover the mirrors in the *shivah* home, from the moment of death to the end of *shivah*. While the custom is of uncertain origin, its practice is universal and thoroughly appropriate to the spirit of *avelut*.

A variety of reasons have been advanced for the custom of covering the mirrors:

1. Judaism teaches that man is created in the image of God and that he derives, from resemblance, his dignity and his value. Supplementing this concept is the idea that the death of one of God's creatures diminishes the very image of the Creator Himself. Man's demise represents a disruption of the relationship between the living man and the living God. If the dignity of man is the reflection of his Creator, the image of the Creator Himself can be said to shrink with the death of

His creations. At the time of the destruction of the image of God, represented by the deceased, the mirror—which serves to reflect man's "image"—ought not to be used.

2. When death strikes, the mourner should contemplate the relationship between God and man, Creator and creature. When, instead, the bereaved dwells vainly on self-adoration, through the use of his mirror, and continues to be concerned with his own image and his own creatureliness, he brings to almost comic proportions the austere moment of tragedy.

3. The mirror occupies an unusual place in the household. It is the object that, more than any other, serves to enhance the attractiveness of man and wife for each other. The silvered glass reflects the external appeal of each of the mates.

Judaism has taken great care to promote a relationship of kindness, concern, courtesy, and even physical desire between a husband and his wife. Nevertheless, with the death of a child or parent or sibling, this intimate relationship must be suspended. One commentator says that the ancient custom observed during *shivah* of *kefiyyat ha-mittah*, the overturning of the bed or couch, served as a means of discouraging marital relations. When the cloud of death settles on a household, the mirror—happy symbol of secure and intimate family living—must be covered, and the mourner must concentrate on the painful loss.

4. It is obvious that the individual, if he were isolated from society, would have little need of the precious reflecting glass. The mirror is the means of achieving social acceptance by enhancing the appearance. The spirit of Jewish mourning, however, is the spirit of loneliness, the mourner dwelling silently, and in solitude, on his personal loss. Social etiquette and appearance becomes terribly insignificant. Covering the mirror symbolizes the sense of withdrawal in *avelut*.

5. The fifth reason is a very practical one. Worship services are customarily held in the home of the bereaved. Jewish law clearly states that one may not worship an image or stand directly in front of one, whether it is a picture or a reflected image in a mirror. That is why mirrors must be covered in this temporary house of worship.

Additional Preparations for the House of Mourning

Several other matters regarding the house of mourning should be remembered. These will be noted here and discussed in further detail later.

1. Arrange with the funeral director for *shivah* benches or stools for all the mourners, even for those who are too ill to sit on them constantly throughout the *shivah*. The mourners also will require slippers that are not made of leather.

2. Ask the rabbi, ritual director, or lay official of the synagogue for a sufficient number of men to constitute a minyan, and for prayer books for all present, men and women, and yarmulkes for the men.

3. Also arrange for chairs for those who will visit during *shivah*.

PRAYERS IN THE HOUSE OF MOURNING

It is desirable to hold daily prayer services during *shivah* in the house of the deceased, whether the death occurred there or elsewhere. It is important to hold these services in the presence of a minyan so that the mourners observing *shivah* can recite Kaddish, which requires a minimum attendance of ten adult males. We thereby demonstrate respect for the bereaved as well as honor for the deceased.

Significantly, however, it is considered by many to be *more* important to hold services in the house of the deceased if he left no mourners, when Kaddish need not be recited and *shivah* not observed. The Talmud (*Shabbat* 152b) records that Rabbi Judah the Prince gathered a minyan to accompany him on a condolence visit to the house of one who died in the neighborhood and left no mourners. After *shivah*, Rabbi Judah saw the deceased in a dream and learned from him that he was comforted and set at ease because of the presence of the minyan. Therefore, if there are two deaths that have occurred in a community that can provide but one minyan, and one of the deceased left mourners, whereas the other did not, the service should be held in the house of the deceased who is *not* being mourned.

1. If the mourners are able to borrow a Torah scroll, they should do so, but must provide a clean and honorable place in the home for it. It will be read at each service on Mondays, Thursdays, and Saturdays (mornings or afternoons, when the mourners prefer to pray at home).

2. Services need not be held in the home if the deceased was a child of less than one year of age. In places where such services are held, however, they are held solely in honor of the bereaved, so that they may remain at home during *shivah*.

3. A male mourner himself is counted as part of the minyan.

4. A mourner may lead the service himself. Although some local customs discourage this, the weight of scholarly opinion urges the mourner to do this. As a practicing rabbi, I know this custom to be a wonderful spur for mourners to learn to lead daily services.

5. If no minyan can be gathered, should the bereaved leave the house of *shivah* to attend services with the congregation, or should they pray at home? While there has been rabbinic controversy regarding this matter, much depends on the commitment of the mourner in observing the *shivah*. If leaving the home for services will tempt him to engage in other activities while he is out-of-doors, it is better that he not attend congregational services. If, however, he will not abuse this leniency, the mourner should not be deprived of the privilege of reciting the Kaddish and praying with a minyan. However, he should first make every effort to secure a minyan at home for both morning and evening services. If this is not possible, the minyan should be secured for at least one service, morning or evening, and he then can attend the synagogue for the other service. Failing this, he should keep in mind the requirements of *shivah*, and should go to the nearest synagogue for services, both morning and evening. At the synagogue, on weekdays, he should not sit in his regular seat,

so that he can, with his own body, signal the radical change in his personal status during mourning.

CHANGES IN THE ORDER OF THE SERVICE
๛

Following are several changes in the order of the prayer service that pertain to the entire minyan when it is held in the house of the mourner.

Daily Services

Tachanun is not said; El Erech Apayim, Lamenatze'ach, and Va-Ani Zot Beriti in Uva le-Tziyyon are not said. Titkabel in the full Kaddish recitation is not said, according to some. Many local customs do require its recitation.

Psalm 49 is recited after every morning and evening service in the house of mourning. Some traditions also urge this recitation after the Minchah service. On days on which Tachanun is not recited, Psalm 17 is substituted. On the Sabbath, *chol ha-mo'ed*, and Purim, this psalm, too, is omitted.

Friday Evening Services

Hodu after the Minchah (afternoon) service should not be recited by the mourner. Lekhu Nerannenah and the introductory psalms are omitted from the Sabbath eve service. The service begins with Mizmor Shir le-Yom ha-Shabbat (Psalm 92). Berakhah Me'ein Sheva is not recited. Shalom Aleikhem should not be recited at the table, but *zemirot* (Sabbath table songs) may be sung.

Sabbath Morning Services

The mourner may not receive an *aliyyah* (the call to recite the blessing over the Torah) at home or in the synagogue. On weekdays, he must refuse the honor even after having been called publicly. On the Sabbath he should avoid receiving the honor even if he is a *Kohen* or a *Levi* (Levite), but if there is no other person available, or he is mistakenly called, he should accept the honor. His refusal of an *aliyyah* on the Sabbath would be considered public mourning, which is forbidden. The mourner may be called to raise or tie the Torah, or to remove and replace it in the Holy Ark, on the Sabbath and on weekdays.

If the mourner was dangerously ill and has recovered, he may recite the blessing of gratitude, the Birkhat ha-Gomel, before the entire minyan, but without receiving an *aliyyah*. Av ha-Rachamim is recited at this home service.

Sabbath Minchah Services

Va'ani Tefillati is omitted and Tzidkatcha is recited, although it is the equivalent of Tachanun, which is omitted on weekdays.

Conclusion of the Sabbath

Vihi No'am is not recited, according to some customs; Ve-Yiten should be recited. Havdalah should begin from the blessings themselves, omitting the introduction, Hineh, if the mourner recites it himself.

Holidays

On holidays, if the mourner is a *Kohen*, he should not participate in the Birkhat Kohanim (the Priestly Blessing), and should leave the minyan prior to its recitation.

Hallel

The Hallel is not chanted in the house of mourning because it speaks of joy, which is not consonant with the spirit of mourning. It also includes the phrase, "The dead shall not praise Thee," which is considered a mockery of the deceased, who cannot, in fact, rise to God. A consensus of rabbinic opinions and different customs provides the following guidelines:

1. On Rosh Chodesh, if the service is held in the house of the deceased, Hallel should not be recited at the service proper, but individuals who attend, and are not mourners, should recite it in their own homes. If the service is held in the house of the mourner, which is not the house of the deceased, the mourner should absent himself while the remainder of the minyan recites the Hallel.

2. On Hanukkah and other holidays, all the members of the minyan *must* recite Hallel individually after the service, if they have not already done so. Likewise, if Hallel is to be said on a holiday that is coincident with the last day of *shivah* (when at the conclusion of services the *shivah* terminates), Hallel should not be recited at the service proper, but everyone must recite it later, individually.

Avinu Malkenu should be recited during the Ten Days of Repentance.

LEAVING THE HOUSE DURING *SHIVAH*

The most characteristic tradition of Jewish mourning is going home—withdrawing from society following the death. The Hebrew word for mourner is *avel*, which means one who withdraws. He does not mix socially, participate in joyous events, or take pleasure trips during this time.

The tradition of staying at home is based, generally, on two reasons. First, a practical reason: If the mourner is prohibited from doing business or experiencing pleasure, home is the most logical place to be. Second, it has positive, curative value: mourning is an in-depth experience in loneliness. The ties that bind one soul to another have been severed, and there is a gnawing sense of solitude. To remain incommunicado is symbolic; the mourner expresses grief over the total disruption of any further communication with someone he loved. There are moments in life when a person has a right, even an obligation to be alone. This is such a time.

The mourner, therefore, remains at home during the entire

period of the *shivah*. It then becomes the moral duty of the Jewish community to come to the door of the bereaved and to comfort him with words of praise for the deceased, drawing him out of his loneliness and into the social structure once again.

Following are some details of the law of staying at home during *shivah*:

1. If there is a compelling need for the mourner to leave the home for the purpose of fulfilling a mitzvah that he *personally* is obligated to perform, he may do so. For example: the circumcision of his son, or the purchase of *tefillin*, where others cannot help him.

2. The mourner may not leave the house to participate in a mitzvah that can be accomplished without his presence, such as attendance at a Bar Mitzvah, circumcision of the son of a relative or friend, attending a wedding ceremony, or paying a condolence call upon other bereaved.

3. If there is no available place for the mourners to sleep in the house of *shivah*, or if mourners are needed at their own homes (especially if one of the mourners is the mother of young children), they are permitted to leave the house of *shivah*. The same applies to the bereaved that want to sit *shivah* at home so that personal friends and neighbors may visit—they can leave the house. But mourners should do this in the manner described below.

4. If during the *shivah* another one of the seven close relatives dies, the mourner may leave the house to attend the funeral—by following the procession inconspicuously, always remaining at the periphery of the cortege.

5. If the mourner is needed in order to make funeral arrangements or to act as a pallbearer, he is permitted to attend a funeral even during the first day of *shivah*. If he is not needed for these duties, he may not attend another funeral until the third day of *shivah* (that is, the second morning after interment).

6. On Tishah be-Av and Purim the mourner should attend congregational services.

7. On the Sabbath, if a minyan and Torah scrolls are not easily available, he should worship at the synagogue, as well.

8. If there is no minyan able to come to the home and if, in accordance with the qualifications stipulated above, he chooses to attend Sabbath services, he should worship at the closest synagogue. Preferably, he should proceed alone, or in the company of other mourners. On weekdays, travelling by car is considered being alone. The distance required to travel is of no consequence. The mourner may not use this occasion to do *anything* other than to attend services.

9. The urgency requiring the mourner to leave home for personal, business, or professional purposes, or for other special emergencies, will be considered in a special chapter below, on work during *shivah*.

10. A mohel may leave the house to perform a circumcision, because this must be performed specifically on the eighth day after birth. If there is no other mohel available, he may perform it even on the first day of his *shivah*. If there is another mohel available, but only the mourner's services are desired, he may indeed perform the circumcision, provided it is to take place after the third day of the *shivah* period.

11. A *Kohen* required for a *pidyon ha-ben* follows the same regulations as for the mohel.

12. The mourner may be asked to serve as *sandak* (one who holds the child during circumcision) at a bris after the third day, but it is inappropriate to make such a request of him. A person in mourning surely will have ambivalent feelings about accepting this honor.

Every effort should be made by the mourner not to leave the house of *shivah* until the third day—that is, the second morning after interment. He should make every effort to leave only after dark. If this proves impractical he may leave during daylight hours, but should proceed as inconspicuously as possible. He should not wear leather shoes, even out-of-doors. If this is impossible, he should place some pebbles or sand in his shoes, as a constant reminder that he is in mourning.

SITTING *SHIVAH*

A universal, ancient tradition requires that mourners, during *shivah*, not sit upon chairs of normal height. Until only recently it was customary for mourners to sit directly on the floor, which expressed radical depression and the departure from normal life. The Bible tells us that when Job suffered a succession of disasters he was comforted by friends who sat with him "to the ground" (Job 2:13). It is, almost in a literal sense, an adjustment of one's body to one's emotional state, a lowering of the human frame to the level of his feelings, a symbolic enactment of returning to the earth that swallowed his beloved.

The mourner today sits "to the ground," in the Biblical phrase, by sitting *closer* to the ground on a wooden stool, hassock, or footstool, or on a mat or several pillows. The material the mourner chooses to sit on is unimportant. Primarily, the tradition stipulates, he must sit on a level lower than that of normal seating height, and whether the seat is comfortable or not is irrelevant. If he desires, he may put a cushion on the stool. Sleeping on a bed of normal height is permitted.

Following are details of the tradition of sitting *shivah*.

1. One need not "sit" at all during *shivah*. The mourner may stand or walk or lie down. The tradition is concerned only that when the mourner does sit down, he should sit on a stool of lower height than usual.

2. Elderly people, the physically weak, and pregnant women may sit on normal seats. However, they should make an effort, whenever practicable, to sit on a low stool when people come for short visits to comfort the bereaved. This demonstrative bereavement is an important aspect of the tradition of "sitting," and should not be taken lightly.

3. The mourner should not rise from his seat out of respect for any visitor, no matter how important the visitor is, whether he is a renowned scholar, an eminent public personality, or a government official.

4. If the mourner wishes to sit on a porch or terrace or in the backyard, he may do so, provided he sits on a low stool.

WORKING AND DOING BUSINESS

One of the fundamental laws of Jewish mourning, over three thousand years old, is that mourners do not work or do business during *shivah*.

Judaism, unlike many ancient and some modern cultures, endows labor with dignity and considers commerce a proper activity of man. However, work must never so dominate a man that he becomes a mere cog in society's wheel. The dimensions of man's personality should include his profession or labor or business, but must transcend them. He must be able to experience life's great moments as an authentic human being, and not restrict his horizon to his career. Hence, Judaism demands that at moments of great joy or great grief—both of which require concentration and undisturbed meditation—we refrain from our daily pursuits.

The prophet Amos records God's words: "And I shall turn your feasts into mourning" (Amos 8:10). The Sages comment, "as on festivals labor is prohibited, so in days of mourning." The work prohibition during mourning is not similar to that of the Sabbath but to that of *chol ha-mo'ed*, the intermediary days of Pesach and Sukkot. The tradition wisely noted the different motivations for the work prohibition on festivals and during mourning, and these differences are reflected in the laws of *avelut*.

Following are the basic laws of the work prohibition during *shivah*. We must realize that because of the many possible situations and the variety of personal and business obligations, the specific decision of a rabbi may be required. There are a number of contingencies in this law, and only a competent, learned authority can weigh the human need and the religious requirement in order to make a valid decision.

Generally, the law states that one may not do any manner of skilled or unskilled labor, manage any business enterprise, or direct any investment of monies, by himself or through agents, for all of the days of *shivah*. Included in this prohibition are all those who are fiscal dependents of the mourner and his immediate domestic help, whether they are Jewish or Gentile. A child of a mourner, who is not himself in mourning, even if he is past the age of Bar Mitzvah, may work during *shivah*, but only if the profits go to the child, not to the parent. Those who are economically independent of the father are not at all affected by the *shivah* restrictions.

1. If the mourner is an employee—either a manager, executive, craftsman, or laborer—he may employ another person to work on his behalf. The employer is not expected to suffer because of the bereavement of an employee. Likewise, a mourner, if he is a tenant farmer, may designate a replacement so that the percentage of the owner's profit should not be lost. Under ordinary circumstances, however, those who are self-employed may not similarly engage replacements to function on their behalf.

2. If a mourner is the employer, the employees should be allowed to work during their owner's observance of *shivah*. They are considered to be working for their own profit, even though the mourner profits thereby as well.

Similarly, one who is a tenant farmer in the fields of a mourner, either on a percentage or rental basis, or for a stipulated share of produce, may continue working, as he is doing so for his own benefit, even though profit accrues to the mourner as well.

3. If the mourner contracted work to others before the death occurred, the workers may continue to do their labor, but it should not be performed on the premises of the mourner. However, the mourner may not contract for new work during *shivah*. These principles hold only for portable items; contract work on stationary items, such as building construction, may not be done at all by anyone during *shivah*, under ordinary circumstances.

4. A day worker, one who gets paid by the hour rather than by the piece, may not, under ordinary circumstances, work for the mourner during *shivah*.

5. If the mourner has agreed to do contract work for others, he may arrange to have it completed through others but not on his own premises.

The mourner may accept contract work during *shivah* for the period after *shivah*, but should not enter into written agreements or contractual arrangements at this time.

6. Items that the mourner rented to others before *shivah* may be used by them without restriction. He may not renew the rental during the *shivah*, unless it is on a continuous renewal basis and the matter cannot wait until after *shivah*.

7. Retail stores should be closed during *shivah*, under all ordinary circumstances. This rule applies to stores individually owned or owned in partnership. The details of this law are complex:

- The partner of the mourner, in this case, will, unfortunately, be adversely affected. He may do work for the business in private, but not publicly and not in the place of business. If the mourner is the major partner, and the business is named after him, even private work done for it by the other partner is not permitted. If the mourner is a silent partner, the opinion of many scholars is that the other partner may continue normal operations.
- If the partnership owns more than one store, and each partner manages one, only the store managed by the mourner needs to be closed.
- If one of the partners himself dies, the partnership is considered suspended, and the business may operate normally, unless it was explicitly stipulated, previously, that the children will inherit the deceased's portion of the business. If it was not explicitly stated, the store need not be closed at all (except in honor of the deceased, if so desired by the surviving partner).
- If they are partners merely in the rental of store space, but individually own separate businesses, the partner need not close his part of the store. In fact, in such a case, if the family is in need, the mourner may have others work in his portion of the store, since it is already open and not specifically open for the mourner. (See the following section on when work is permitted.)

8. Housework, such as cooking and cleaning, may be performed during *shivah*, but only such work as is necessary for that specific household. This applies not only to the man or woman doing chores for the family, but also if the residence is located in a commercial establishment, such as a restaurant or hotel, for customers who eat or sleep there. While this is technically not considered labor, it should be avoided in ideal circumstances. Likewise, mourners who work as housekeepers, bakers, or waiters may, in critical circumstances where the labor is absolutely required, perform their appointed tasks. However, they should not do so until after the third day, and they should not leave the premises of their employment until the conclusion of *shivah*.

9. A physician may attend to those of his patients who need his personal services during *shivah*, even if other physicians are available. Of course, the doctor should use his discretion as to whether or not he needs to be in attendance. If there is any doubt in his mind, the physician definitely should attend to his patient.

10. If the mourner was engaged in his business and, for some reason, he did not learn of the death, there is no obligation to inform him immediately of the tragedy. (It should be understood that keeping such news from a child or parent triggers other major risks.) So long as he himself is not aware of the death, the members of his family are not forbidden to work. He and his family may continue business activity until they are made aware of the death. If the mourner is away from home and is notified by his family by letter or telegram, they should estimate the time of his receiving it, at which moment he becomes a mourner and his place of business must be closed by them.

WHEN IS WORK PERMITTED?

There are cases that, by their very nature, must be considered exceptions to the normal rules of mourning because of the severe hardship they may entail.

These exceptions fall into three categories:

The Needy

No one is expected to suffer unduly as a consequence of observing the traditions of Jewish mourning; Judaism therefore provided relief from the strictness of selected laws when they conflicted with serious human need. By the same token, the needy were not simply lumped into an exclusive class, giving them complete exemption from *all* the laws of mourning. Such economic burdens that developed from strict observance of the laws were relieved in accordance with the clear provisions of the Jewish tradition. But the remainder of the mourner's obligations, not pertinent to this exigency, remained in full force.

The following laws apply to indigent mourners. Poverty is defined, in terms of the laws of mourning, as those unable to earn their income unless they work each day.

1. The indigent mourner, even if he or she must borrow money or accept charity, must observe the first three days of mourning and not work on the day of interment, the following day, and until a short time after sunrise on the third day.

2. After the third day he or she may work, but should do so privately and inconspicuously if possible and, more appropriately, in a home office. They may work for the family in the home. The mourners may work after the third day even if charity or loans are offered them but they refuse to accept this assistance because it represents a compromise of their dignity.

3. If there is no possibility of their receiving charitable assistance, they may work even on the very first day, but should try to perform such work inconspicuously.

Extensive Financial Loss

Abject poverty is grounds for exemption from the restriction of work during *shivah,* as is the probability of incurring a severe business loss. Understandably, each person will tend to evaluate the extent of his loss exaggeratedly. The deeply grieved may look lightly upon the possibility of losing their employment. Those who grieve mildly may consider a half-week's wages a major setback. A religious authority should therefore make the judgment in such a situation.

The following matters will be taken into consideration:

1. Will the mourner lose much trade to competitors if the store is closed?

2. Does the *shivah* fall during the busy season?

3. Are the goods that will remain unsold because of the *shivah* restrictions perishable? Is it possible they may be rendered nonmerchandisable or lose significant value after the *shivah*?

4. Will the purchase price of materials that may not be acquired during *shivah* rise if the purchase is delayed?

5. Is there a possibility of losing his job if the mourner does not work for the entire week?

6. Will employees have to be paid while they sit idle while the employer is mourning? Will rented items, such as delivery trucks, have to be paid for, although they will not be used?

7. Will the cessation of business activity cause an irretrievable loss of capital investment?

8. Will there be a major loss of profit if normal business is not conducted? The rabbi will have to decide judiciously, for example, if one is a casual investor in his spare time for additional income and the loss will be relatively mild, or if the mourner derives his major income from his investments and will face a serious financial crisis.

9. Will another person suffer financial loss as a result of the mourner's *shivah*?

10. Are the administrative aspects of the business, such as billing, etc., so time sensitive that if they are delayed payment may never be received?

11. Finally, and most important: will an extensive financial loss result in any way, to anyone, because of the full observance of mourning laws?

In cases where the hardship is adjudged to be severe, the mourner should abide by the following scale of preferences:

1. He should try to have others do the work in his stead.
2. He should attempt to delay the work until, at least, after the third day.
3. If he must work, he should strive to accomplish his work inconspicuously. If at all possible, it should be done at night, and *shivah* should be observed during the day.

Only under exceptional circumstances may the work be done by the mourner himself, or before the third day, or in public. This is true for the professional, the CEO, the employee, the self-employed, the shopkeeper, or the artist.

Public Urgency

Personal mourning also should not intrude on the conduct of public affairs. Thus, the Talmud guards against the cessation of public Torah studies when the teacher is required to observe *shivah* at home. It insists that another person teaches in his stead, and if that is not possible, it allows the mourner to perform his normal duties. Public need received priority, and any disruption of this need was considered an exigency. In the category of public need are included the following:

1. A rabbi, in a professional capacity, may decide points of religious law during *shivah* if there is no other available rabbi who can decide these matters. If there is a wedding ceremony at which there will be no music played, and the rabbi is the only qualified person available, he may perform the ceremony in as inconspicuous and quiet a fashion as possible.
2. The teacher of religious studies, if there is no available substitute, should not cancel classes during *shivah* but should continue teaching himself. If this can be done in his home, it is preferable. This does not apply to a teacher of secular subjects.
3. A *shochet* (one trained to slaughter kosher animals) of a small community, which depends on him for daily meat, may perform his duties after the third day so that the community

need not go without meat on the Sabbath. If there is no other *shochet* he may go back to work even during the first three days. (This usually is of little concern in our day of prepackaged frozen kosher meats to be found in supermarkets.)

4. The *shammash,* or ritual director of the synagogue, may perform his work during *shivah* if he personally is needed to arrange the sanctuary and prepare for the Sabbath, or care for the burial of the dead, and there is no other person who can function in his stead.

5. A scribe may write a Jewish bill of divorce if there is a possibility that one of the couple may otherwise renege on the agreement or that the proceedings may be disrupted because of his absence.

6. The mohel for the circumcision and the *Kohen* for the ceremony of *pidyon ha-ben* likewise should perform their duties if there is no substitute.

7. Community officials, who are personally indispensable at the time of *shivah,* may perform their duties if they can find no adequate replacement. Similarly, military personnel, policemen, emergency medical personnel, and firemen, during times of emergency when their participation is necessary for the public good, may perform their duties during *shivah.*

It cannot be repeated often enough that the decision to curtail the practice of *shivah* should not be made by laymen or well-wishers; by "knowledgeable" relatives; by cantors, sextons, or Jewish administrators; or by funeral directors. It is to be decided by duly ordained rabbis, thoroughly steeped in the law and aware of the problems of the day.

WEARING SHOES

The comfort of wearing leather shoes is denied the mourner during *shivah.* As on Yom Kippur, leather footwear may not be worn. The stockinged feet or the wearing of soft shoes during bereavement is symbolic of personal mortification, and also a disregard of vanity and comfort in order to concentrate on the deeper meaning of life. The Torah records that the prophet Ezekiel was told to remove his shoes while he was mourning. This single act more than any other symbolizes for the Jew the formal acceptance of mourning.

1. Shoes made of materials other than leather may be worn, and it is not necessary to walk around in stockinged feet. Shoes made of cloth, reeds, hair, or wood are permitted, so long as they are not covered with leather and the soles are not made of leather. Rubber or plastic shoes may be worn even if the laces are made of leather, as the laces are not used to cover the foot. While shoes made of imitation leather with rubber soles are permitted according to Jewish law, their appearance is so close to leather it might mislead people into believing that the mourner is not properly honoring the deceased. Such shoes should be avoided if possible.

2. A pregnant woman or a woman shortly after birth, a sick person or one subject to illness because of the cold, certainly one who suffers from foot ailments, skin disease, or one who has chronically weak legs needing the support of structured leather, may wear leather shoes. Even in such cases, it is preferable, if possible, not to wear these shoes in the presence of visitors during *shivah*.

3. One who is permitted to leave the house during *shivah* for official government business or other important public appearances may wear leather shoes outdoors but should remove them when he returns home. One who has no minyan at home and wants to travel to services may wear leather shoes in transit, if no other socially acceptable, permissible shoes are available, but he must remove them at the synagogue and upon returning home.

GREETINGS AND GIFTS

With the shocking disruption of normal life caused by a death in the family, the standard forms of social intercourse, its niceties and graces and minutiae of etiquette, are without significance. The mourning heart has no patience for these formalities. Jewish tradition disdains all types of greeting during *shivah*.

The Sages, who consistently demand that one greet all men graciously and courteously, regarded greetings as out of place when spoken by, or to, the mourner. It is absurd to say to a man, deep in anguish over someone he loved, "Hello. How are you feeling?" How should he feel? This not only is a question that cannot be answered; it indicates a touch of mindlessness. (All you need do is add "today" to that greeting, and it takes on a different coloration.) The *shalom aleikhem*s, the hellos and goodbyes, are hollow and purposeless to the despairing heart. As Maimonides taught, we should strongly discourage the petty small talk and lightheartedness of thoughtless visitors. The rejection of greetings at this time, far from betraying a lack of cordiality, issues from a profound insight into man's nature and a deep compassion for his predicament. This tradition, as so many other laws of bereavement, originated with Ezekiel. God tells Ezekiel (24:17): "Sigh in silence." Indeed, how can one mourn more eloquently than by "sighing in silence"?

The Sages offer a second reason for avoiding the standard greeting of *shalom*. *Shalom* is one of the names of God, and greeting in the name of God at a time when God has taken a close relative could conceivably be, in the view of the mourner, an intimation of scoffing. It also may trigger an instinctive invitation to question God's justice, at a time when one is required to proclaim God's justice, as in the Tzidduk ha-Din prayer.

Traditionally, therefore, Jews do not extend greetings to the mourner. The visitor enters the door, usually left slightly ajar precisely to avoid the first meeting and greeting, and sits down, without fuss and bother, to share in the grief of his neighbor.

1. During *shivah* the mourner should not extend greetings to visitors, and they should not bid him *shalom*.

2. If, during the first three days, visitors unaware of this custom extend greetings, the mourner may not respond to

the greeting. He should indicate, graciously, of course, that as a mourner he is not permitted to do so. After the first three days he may respond to the greeting out of courtesy, but should do so in an undertone, to pay respect to both the person and the tradition.

3. After *shivah* he may initiate a greeting and respond to one. Customarily, however, the mourner is not greeted with *shalom* for the full year of mourning in the case of a parent's death and for the thirty days after the death of other relatives.

4. If a large contingent of people visits as a group, such as, for example, representatives of an organization, the mourner may bid them farewell. Special respects are accorded to a large number of people.

5. On the Sabbath, the mourner may greet others with *Shabbat shalom,* and they may respond. As to whether others may initiate greetings, there is a difference of opinion, and the mourner should follow the practice of his own community.

6. May visitors greet each other in the house of mourning? It is considered in poor taste even to utilize the word *shalom* in the house of mourning, especially since one must then differentiate between the greeting spoken to the bereaved and that spoken to the comforters.

7. Other forms of greeting to the mourner (not using the word *shalom*), such as "good evening," etc., also should be avoided. Merely sitting beside the mourner is sufficient. If one desires to approach the mourner directly, the mention of his name alone is indicative of both courtesy and the compassion for his bereavement. Visitors may greet each other but should avoid using the word *shalom*.

8. The religiously proper way to bid farewell is to use the Hebrew phrase, *Ha-Makom yenachem [otecha* for one male, *otach* for one female, *etchem* for many mourners, *etchen* for more than one female mourner] *betokh she'ar avelei Tziyyon vi-Yerushalayim.* One may use the translation, as well: "May God comfort you among the other mourners of Zion and Jerusalem." It is, after all, God alone who can provide the only valid, lasting comfort at this moment of anguish. God, in this phrase,

119

is referred to as *Ha-Makom*, which ordinarily means "The Place." It implies that the omnipresent God—who is everywhere at every time, was present at the birth and death, and is now present in the house of mourning—knows the grief that is suffered by the mourners. He is the God who will grant comfort.

9. There is no reason why the visitors should not wish the mourner well: that he be blessed with good health and strength, that in the long future he be shielded from great sorrow, and that he be granted long life, or other appropriate blessings. By the same token, the mourner may extend these good wishes or *mazal tov* for some happy occasion to those who visit. It is spiritually and psychologically valuable for the mourner to demonstrate concern for others—for their sorry plight or their good fortune—although he is himself steeped in the despair of his own difficulties.

10. To bring expensive material gifts to the mourner is not only in poor taste but also in violation of the traditional custom. The avoidance of sending gifts is in a class with avoiding greetings. It expresses only the superficial joys of friendship at a time of profound personal disorientation. Traditionally, the meal of condolence was an appropriate gift of consolation. Similarly, bringing food to alleviate the mourner's need to cook is in keeping with the spirit of *avelut*. A gift to charity in honor of the deceased also is a meaningful gesture. Thoughtful visitors will follow these suggestions.

PERSONAL HYGIENE AND GROOMING

"Cleanliness is next to Godliness" is a mantra of modern Western society. In Judaism, the washing of hands must have been a major factor in avoiding medieval plagues. In mourning observances, *halakhah* considers hand washing not only as a need but as a potential source of enjoyment, in which case it is not consistent with mourning. How does Jewish law manage this apparent contradiction?

Bathing

As personal pleasures are denied the mourner in all his other activities during *shivah*, so the mourner may not bathe or shower for pleasure. The Jewish tradition has always emphasized the urgent requirement of washing, and it has never compromised its age-old insistence on the need for total cleanliness. But the Sages of the Talmud realized that sometimes washing also was done for comfort, and this is not in keeping with the spirit of mourning.

In having to judge where cleanliness ends and comfort begins, the Sages maintained that the bathing of the whole body and the use of hot water were sources of pleasure, and not necessarily essential to the basic cleaning process. While they rejected washing of the whole body at one time, as in a pool, bath, or shower—and in hot water—they did permit the washing of separate parts of the body or head and face, and in cool water.

1. One who is ill, or perhaps a woman before or after giving birth, or anyone else who feels his health requires him to bathe in warm water may do so even during *shivah*, on the direct advice of a physician. He should prepare his bath, however, in as inconspicuous a manner as possible.

2. One who is very sensitive, *istnis*, and is accustomed to showering every single day, and experiences discomfort at having to forgo that necessity (not for him a luxury), may shower even during *shivah*. He should be careful to do so inconspicuously. In general, in our society, people who customarily shower several times a week, and experience discomfort when they are prevented from doing so, may shower during *shivah*.

3. If one becomes dirty, he should remove the dirt with soap and water.

4. A woman should not perform immersion in the mikvah during *shivah* since, in any case, she is prohibited from marital relations during *shivah*.

5. Children under Bar/Bat Mitzvah age may wash, as they are not obligated to observe the laws of mourning.

The Use of Cosmetics

The use of cosmetics to enhance one's appearance not only is acceptable in Judaism but desirable, especially if it helps in matters of matrimony and family. Below are halakhic concerns about their use by mourners.

1. As mourners must refrain from bathing, so must they, male or female, refrain from using oils, soaps, perfumes, colognes, and hair cream, even if they are to be used only for parts of the body or for the hair. Certainly, if soap or oil must be used to remove sweat or dirt, it is permissible. Makeup, including foundation, eye shadow, blush, powder, lipstick, mascara, and nail polish, should also be avoided as these obviously are for cosmetic purposes and not for cleanliness. If the cosmetics are required to cover a wound or such, the mourner's needs are perfectly understandable.

2. If the mourner is engaged to be married, or has a significant other, she may feel that the cosmetics are critical for her appearance in terms of socializing, with the ultimate goal of marrying. The law is that she may use the cosmetics even during this period of mourning, but she should use them sparingly. The same rule applies if she is recently married and feels this way. The rabbis were very protective of a woman's sensitivities and would not allow anything at all to disrupt a possible *shiddukh* (betrothal), a marriage, or even strain the relationship of married people.

3. If there are medical reasons for applying oils or ointments of any kind, they should of course be used.

Haircutting

The Talmud, in describing the origin of the prohibition of haircutting for the mourner, cites the command of God to the sons of Aaron that they not prevent their hair from growing. From an analysis of the Biblical text, we can determine that the duration of the prohibition is thirty days.

Allowing the hair to grow is another indication of the withdrawal of the mourner from society. It is part of the general mourning pattern of forsaking personal appearance and grooming at a time of great personal loss. Such reactions are well known to anthropologists. One of the principal characteristics of the hermit was the unrestrained growing of hair. Similarly, the ancient Nazirite, who was a spiritually inspired rebel against the sinfulness of society, did not cut his hair, expressing a rejection of civility.

In our contemporary community many youngsters, who arc not in the least spiritually inspired, demonstrate their rebellion by letting their hair grow excessively long. It is an act of abandoning accepted norms and withdrawing from rigid rules of society. While the mourner is never asked to become a recluse—religious or social—he nevertheless is in a state of social withdrawal. He does not go to business or parties; he does not even go out-of-doors. IIe does not wish to be bothered with the social amenities of "hellos" and "good-byes." IIe allows his hair and beard and nails to grow in a spirit of abandonment because life's tragic twists and turns have demoralized him. Only upon his emergence from deep despair, when relatives or friends begin to comment on his unkempt appearance, does the mourner begin to groom himself again.

In ancient times, when the normal custom of society was for men to grow long beards, withdrawal from society was symbolized by shaving, as in Jeremiah 41: "The people came from Shechem . . . with shaven cheeks and rent clothing." Today, in a society of the clean-shaven, the mourner withdraws by allowing his hair and beard to grow. As we noted in the section on personal hygiene, however, the mourner is not expected to look unkempt and disheveled and may, therefore, comb his hair in accordance with the minimum acceptable standards of social living.

From these principles the following traditions derive:

1. When mourning for relatives other than parents, haircuts are not permitted until the end of the thirty-day period, the *sheloshim*.

2. Optimally, those in mourning for a parent should not cut their hair for twelve months. However, the law provides for the principle of "social reproach." This means that those

in mourning for parents may cut their hair after the thirty days at the first instance of even mild reproach or criticism by friends or neighbors. Immediately after this social reproach, the mourner is permitted to get a haircut. But, he may not do so before the thirtieth day after interment, even if he is reproached.

This reproach does not need to be a critical remark but only an observation: "Why is your hair so long?" (In our very tolerant society, that question may never be asked!) And the comment is valid whether it comes from a Jew or non-Jew. In fact, the social reproach does not even have to be articulated. If the length of the hair is so marked that he would be called an eccentric, he is permitted to get a haircut immediately after *sheloshim*.

3. A festival occurring after *shivah*, but during *sheloshim*, which ordinarily cancels the remainder of *sheloshim*, allows a mourner for relatives other than parents to get a haircut prior to the onset of the holiday, toward evening. On Pesach this should be done before noon.

For mourners of parents, the festival before the end of *sheloshim* does not suspend the prohibition of getting a haircut. However, after the *sheloshim*, the festival takes the place of social reproach, and allows the mourner to get the haircut toward evening before the onset of the holiday.

The onset of the Sabbath is no reason for the mourner to take a haircut.

4. The female mourner may set her hair. The Sages were more lenient with regard to a woman's appearance. Also, they understood that people tend to focus on a woman's appearance on "dressy" occasions.

5. Marriage is no reason for self-abandonment. It does not confer upon husband or wife the option of being disheveled. Therefore, Maimonides and other major authorities permitted a married woman to have her hair cut after *shivah*. The recognized custom, however, is to wait until after *sheloshim*.

6. The coloring and cutting of hair at the beautician's before the thirtieth day is not sufficiently important to exempt a woman from the laws of mourning. But having a beautician wash and set her hair, or her wig, is permitted after *shivah*.

7. If the mourner is a political figure and must make an important appearance during the thirty days, he should consult a rabbi as to whether he may take a haircut. Likewise, one who is obliged to appear in court, or before a distinguished, generally non-Jewish, body, or before important business leaders who have no knowledge of Jewish law, might be at a disadvantage. His unkempt appearance might seriously damage his cause or his business. He should request rabbinic advice regarding taking a haircut.

8. A mustache may be trimmed after *shivah* if its growth interferes with eating in any way.

9. Hair combing is entirely permissible during *shivah*, for both women and men. Neatness, as cleanliness, need not be ignored during *shivah*. It is entirely in keeping with the dignity of the deceased to honor him through the observance of the law, and also by a display of respectability and neat appearance despite the fact that one is in mourning and is not clean-shaven.

Shaving

Shaving generally follows the laws of haircutting: Theoretically, for relatives other than parents, shaving is permissible only after thirty days, and for parents, not until the mourner experiences the social reproach *after* the *sheloshim*. However, it should be realized that this law obtained in a predominantly beard-wearing society.

In the modern, Western world, where the clean-shaven face is standard, the estimated time for social reproach in regard to shaving "can hardly be longer than a few weeks," according to the great sage Noda bi-Yehudah (Rabbi Ezekiel Landau), writing in the eighteenth century. After this time, the thornlike cheek bristles would surely cause the mourner anguish, and shaving would be in order. In our world of electric shavers and ultraistic neatness in the business environment, the time is surely much shorter. Indeed, in the 1930s, the author of the Kol Bo on mourning had already decided that those who shave daily and who need a smart appearance for parnassah, their business or profession, may shave after *shivah*.

There is, however, less permissiveness to shave because of an appearance before a group of knowledgeable and observant Jewish people. So, too, if the mourner attends the circumcision of his son, there is no reason to violate the mourner's practice of haircutting or shaving.

Laws that flow from this understanding are as follows:

1. The occurrence of a festival after *shivah*, before the *sheloshim*, permits the mourner for relatives other than parents to shave before the onset of the festival.

2. Even a mourner for parents, if he must represent the Jewish community in some endeavor, as was noted in the previous section on haircutting, may shave.

3. A groom, on the day of his wedding, may shave.

4. If hair growth causes or aggravates a skin condition, the mourner may shave.

5. If, after *shivah*, business policy would strictly mandate a neat appearance, a rabbi will permit shaving.

Nail Trimming

The male mourner may not trim his nails with scissors or a nail file during the *sheloshim*. The female mourner who requires the trimming of her nails, such as for ritual immersion, or if they have grown to abnormal length, should preferably have a manicurist trim them after *shivah*. If the mourner prefers to do them herself, she may do so, using a file or scissors or other instruments.

LAUNDERING AND WEARING NEW CLOTHES

The principle of avoiding pleasure during mourning also applies to the prohibition against laundering and against wearing freshly laundered or dry-cleaned clothes during *shivah*. The mourner must deny himself certain pleasures while continuing to exercise normal standards of hygienic care and personal dignity. After *shivah* but during *sheloshim*, he may wear such clothes but preferably after someone wears them for a few minutes or even after slightly crumpling the pressed creases.

One of our quiet delights is getting dressed in freshly laundered and cleanly pressed clothes. A feeling of refreshing newness prepares you for the toil of the day and generates a healthy frame of mind. Thomas Carlyle, the nineteenth-century Scottish essayist, said that the first impulse of man is ornamentation or dressing-up. Thus, we have the halakhic practice of dressing up for the Sabbath, what in Western jargon is called "Sunday best."

This spirit of newness and a fresh start contradicts the mental attitude of the mourner, whose mind is gripped by the "end of days" and times gone by. The mourner looks not forward, but backward to the past, one portion of which has just been closed shut. It is a past lived in relationship with someone close to him, with whom he was emotionally intertwined, and who is now deceased. The days of mourning are filled with review, not with plans; with a relationship ended, not with a new beginning; an era terminated without a hint of beginning again. In such a mood, a simple pleasure like a newly pressed shirt is out of place. A new suit or dress is an affront to the mourner's inner spirit.

While newly washed and tailored clothes may not be worn, wearing clean clothes is mandatory. If the only clothes available are soiled, they must be washed and then worn. Tradition permits the mourner to wear freshly washed clothes for cleanliness, if no others are available, not for pleasure.

Laundering

Two laws are involved in the laundering of clothes during *shivah*:

1. The mourner may not wash clothes, even if only to soak them in plain water or prepare them for wearing the week after; this is considered "work" and prohibited during the *shivah*. The only exception is infant's clothing, when there is no one else available to do it.

2. The mourner may not wear freshly laundered clothes that have been washed by someone else during *shivah*, or even before the death.

- The mourner is not permitted to wear freshly laundered or freshly pressed clothes during *shivah*. He should wear clean clothes that were worn to the funeral, or at any time previously, but by no means clothes that are soiled.
- If the clothing becomes soiled, he should wash out the dirt, and if that proves difficult he should change the garment.
- Shirts, blouses, trousers, underclothes, socks, stockings, or other garments that touch the body and are liable to absorb sweat and bodily odor may be changed when necessary, even during *shivah*.
- Handkerchiefs and bed sheets follow the law of underclothes referred to above. A freshly washed tablecloth may be used for the Sabbath, when there is no public mourning, but may not be used on weekdays.
- In honor of the Sabbath, a freshly washed shirt and simple Sabbath outer clothing may be worn. Underclothing, however, should be changed as necessary. Publicly, the mourner dresses up for the Sabbath. Inwardly, he remains himself, in mourning, even on the Sabbath.
- New clothes may not be worn during *shivah*, even on the Sabbath.
- After *shivah*, but during *sheloshim*, the mourner may wash his clothes in hot water (without detergents) and iron them. If a mourner must wear new clothes, he should have someone wear them for a few minutes so that they will no longer be considered new. The mourner may wear underclothes without any of these restrictions.

New Clothes

Simple things can spike our sentiments. New clothes make us feel refreshed and give us satisfaction. During *avelut*, their use is circumscribed by the *halakhah*.

1. During *sheloshim* one may not wear new clothes, even if

he dyes them, changing their original color.

2. Even mourners for relatives other than parents may not wear new clothes until after *sheloshim*. Exceptions may be made under certain conditions that should be evaluated by a rabbi.

3. Technically, mourners for parents may wear new clothes after *sheloshim*. However, common Jewish usage urges them not to buy new clothes during the entire year. Therefore, if the mourner finds it necessary for some reason to buy clothes, or if his friends issued what we call "social reproach," or if a festival is approaching, the mourner may purchase new clothes. In this case, however, as in the case of mourners for relatives other than parents during *sheloshim*, he should have the new clothing worn for a short while by a friend or relative.

MARITAL RELATIONS

The principle of avoiding pleasure during mourning includes the act of sexual union during the observance of *shivah*. However, this is unlike the prohibition of cohabitation during menstruation and the seven days of purification that follow—during those days, husband and wife must remain physically separated. The traditions of mourning prohibit intercourse because of the sense of joy it produces, not because of any inherent ritual impurity in the mourners. Although the law does not condone physical demonstrations of affection, the whole tradition implies that nonsexual intimacy and personal affection can bring great spiritual and psychological support to the mourner.

On the Sabbath, even though public mourning practices are suspended, the prohibition of marital relations remains in force.

The prohibition holds also for festivals, even if the death occurred during the festival and *shivah* does not begin until after the end of the holiday. Sexual congress is not permitted in that case from the time of death through the end of *shivah*, despite the fact that *shivah* actually begins later.

This law is based on the principle that while on the Sabbath and holy days public mourning practices, such as the wearing of shoes and the rent garment, are not permitted, the prohibition of intimate practices, such as marital relations, is continued at all times. The joyous nature of the holy days does not alter the terrible shock of death that struck the soul of the mourner. Nonetheless, the holy days call on the Jew to celebrate the spiritual delight in the eternal partnership with God.

STUDYING TORAH

Studying Torah is not permitted during *shivah*, because it is considered a source of joy. As the Bible itself expresses it, "The laws of God are right and rejoice the heart" (Psalms 19:9). Torah study becomes not only a source of joy, but also a means of distraction to a mourner who is sunk in despair. Such enjoyment, even from a holy source such as Torah study, is prohibited during the initial mourning period. While the bereaved may not study Bible, Prophets, Talmud, or Midrash, he may read the Book of Job, the story of the classic mourner. He also may read the penetrating poetry of anguish, the Book of Lamentations (that is read on the ninth of Av, when we commemorate the Temple's destruction), and also parts of Jeremiah that foretell doom. He also may read the laws of mourning and study books on ethical behavior.

However—and this is so very characteristic of the Jewish tradition of Torah learning—he should not study these in depth. The reason: because he may discover a new interpretation or glean a new insight into the profound depths of the Torah and Talmud, and this would bring him sublime joy, a sensation well known to those who love scholarship.

A fascinating exception to this law is cited in the Jerusalem Talmud, which says that one who has an unquenchable desire to study may in fact do so. But the question is posed: The purpose of the prohibition is to deny the mourner the delight of learning that this man, who deeply yearns for such study, will surely derive; should it not be prohibited? The answer offered is that an exception is made in this case as it is for one who becomes sick from observing the laws of mourning and who is, therefore, exempt from these laws! The law forbids pleasure; it does not command pain. The Talmud recognized that it is entirely possible that one who yearns so deeply to study can become physically ill if he is prevented from doing so. In such a case, it ruled, he is permitted to study.

Further, a question arose as to whether a scholar who finds a new interpretation, and is excited by his discovery, may put it into writing. The simple reply must be that writing is not a permissible form of work to the mourner, just as it is not permissible on *chol ha-mo'ed*, the intermediary days of Passover and Succot. However, in regard to writing new insights into Torah, it is to be equated with a man who, normally forbidden work during *shivah*, is permitted to do so if he will otherwise experience an irretrievable financial loss. By being prohibited from writing, the ideas may be forgotten, and it is, therefore, considered an irretrievable loss!

"How goodly are thy tents, O Jacob, thy study halls, O Israel!" (Numbers 24:5). We stand amazed at the rich tradition to which we are heirs, and also depressed by its gross neglect in our times. Can such a glorification of mind and soul be found on any page of world literature? Are there Boswells sufficient to chronicle the biographies of so many poor laborers who yearned for study? Are there historians wise enough to analyze the magnificent consolation that Torah brought to a people willing to endure any deprivation, even death itself, for its sake?

From the intricate laws of mourning we catch a glimpse into the eternal law of Jewish life—the love of Torah.

May a mourner teach, if teaching is his profession? As we said, one who is needed to teach a group of people Torah, when there is no one to replace him, may continue to teach during *shivah*. Likewise, one may teach youngsters Torah, if there is no other qualified teacher available, even on the very first day of mourning.

It is forbidden to keep students from study, even if the

mourning laws must be suspended temporarily for this purpose. In addition, a parent who is accustomed to teach his own children should not sacrifice seven whole days of Torah study but should continue to teach them during *shivah*. While the mourner may teach in such circumstances, he should do so in as inconspicuous a fashion as possible and should make some noticeable change in style that, while perhaps insignificant in itself, will convey the fact that teaching is an exception to the laws of mourning.

COMFORTING THE BEREAVED

A sacred obligation devolves upon every Jew to comfort mourners, whether related to them or not, and whether the mourner was a close friend or only a passing acquaintance. In Judaism, exercising compassion by paying a condolence call is a mitzvah, considered by some of our greatest scholars to be Biblically ordained. The Bible records that God visited Isaac: "And it came to pass after the death of Abraham, that God blessed Isaac, his son" (Genesis 25:11). The sages infer from this verse that God Himself comforted the bereaved Isaac.

It is a man's duty to imitate God: as God comforts the bereaved, so man must do likewise. Consolation is considered a Godlike action that the children of Israel must perform. When, following the destruction of Jerusalem and the decimation of the Jewish people, Isaiah proclaimed God's message, "Comfort ye, comfort ye My people" (Isaiah 40:1), it was not merely a recommendation from on high but a specific mandate obliging the prophet to bring consolation to his people.

The fundamental purpose of the condolence call during *shivah* is to relieve the mourner of the intolerable burden of intense loneliness. At no other time is a person more in need of such comradeship. *Avelut* means withdrawal, a personal and physical retreat from social commerce and the concern for others. It is a loss that the mourner alone has suffered. All the traditions of mourning express this troubled loneliness in diverse ways, covering the spectrum of social life—from the excessive growing of hair in indifference to social custom, to the avoidance of greetings, the minimum social courtesy.

Recognizing this state of mind, the visitor comes to the house of mourning, silently, to join the bereaved in his loneliness, to sit alongside him sorrowfully, to think his thoughts and to linger on his loss. The warmth of such human presence is inestimable. Practiced as the tradition prescribes it, true consolation is a distillation of empathy. The effect of such visits by friends and relatives—some long forgotten, others who may rarely have paid the mourner any attention at all—is the softening of loneliness and the relief of the heavy burden of despair. It is an affirmation that the world at large is not a hateful and angry place, but a warm and friendly one. It is beckoning with open arms for the mourner to return to society. Comforting the mourners, says Maimonides, is *gemilut chasadim*, a genuine kindness—to both the dead and the living.

The purpose of the condolence call is not to convince the mourner of anything at all. This is the time for accompanying him on his very own path, not for argumentation or debate. It is time for contemplating disaster. While the mourner himself may want to discuss it, it is not the prime purpose of the visit to relieve his fears for the future or his guilt for the past. Nor is it proper (indeed it borders on sacrilege, say the Sages) to impress upon the mourner the inevitability of death, as though to doubt the true purpose and justice of a decree that God issued, but that He would change if only He were free to do so. It is not seemly, perhaps it is even entirely useless, to assure the mourner that others have suffered similar tragedies or worse fates, as though by right he should be less despairing. "It could have been worse," is cold consolation. This is a time for subjectivity, for an intensely personal evaluation of life, and the mourners should not be deprived of this indulgence. Some of the importuning of visitors that "life must go on," and that the mourner should be "thankful that worse did not occur," are well meaning, but hollow and sometimes annoying expressions.

The strategy of true compassion is a blend of presence and

silence, the eloquence of human closeness. Sad, muttered words are clumsy openers of the heart compared with the whisper of soft eyes. The comradeship demonstrated by a facial expression speaks volumes that ancient bards could not match with mere words, no matter how beautiful. It fulfills at once the mourner's desperate need for both companionship and privacy. It was, therefore, an old custom, unfortunately lost to our generation, for visitors to sit silently on the earth with, and like, the mourner who sat there. How magnificent is this expression of compassion.

Therefore, the first principle of comforting the mourner, found in the major codes of Jewish law, is that one should be silent and allow the mourner to speak first. In many Jewish communities in ancient days, congregants accompanied the mourner as he walked home from synagogue on the Sabbath or holiday, and there they sat with him. How warm the physical presence of other human beings is. How it relieves the sharp sting of tragedy. The classic mourner, Job, visited by three friends, sat with them for seven days and no one uttered a sound. Ecclesiastes (3:7) notes that there "is a time to keep silent and a time to speak." The Midrash (*Kohelet Rabbah* 3:9) records that the wife of Rabbi Mana died. His colleague, Rabbi Avin, came to pay a condolence call. Asked Rabbi Mana, "Are there any words of Torah you would like to offer us in our time of grief?" Rabbi Avin replied, "At times like this the Torah itself takes refuge in silence!" Indeed, the Talmud codifies this emphasis on silence by the mourner in unusually forceful terms (*Mo'ed Katan* 15a). It categorically prohibits the mourner from studying Torah—remarkable for these expounders of the Torah—because Ezekiel, the prophet (24:17), says: "Sigh in silence." Speech leads to enjoyment, and certainly Torah study.

It is in this spirit that Maimonides cautions visitors not to speak too much. Somehow, words have a tendency to generate frivolity, so contrary to the spirit of *shivah*. Jewish folk wisdom notes: True reward comes to one who is silent in the house of mourning and voluble in the wedding hall.

It is true, of course, that it is exceedingly difficult to comfort with warmth and hope and compassion while sitting relatively silent. Perhaps that is the reason for the parting phrase of consolation, "May God comfort you among the other mourners of Zion and Jerusalem." For only God can thoroughly comfort, as He consoled Isaac after his father Abraham's death, as He comforted the other mourners of Zion after the tragic destruction of the ancient Temple, and as He has comforted those who suffered in crusades and pogroms and the Jewish exiled of every age. If the visitor feels uncomfortable in the tension of silence, he should of course talk to the mourner—but little and wisely.

When to Pay a Shivah Call

Making a *shivah* call to console mourners is a sensitive matter that requires forethought. When and how to do this is very important.

1. One may visit the mourner by day or by night.
2. Some rabbis held that the visit should be delayed until the third day after interment. The mourner's wound is fresh, the deceased is constantly in his mind, and most prefer to agonize in private. However, if for some reason this delay cannot be arranged, the visit may be made even on the very first day. Other rabbis held that consolation visits could begin as soon as mourners begin *shivah*. Actually, comforting the bereaved begins at the cemetery when the mourners leave the grave passing through parallel rows of friends and relatives.
3. Visitors do not customarily pay condolence calls on the Sabbath or holidays, because these are days when one does not mourn publicly. However, the mourner may receive company and condolences on these days. There may be *shivah* visitation on *chol ha-mo'ed*, Rosh Chodesh, Purim, and Hanukkah.
4. If one did not visit during *shivah*, one can express condolences anytime during the twelve months upon meeting those bereft of parents and during the thirty days for those bereft of other relatives.
5. Condolence calls may be paid mourners who needed to return to business during *shivah* (if it was proper to do so) the same as to other mourners. If the mourner returned to work

in violation of the tradition, he need not be visited, as he has denied himself the comfort of religious consolation.

Etiquette at the House of Mourning

The purpose of the visitor's presence and speech during the *shivah* should not be designed to distract the bereaved. It is altogether fitting, and entirely proper, to speak of the deceased, his qualities, his hopes, and his loved ones.

1. There should be no greeting, either of welcome or farewell. Details of this law are found above.

2. It is customary not to speak until the mourner does.

One should not speak too much and monopolize the discussion. Conversation in the house of *shivah* should be in the nature of a response to the mourner.

One should address the mourner's anguish, not distract his attention from it. Far from recalling the anguish that surely has not been forgotten, it gives a bereaved person the opportunity to reminisce and to express his grief aloud. Psychologists assure us that the mourner very often desires to speak of his loss. Dr. Eric Lindemann, in his *Symptomatology and Management of Acute Grief*, says: "There is no retardation of action and speech; quite to the contrary there is a push of speech, especially when talking of the deceased." Both the mourner's words and his tears should not be avoided or suppressed. It is analogous to the world of nature, where animals heal themselves by licking their wounds.

There really is no need in these pages to chastise those who believe that joking and humorous remarks or frivolous tales will relieve the bitterness of the mourner's feelings. This all too prevalent type of "socializing" in the house of mourning is a constant reminder that coarse souls know no bounds.

3. One should not urge the mourner to "sit" on the *shivah* stool, as this innocent remark may imply to the mourner that he "remain" in grief. It may possibly cause resentment.

4. The visitor should, by all means, be sensitive to the mourner's feelings, even if this means leaving early so that the mourner can have a rest from the barrage of good advice

and well-meaning instructions. There is a time for all things, the Bible tells us, and surely there is a time for leaving the house of the bereaved. Visits should never be unduly prolonged, in the mistaken belief that one's presence brings an unusual degree of relief.

5. Upon leaving, the visitor should recite the phrase in Hebrew or in English or both: *Ha-makom yenachem etchem betokh she'ar avelei Tziyyon vi-Yerushalayim,* "May God comfort you among the other mourners of Zion and Jerusalem." (The varied Hebrew text for masculine and feminine, singular and plural is found on page 119.)

Behavior during the Condolence Call

It sometimes is awkward to respond to condolence. The law provides some guidelines.

1. The mourner should not respond to even well-meant greetings during the first three days (see "Greetings and Gifts").

2. The mourner does not need to rise to greet any guest, no matter his stature, and the mourner should not feel compelled to obey the little niceties of good form at this dreadful time. Visitors will understand.

3. The mourner should sit when people comfort him as they are about to leave. However, especially during prolonged visits, he need not sit all the time but may stand and walk as he desires.

4. At mealtime, in the company of guests, the mourner can sit at the head of the table on a lower stool.

PSYCHOLOGICAL SYMPTOMS OF GRIEF

For a clearer and deeper understanding of the dynamics of grief, the visitor should be familiar with the results of a classic psychological study of bereavement. Below is the Lindemann report excerpted and abbreviated by Geoffrey Gorer in his book, *Death, Grief and Mourning*. Dr. Lindemann describes here the symptomatology of normal grief. Although the study was published more than thirty years ago, his characterizations of the grieving process are as accurate today as they were then.

The picture shown by persons in acute grief is remarkably uniform. Common to all is the following syndrome: sensations of somatic distress occurring in waves lasting from 20 minutes to an hour at a time, a feeling of tightness in the throat, choking with shortness of breath, need for sighing, and an intense subjective distress described as tension or mental pain. The patient soon learns that these waves of discomfort can be precipitated by visits, by mention of the deceased, and by receiving sympathy. There is a tendency to avoid the syndrome at any cost, to refuse visits lest they should precipitate the reaction, and to keep deliberately from thought all references to the deceased.

Another strong preoccupation is with feelings of guilt. The bereaved searches the time before the death for evidence of failure to do right by the lost one. He accuses himself of negligence and exaggerates minor omissions.

In addition, there is often a disconcerting loss of warmth in relationship to other people, a tendency to respond with irritation and anger, a wish not to be bothered by others at a time when friends and relatives make a special effort to keep up friendly relationships.

These feelings of hostility, surprising and quite inexplicable to the [participants in the study], disturbed them and were again often taken as signs of approaching insanity. Great efforts are made to handle them, and the result is often a formalized, stiff manner of social interaction.

The activity throughout the day of the severely bereaved person shows remarkable change. There is no retardation of action and speech; quite to the contrary there is a push of speech, especially when talking about the deceased. There is restlessness, inability to sit still, moving about in an aimless fashion, continually searching for something to do. There is, however, at the same time, a painful lack of capacity to initiate and maintain organized patterns of activity. What is done is done with lack of zest, as though one were going through the motions.

The bereaved clings to the daily routine of prescribed activities; but these activities do not proceed in the automatic self-sustaining fashion that characterizes normal work but have to be carried on with effort, as though each fragment of the activity became a special task. The bereaved is surprised to find how large a part of this customary activity was done in some meaningful relationship to the deceased and has now lost its significance. Especially the habits of social interaction—meeting friends, making conversation, sharing enterprises with others, seem to have been lost.

These five points: 1) somatic distress, 2) preoccupation with the image of the deceased, 3) guilt, 4) hostile reactions, and 5) loss of patterns of conduct, seem to be pathognomic of grief. There may be added a sixth characteristic, shown by patients who border on pathological reactions . . . this is the appearance of traits of the deceased in the behavior of the bereaved.

The duration of a grief reaction seems to depend upon the success with which a person does the grief work, namely emancipation from the bondage of the deceased, readjustment to the environment in which the deceased is missing, and the formation of new relationships. One of the big obstacles to this work seems to be the fact that many patients try to avoid the intense distress connected with the grief experience and to avoid the expression of emotion necessary for it. The [male] victims after [a horrendous] fire appeared in early psychiatric interviews to be in a state of tension with tightened facial musculature, unable to relax for fear they might "break down." It required considerable persuasion to yield to the grief process, before they were willing to accept the discomfort of bereavement.

END OF *SHIVAH*

Just as at the commencement of *shivah*, the tradition considers a portion of the day a full day, so at its conclusion the *shivah* terminates in the morning, although it is only a small portion of the seventh day. Thus, if interment took place on

Tuesday before dark, *shivah* ends on Monday morning. The mourner should wait, however, until after morning services. He then receives formal condolences and rises.

If interment took place on Sunday, the *shivah* technically should end on the Sabbath morning. So, indeed, the private observances of mourning terminate on the Sabbath morning after services. Thus, too, the mourner should not accept a Torah honor until the late afternoon Sabbath service. However, the public observances of *shivah* end on Friday, prior to the onset of the Sabbath. For details as to exactly when it ends, see the section on "The Sabbath During *Shivah* and *Sheloshim*." (page 89)

Many follow the custom of having all mourners leave the house and walk outside together for a short distance. This thoughtful move symbolizes a return to the society from which the *avel* has withdrawn.

SHELOSHIM PRACTICES

The *sheloshim*, or thirty-day period, constitutes the complete mourning observances for all relatives other than father and mother. Mourning for those bereaved of their parents terminates at the end of twelve Hebrew months.

The counting of *sheloshim* follows the principles used in counting *shivah*, as detailed above.

1. A portion of a day is equal to a full day. Thus, *sheloshim* ends after the Shacharit service at the synagogue on the morning of the thirtieth day.

2. The period technically commences after interment, not after death. For example, if burial took place on Monday afternoon, *sheloshim* ends four weeks later on Tuesday morning.

3. Unlike *shivah*, a festival does not cancel the *sheloshim* period unless the observance of *shivah* had already ended prior to the onset of the holiday, in which case *sheloshim* is cancelled.

Following is a brief review of the *sheloshim* observances. (For details see the pertinent sections above.)

1. The following practices are observed by all mourners only during *shivah,* and are *not* practiced during *sheloshim*:
   - Sitting on a low stool
   - Remaining indoors
   - Wearing of non-leather shoes
   - Abstention from marital relations
   - Prohibition of work
   - Prohibition of studying Torah

2. The following prohibitions *continue* from *shivah* and are to be observed during *sheloshim* under normal circumstances:
   - Haircutting, shaving, nail cutting, bathing, and the wearing of new clothes or newly laundered clothes
   - Getting married
   - Attending parties

In addition:

- Greetings may be extended by the mourner, but others should not inquire after his *shalom* as, obviously, he is not experiencing peace.
- Gifts, including Purim gifts, are not to be sent to the mourner. On Purim, however, the mourner is obligated to send gifts to others, as prescribed by tradition.

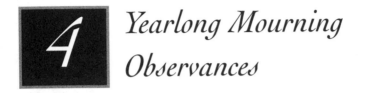# 4 *Yearlong Mourning Observances*

TWELVE MONTHS COMPLETES the full mourning period for those bereft of their parents, just as thirty days concludes the mourning period for other relatives. It should be noted that the counting of the twelve months does *not* follow the rules used in the counting of *shivah* and *sheloshim*.

COUNTING THE TWELVE HEBREW MONTHS

Following are the differences between counting thirty days and counting twelve months.

1. When counting the twelve months we do not subscribe to the principle that a portion of the day is equal to a full day and that, therefore, a portion of a month is equal to a full month. We must count twelve full months.

2. The counting of the twelve months begins from the day of death, not from the day of interment as in counting *shivah*. One who died on the first day of the Hebrew month of Tevet is mourned until the end of the first day of Tevet of the following year. If death occurred on the second day, he is

mourned through the second day of that month next year, and so on, provided this is for a twelve-month year (see below).

3. The duration of mourning observances is not one year, but twelve months. In a leap year, when the Hebrew calendar adds one full month, called Adar Sheni, only twelve months are observed, not the thirteenth that is added to make the leap year. This applies to all mourning observances except Kaddish, which is recited for only eleven months as will be described below.

Survey of Observances

Following is a brief survey of the observances of the twelve-month period for mourners of parents.

1. Haircutting, technically prohibited for twelve months, is permitted upon the occasion of social reproach after the *sheloshim*.

2. Similarly, wearing new clothes is permitted upon "social reproach" after the *sheloshim* and after being worn for a brief period of time by others. Without the above two conditions, it is halakhically a twelve-month observance.

3. The mourner should find a new seat for weekday prayers in the synagogue. On the Sabbath, he should sit in his usual place, to avoid overt mourning practices on this holy day.

4. The mourner should, in general, pay closer attention to educational, charitable, and religious matters; these, the Sages say, are the most eloquent tributes to the teachings of the deceased parent. Thus, it has become customary for the mourner to study a portion of the Torah, Mishnah, or Talmud before or after daily services. He also should learn to lead all or part of congregational services.

5. Regulations pertaining to the recital of Kaddish and participation in joyous celebrations will be treated in the following sections.

HISTORY OF THE KADDISH

The Kaddish is a vigorous declaration of faith. It is one of the most beautiful, deeply significant, and spiritually moving prayers in the Jewish liturgy. It is an ancient Aramaic prose poem, a litany whose word-music, strong rhythms, stirring sounds, and alternating responses of leader and congregation hypnotize listeners. The Kaddish is an echo of ancient Job, reverberating in the prayer book: "Though He slay me, yet will I trust in Him" (Job 13:15).

It is a call to God from the depths of catastrophe, exalting His name and praising Him, despite the realization that He has just wrenched a human being from life. Like the Kol Nidre prayer of Yom Kippur, the Day of Atonement, the significance of the Kaddish usually is taken for granted. It is a response from the subvaults of the soul—a primitive, mesmerizing response to the sacred demand to sanctify Almighty God. Its passionate recitation has inspired a healthy, vigorous expression of strength, surprising for a time of deep sorrow.

The Kaddish appears in the traditional services no fewer than thirteen times a day. It is recited at the conclusion of all the major prayers and at the conclusion of the daily prayer services. It also serves as a transition at every turning point in the service. It is recited after a Talmud study period, at the cemetery after burial, at services during the year of mourning, and at every yahrzeit. The Sages said that one who recites the Kaddish with inner strength and conviction will merit the annulment of any severe Divine decree that may be directed against him. In fact, the Sages contend that the whole world itself is maintained because of the recital of Kaddish, which redeems the deceased from possible perdition.

The Kaddish was considered so vital to the religious life of the Jew that it was recited in Aramaic, the spoken tongue of the Jewish masses in ancient times, in order that every individual could understand it. In testimony to its continuing power, it is recited in that language to this very day. Another

144

reason suggested for the use of the common Aramaic language is that Kaddish functioned as an educational device. It taught that the daily, secular life must be infused and interpenetrated by sanctity, the epitome of which is expressed in the Kaddish.

Inevitably, the Kaddish became so popular that the Sages actually had to forewarn the people lest they come to rely on it as on some magical power. It was feared that they would increase the number of Kaddish recitations, possibly leading to the undesirable consequence that a prayer for the dead might become central to the worship of God.

For all its majesty, grandeur, and importance, the origins of the Kaddish are beclouded in the obscurity of our ancient religious tradition. From the sparse, yet emphatic, references to the Kaddish in the Talmud, it is evident that the recitation of the essence of the Kaddish—*Yehe sheme rabba*, "May His great name be blessed"—was so well established a custom that its origin and significance simply were taken for granted. It is probable that the Kaddish was formulated after the destruction of the first Temple and was recited primarily after a lecture or discourse on a Torah theme. It then slipped easily into the worship service into which its themes and responses fitted admirably.

There arose five variations of the basic Kaddish that embodied the "*Yehe sheme rabba*," the central core of every Kaddish.

1. The abbreviated form called the Half Kaddish, follows minor portions of the service, sounding a transitional theme.

2. The Full Kaddish is used to terminate major parts of the service and, thus, includes the prayer beginning Titkabel, asking God to accept the heartfelt words just uttered.

3. The Rabbis' Kaddish is used as an epilogue to the study of rabbinic literature and contains the rubric Al Yisrael, a prayer for the welfare of students of Torah—and of all Israel—in the hope that they may devote themselves uninterruptedly to their sacred tasks.

4. Originally, only scholars and students who understood the deeper meaning of the Kaddish appreciated its significance. In the tractate *Soferim*, an early medieval geonic docu-

ment, we are told that it came to be used as solemn recitation at the end of the *shivah* period, when mourning the death of a scholar. Then, Kaddish began to ride the crest of popularity. In order to avoid embarrassing distinctions between a true scholar and a learned layman, it came to be used for all who died and by all, especially youngsters, who did not even know how to recite the prayers or study the Oral Law. It then began to engage the minds of all Jews, knowledgeable or illiterate, and it was recited at the closing of every Jewish grave.

Thus, a fourth form of Kaddish arose, the Burial Kaddish, which adds a prayer for the resurrection of the dead and the restoration of the Temple. It soon became associated with the deepest human emotions.

5. Then a fifth and final form of Kaddish, the Mourner's Kaddish, was incorporated into the service. It was recited for the first year after interment, making it the primary prayer for the Jewish bereaved of every age. Although nothing in the Mourner's Kaddish explicitly refers to the grave, the dead, or to life after death, the recitation of the Kaddish and its cadences were so well patterned to the mood of the mourner that it became a cherished part of the whole Jewish people.

Please see Appendix One for the complete Burial, Mourner's, and Rabbi's Kaddish.

FUNCTION OF THE KADDISH

The Mourner's Kaddish performs two pragmatic functions: it blends in with the internal spirit of the mourner, imperceptibly healing his psychological wounds; and it teaches the mourner vital and profound lessons about life and death, and the conquest of evil. It is, therefore, no accident of spiritual history that the Kaddish has become so important to those stricken with grief, and that, in the course of time, it went on to become the hallmark of bereavement.

The Kaddish as Consolation

As far back as ancient times, the Kaddish was associated, albeit indirectly, with consolation, *nechamah*. In the earliest source dealing with the Mourner's Kaddish we find that the leader of the service proceeded to the rear of the synagogue, where the mourners were congregated, and publicly comforted them with the mourner's blessing and Kaddish. It should be noted that the Kaddish recitation coincided, and was precisely coterminous, with the twelve-month time traditionally provided for comforting mourners of parents. (Only later was this period reduced to eleven months.)

In a spirit of consolation and surrender, this beautiful litany begins with the admission that the world that is known only to God remains mysterious and paradoxical to man. It ends with an impassioned hope, expressed in the words of the friends of Job as they sought to comfort him, *Oseh shalom bimromav*, that He who is sufficiently mighty to make peace among celestial bodies can also bring peace to all mankind.

Finally, we pray to achieve, in the words of the Kaddish, the *nechemata*, the consolation of all of the Jewish people, not only for their dead, but also for the destruction of their ancient Temple and their holy city, Jerusalem. Indeed, many rabbis maintain that the Kaddish finds its origin in the prayer composed by the men of the Great Assembly for the consolation of the population following the destruction of the First Temple and their subsequent exile. In fact, it is in response to this historic tragedy that Ezekiel first cries out the words from which the opening line of the Kaddish is drawn: (Ezekiel 38:23) "I have exalted and sanctified My name and I have made it known in the eyes of all nations, and they shall know that I am the Lord." The Master of all will bring His people salvation.

Besides the concepts found in the Kaddish, the very words offer implicit comfort. Because of the accentuation and repetition of the positive thoughts of life and peace, these values become impressed on the bewildered and those with saddened hearts. It transfers, subliminally, the fixed, inner gaze of the mourner from the departed to the living, from crisis to peace, from despair to hope, from isolation to community.

Indeed, the very fierce moment when man's faith is most shaken, when likely he feels defiant against God for the death that has befallen him, he rises to recite the praises of the Creator. *Yitgadal ve-yitkaddash* . . . "magnified and sanctified is He who created the universe." All the laws of nature operate in accordance with His will. Just at the time when man's focus is on the Kingdom of Heaven, the world of the dead, the destination of the departed, the Kaddish quietly, almost imperceptibly, transfers his gaze to God's kingdom on earth, among the living—*ve-yamlich malkhuteh, be-chayyekhon u-ve-yomeikhon.* "May He establish His kingdom during your lifetime and in your days." Man's vision is blurred by images of a limp frame, by shrouds and coffin and grave, by the ultimate decay and decomposition of the human being. The Kaddish beckons him to stand on his two feet and fills his mind with the constant, hypnotic repetition, morning and night, of the words *chayyim* and *yamim* and *olam,* "life" and "days" and "this world." When the mourner experiences disorientation and disruption, a sense of agitation and conflict and guilt, the Kaddish mesmerizes him with thoughts of eternal rest and quiet. It emphasizes, again and again, the peace that God made in the heavens and the *shalom* that He ultimately will bring to people on earth.

One other major technique of consolation in the Kaddish is the insistence, because it is a prayer of holiness, that it be recited only in public, in the presence of a minyan, never privately. The recitation, nowadays made alongside other mourners, creates a fellowship of the bereaved in a time of profound loneliness and helplessness. It teaches, implicitly, that others have experienced similar pains; that death is a natural, if often untimely, end to all life; that the rhythm of man has followed the same beat since the days when Adam refused to eat from the Tree of Life.

The Kaddish is a comforting prayer, grandiose in its spiritual conception, dramatic in its rhythms and word-music, and profound in its psychological insights.

When Mourners Console the Master

A great Hasidic sage noted that the death of any one of God's creatures causes a gap in the armies of the exalted King. The Kaddish, he said, is recited in the hope that that gap will be filled. It was left to Israel's poet laureate, S. Y. Agnon, to interpret this with a beautiful analogy.

The King of Kings, Almighty God, is not like a human king. When a king of flesh and blood orders his armies into battle, he sees only large effects, massive logistics, and a great goal. He does not know individual men. They are not distinguishable one from the other. In essence, they are human machines that carry weapons and perform a specific function. If this human king loses half a regiment, he sincerely regrets the mass death. But he does not mourn a single individual.

Not so the King of Kings. He is Master of the world, yet cares for each individual life. Men are not machines or ciphers; they are human beings. When God's soldiers die, He mourns each man. When a man dies, His own holy Name is diminished, His own sanctity lessened. His Kingdom experiences a painful vacancy. God suffers just as the human mourner suffers.

When human beings recite the Kaddish, they offer God consolation for His loss. We say *Yitgadal*: Thy name has been diminished; may it be magnified. *Yitkadash*: Thy sanctity has been lessened; may it be increased. *Yamlich malkhuteh*: Thy kingdom has suffered a sudden loss; may it reign eternally.

Agnon's astonishing interpretation of the Kaddish—which sees it as the mourner's attempt to console the Master of all men—is itself a consolation to the bereaved. The knowledge that God cares for every person, and that He suffers in the loss of every one of His creatures made in His own image, is a source of warmth and comfort.

Beneath the surface, the Kaddish expresses a thought basic to an understanding of the Jewish attitude toward life: an acceptance of seemingly undeserved pain and unreasonable tragedy as being the just act—even if paradoxical—of an all-wise God. In ancient sources, Kaddish is found bracketed with the Tzidduk ha-Din, a prayer justifying God's edict. This prayer is recited at the moment of burial and proclaims, "The Lord hath given and the Lord hath taken. May the name of the Lord be blessed."

The Kaddish echoes this theme: "Let His great name be blessed forever and to all eternity." It is the recognition that Almighty God knows our innermost secrets; that He reliably and justly rewards and punishes us; that He knows what is best for mankind; and that all His actions are for the eventual benefit of the whole human race. It is only by virtue of this acceptance of death as the just and inexorable terminus of life, that life can be lived to its fullest. It is only through the difficult, but necessary, acknowledgement that only the Creator understands the design of creation, that we avoid becoming disabled by the dogged questioning of imponderables that can wear out our very existence. That is why we recite in the Kaddish, "May His great name be magnified and sanctified, in this world that He has created in accordance with His will." It is a world whose ways bypass our understanding and conforms only to His will. How can our limited intellects fathom His exalted greatness or plumb the endless depths of the Divine mind? If tragedy strikes, if our families are beset by evil circumstances, we have faith that the just God has acted justly. "Where were you," God thunders at Job out of the whirlwind, "when I created the world?"

SIGNIFICANCE OF THE KADDISH

Kaddish probes even more deeply into a hidden nerve. Beyond the psychological healing that it encourages, beyond educating the mourner to adjust to tragedy, is there not some mysterious influence, some wondrous power that affects so marvelously the soul of the mourner? How does Kaddish relate to mourning for parents?

A Reflection of Parental Esteem

Kaddish is a spiritual handclasp between generations, one that connects two lifetimes. What better consolation is there for a mourner than the knowledge that the ideas and hopes and concerns and commitments of the deceased continue on in the life of his own family? The child's recitation of Kaddish represents a continuation of that life, and in that sense, it snatches the deepest worth of the individual out of the cavernous jaws of death.

How does that happen? Jewish tradition recognizes the important influence of a mother and father upon the son or daughter during the lifetime of the parent. The "merit of the fathers" is a bold and important theme in rabbinic literature. We should remember that, collectively, the Jew asks God for mercy because of the righteous deeds of the patriarchs and matriarchs of old whose descendants we are. Tradition recognizes also that the sins of parents—impure motives, ill-gotten wealth, purposeless living, and so on—may make themselves felt in the lives of children for many generations. The child's psyche indelibly bears the imprint of the parent, whether we think it just or not. For all that, however, Jewish thought never considered the parent able to redeem an erring son by virtue of his own good deeds before God. Abraham and Sarah could not save their wayward son, Ishmael. Isaac and Rebecca could not save their avaricious son, Esau.

Curiously, though, in the complicated calculus of the spirit, the reverse is possible! The deeds of a child can redeem the life of a parent, even after the parent's death! It is a neat reversal, a "merit of the children." The ethical, religious, and social virtues of children place haloes on their parents. The Talmud declares, *bera me'zakeh aba*, the son or daughter endows the father or mother. Elsewhere, Rabbi Simeon bar Yochai says, *mah zar'o ba-chayyim, af hu ba-chayyim*, so long as the children live, so long does the parent live. They who leave worthy children do not die in spirit. Their mortal remains are interred in the earth, but their teachings are energy that remain dominant on earth.

While no individual can intervene decisively with God in behalf of the life of another—neither a parent for a child, nor a child for a parent—a person surely may modify the significance of another person's life and grant it meaning and value. As the tree is judged by its fruit and the artisan by his product, so a parent achieves personal significance by the moral and intellectual success of his child. David left a son worthy of himself; the Talmud refers to David's death as "sleep," indicating his continuity in life. Of Joab, who had no son who could inherit his greatness, the Talmud says, "he died," implying finality. The reflection of the child upon the parent is true in life, and it is true after death as well.

It is precisely in this regard that Kaddish reaches its deepest level. Kaddish serves as an epilogue to a human life as, historically, it served as an epilogue to Torah study. Was that life marked primarily by goodness and dignity and nobility or by shame and disgrace, folly and weakness? In either case, the Kaddish is effective. The Sages state that a child's recitation of Kaddish confirms a parent's life of goodness on one hand, or effects repentance for a parent's life of sin, on the other.

The rabbis have long declared that a person is obligated to honor parents in death, as well as in life. Kaddish is the verbal demonstration of a deep and abiding honor that Jews were bidden to give parents since the day the fifth commandment was pronounced on Sinai. The very duration of the Kaddish recitation for parents is ample testimony to that respect. Because the wicked soul is said to undergo judgment for a full year, the child, in reverence for his parent, ends the Kaddish a month earlier, at eleven months, bearing witness, in one month's eloquent silence, to the goodness of those who bore him.

It is not the recitation of Kaddish alone that is emblematic of a parent's teaching; it also is the fact that the mourner elicits a response of holiness from others, causing others to proclaim the greatness of God with him—which the Sages term, *kiddush ha-Shem*, sanctification of the Name. The mourner announces, "May His great name be magnified and sanctified," and his neighbors respond, "Let His great name be blessed forever and to all eternity." The mourner continues, "Blessed, praised, glorified, and exalted; extolled, honored, magnified and lauded is the name of the Holy One, blessed be He," and the congregation replies, "Blessed be He." The Kaddish is thereby made into a public sanctification of God's name. It is a self-contained, miniature service that achieves the heights of holiness; this spiritual triumph reflects on the life of mother and father, and dramatically confirms the correctness of their teachings.

If, on the other hand, parents have strayed or sinned and have desecrated the name of God (*chillul ha-Shem*), the Kaddish, which is the sanctification of the name (*kiddush ha-Shem*), is considered as though the deceased repented, and redeems the deceased from divine retribution. Kaddish is not an explicit prayer for this redemption of parents, but its recital is an indication that good has nonetheless come from them and is redemptive.

The fundamental and most frequently recorded incident regarding Kaddish is the mystical vision of the great sage, Rabbi Akiva. This incident can be found in numerous sources: the Talmud, the Midrash, Zohar, and other literary works, which attests to its wide acceptance and popularity. Rabbi Akiva had a vision of a well-known sinner who had died and was condemned to intolerable punishment. The sinner implored the rabbi to have his surviving son recite the Barekhu and Kaddish— this would redeem him. The rabbi rushed to teach the youngster these prayers. As soon as the youngster recited the Kaddish, he saved his father from perdition. A child endows a parent!

Moreover, this concept of the "merit of the children" is associated historically with the central core and response of the Kaddish. Tradition records a dialogue between Jacob, the old patriarch, and his twelve sons. Jacob was anxious about the future. He was not sure his children would not follow in the wicked footsteps of their uncle, Esau, or perhaps their great-uncle, Ishmael. Would one of his sons defect from the faith of his fathers? When in great consternation Jacob confronted his sons with this worry, they declared, "Hear O Israel [Jacob], the Lord our God, the Lord is one." With great relief at being assured of the merit of his children, Jacob responded in full gratitude, "Blessed be His name whose glorious Kingdom is forever and ever." This response has been enshrined as the verse immediately following the first line of the Shema: *Barukh shem kevod malchuto le-olam va'ed*. In its Aramaic form it is almost identical with the central response of the Kaddish, *Yehe sheme rabba mevarakh le-alam u-le-alemei alemayya,* "May His great name be blessed forever and to all eternity." The Kaddish is a firm handclasp between the generations!

When death stalks our homes, it brings an end to physical life. The current is cut off. That is all. But the spirit is mightier than the grave. The thoughts and emotions, ideals and attitudes of the heirs, attest to the undying influence of the dead. The recitation of Kaddish is a public demonstration that a parent's life was not lived without furthering, in some sense, the cause of good. It is no exaggeration to say that the spiritual handclasp of the Kaddish has helped assure the continued survival of the Jewish people, the Jewish religion, the synagogue, and its major institutions.

KADDISH OBSERVANCES

The bounty of religious values and ideas that we derive from the Kaddish will come to us only if the Kaddish is observed according to the conditions framed by the *halakhah*. It is much like a river that surges between the banks on both sides. Remove these banks and the water dissipates in a random flooding of the surrounding fields. Gone are its force, its power, and its beauty. This is true with most religious observances. If Kaddish could be said by anybody at anytime, ultimately it would be said by nobody at no time. If the reader would like a graphic glimpse into the awesome power of Kaddish, he or she need only listen to Leonard Bernstein's magnificent composition, called *Kaddish.*

Following are the banks of that perpetually moving and powerful prose poem.

The Time for Kaddish

The Kaddish is recited at every prayer service, morning and evening, Sabbath and holiday, on days of fasting and on days of rejoicing.

1. While Kaddish must be recited on these days, the mourner may not violate basic religious practices in order to say the Kaddish. Thus, if one is not within walking distance of a synagogue and would have to ride on the Sabbath—a violation—it is more valuable, both in terms of respect for the deceased and the keeping of the law, to pray at home. In such an instance, the Kaddish would have to be omitted for lack of the necessary quorum. Indeed, several congregations actually do not permit the recitation of the Mourner's Kaddish on Sabbaths and holidays precisely to discourage travelling to the synagogue for that purpose. Compared with the Sabbath, Kaddish is of lesser religious weight. Respect for parents and concern for them, even in death, while highly commendable, should not cause someone to violate the ancient and hallowed religious tradition. The mourner does not determine which is a more sacred observance. Jewish tradition sensitively balances the scale of religious values by which man lives, securing the eternity of the Jewish religion.

2. The Burial Kaddish recitation begins immediately following the closing of the grave. The Mourner's Kaddish begins later, at the first prayer service, usually the Minchah prayer service, recited upon returning from the interment.

3. The period for which the mourner recites Kaddish for parents is, theoretically, a full calendar year. The deceased is considered to be under Divine judgment for that period. Some communities, therefore, adhere to the custom that Kaddish be recited for twelve months in all cases. However, a full year is considered to be the duration of judgment for the wicked. Because we presume that our parents do not fall into this category, the practice in most communities is to recite the Kaddish for only eleven months. Even on leap years, which last thirteen months, the Kaddish is theoretically recited for only twelve months. We subtract one month—and one day— so that we terminate Kaddish in time to allow a full thirty days before the end of the twelve-month period. Thus, if we begin on the eighth day of the Hebrew month of Cheshvan, we end the recitation of Kaddish on the seventh day of Tishre.

4. If a parent insists that a child recite Kaddish for the full twelve months, there surely is no reason not to obey the par-

ent. If a child feels this might bring public dishonor to his parent, he should recite only the Rabbis' Kaddish in the twelfth month. This is a practice that might be worthwhile encouraging in every case for all parents.

5. The eleven-months-minus-one-day is calculated from the day of death—especially if burial took place on the same day or the next. However, a significant number of authorities say the first yahrzeit should be observed on the date of burial, especially if burial occurred several days after death. To avoid confusion between the first yahrzeit and all subsequent years, when the yahrzeit is marked on the date of death, I suggest that the first yahrzeit also be observed on the date of death rather than the date of burial.

It is important to Judaism that community custom prevail in matters such as these. Therefore, the *avel* should consult his rabbi to determine community practice.

6. On the last day of Kaddish recitation, it is desirable that the mourner receive an *aliyyah*, a Torah honor.

7. Kaddish for relatives other than parents for whom one is obliged to mourn—son, daughter, brother, sister, spouse— is recited for thirty days according to some customs. Many traditional communities have never adopted this and have limited it to *shivah*. In the case of no surviving son to recite the daily Kaddish, a relative who has lost one or both parents would do well to take upon himself this strenuous responsibility.

Requirement of a Minyan

Kaddish should be recited only in the presence of a duly constituted quorum, which consists of ten males (including mourners) above the age of Bar Mitzvah. Nine adults and one minor do not constitute a quorum for a minyan. However, many rabbis hold that in certain circumstances, when there is absolutely no other opportunity for its recitation, especially if the minor himself is the mourner, he may be counted toward completing the minyan.

While the Kaddish is an intensely personal tribute spoken out of respect for one's own parents, it may not be said privately. It is true that the individual is accorded great value in Jewish ethics, and it is the individual who is commanded, "Be ye holy, for I the Lord your God am holy." However, this service of holiness must be recited only in public so that it can elicit the response of a minyan. Judaism teaches the values of which the Kaddish speaks, peace and life; the struggle to bring heaven down to earth can be achieved only in concert with society and proclaimed amidst friends and neighbors of faith. If the Kaddish were solely an expression of personal remembrance for the deceased, it would be logical to recite it privately—as the Yizkor can be recited. But, since Kaddish is an adoration of God, it must be prayed at a public service in the midst of a congregation—a minyan—of thinking and believing adults.

Indeed, in a historical twist of fate, it is because of this age-old insistence on a quorum for Kaddish that minyanim have been convened in the most unlikely places; that travelers could gather a minyan in Jewish communities all over the world; and that communities have remained united in all the ages of Jewish dispersion. The recitation of Kaddish has united the generations in a vertical chain, father to son, while the requirement to gather a minyan for Kaddish has united Jews on a horizontal plane. Kaddish, miraculously, has brought together parents and children and also man and his neighbors.

MOURNERS OBLIGATED TO SAY KADDISH

The primary obligation to say Kaddish falls upon the child of the deceased. It is he who is required to recite it; he and not his relatives; he and not someone paid to substitute for him. A child brings merit to a parent. In the vision of Rabbi Akiva, it was a son's recitation that saved his father, and it was the child himself who had to learn it for that reason. Not even the Kaddish of Rabbi Akiva himself, the spiritual giant of the age, could be effective.

The son's obligation is just that; it is not a matter of personal preference, nor does it depend on the family situation or the parent-child relationship. It is a clearly defined obligation placed upon the son by tradition, and the son may not shirk this sacred duty. Indeed, in past generations, an only son was frequently referred to by his parents as the *kaddishel*, the "little Kaddish." One simply may not appoint an agent to fulfill a personal religious obligation. As one may not ask a relative or pay a stranger to fulfill the obligations of the fifth commandment, to honor one's parents, so one may not hire an intermediary to recite Kaddish for parents after death. The prayer without the person is bare.

Minor Children

The obligation to recite Kaddish devolves upon a child even if he is a minor (not having reached Bar/Bat Mitzvah age). It is worthwhile to emphasize *especially* if he is a minor. There is every indication that the Kaddish was intended precisely for those who could not, or did not know how to, lead services. The simple Kaddish recitation, learned easily in one sitting, enabled the youngster to help the congregation in hallowing the name of God. The Kaddish also is an appropriate psychological method for the child to express his grief and thereby receive consolation that is gradual and lasting, one that will bind him closely to the synagogue for the remainder of his life. In the case of very young children, the matter is best decided by the family in conjunction with the rabbi. The minor, however, should not be asked to conduct the public prayer service, whether or not he knows how.

Adopted Children

It is entirely proper, though not religiously mandatory, for a son to say Kaddish for his adoptive parent or stepparent, especially if that parent has raised him for many years. An adopted son or stepson, naturally, should not be compelled to recite Kaddish if there was no filial sentiment between them. There is a stronger plea for the adopted son to say Kaddish, however, if there are no natural sons who survive the parent. See the section on "Discretionary Mourning."

SHOULD WOMEN SAY KADDISH?

The law reads that the primary obligation to recite Kaddish is placed upon a son—presumably, therefore, not upon a daughter. The Sages realized that Kaddish, which must be recited at services before breakfast and at dinner, could not be made compulsory for all women: this daily, yearlong obligation is not for mothers and wives who must attend to their families on an as-needed basis.

The tradition appreciated the equality of male and female in the realm of emotion and love; however, the Sages saw the folly of legally demanding a woman, whose primary occupation was the family, to be hindered in that vocation by prayer at fixed times. Thus, they did not place the *obligation* to recite Kaddish upon any woman, regardless of her individual circumstance, even if she could manage the obligation to meet the requirements of public prayer twice daily.

This reasoning says that a daughter is not obligated for the daily Kaddish. But may she recite it voluntarily? Is our era not critically different from previous ages? Today, women often are free from laborious household tasks and do not always have families dependent upon them—especially after child-bearing age, when adult children customarily lose their parents—and when numerous women remain single all their lives.

The Sages of centuries past did not mean to imply that there is a difference in the quality of compassion between a son and a daughter. They did not say that only a son, and not a daughter, could bring merit to a parent by saying Kaddish. Indeed, they said precisely the opposite: the behavior of a son and daughter reflect exactly the same merit or shame on their parents. Their recitation of Kaddish is equally effective. This was affirmed in virtually every

Responsum on the subject published through the Middle Ages and into the twentieth century. In light of this, sons *and* daughters were both mandated to observe the entire spectrum of mourning obligations—with the one exception: Kaddish.

Rabbi Yaakov Reischer, writing at the beginning of the eighteenth century, emphatically states (*Sh'vut Yaakov, volume 2, number 93*) that a daughter has every right to say Kaddish—and should do so—in the home where there is a minyan, though not in the synagogue (at that time women did not attend synagogue the way they do today). My late revered teacher, Rabbi Joseph B. Soloveichik, told my brother and many of my colleagues that women recited Kaddish in the "Gaon's *Klaus*," the Vilna Gaon's own synagogue. Rabbi Moshe Feinstein, one of the century's leading decisors, who died in 1986, noted—in a delicious disclosure of a profound truth often made in the off-hand remarks of great scholars—that "a certain lady was in shul today, probably to say Kaddish." A book on the history of the shtetl, *Once There Was A World* by Yaffa Eliach, describes a teenage girl saying Kaddish at the front of the synagogue near the great sage known as the Chafetz Chayyim.

There are very few fundamental halakhic objections to women reciting Kaddish, but a handful of notable rabbis were ardently concerned with them. One objection centered on *kol ishah*, the sexually suggestive sound of a woman's voice, which could derail a male's fragile concentration on his prayers and lure his imagination far from the sanctuary. Another concerned the question of whether, in fact, a woman saying Kaddish in a sectioned-off women's area of the synagogue was halakhically in the presence of a required minyan, formed by ten men.

These are legitimate rabbinic questions, but they are not intractable, and ultimately they can be solved. Realistically, however, these halakhic questions are secondary to the concerns of public policy, which constitutes a larger and more far-reaching matter for the rabbis.

Those who insist on allowing Kaddish only for sons hold that a woman leading the responsive prayer of Kaddish, in the full view and hearing of the congregation, will trigger a breach in the traditional way that Jews conduct their religious and communal activities. Any other decision bears in it the seed of destruction of the synagogue as we know it today.

Curiously, even this question of public policy is more compliant today. Permitting a woman to say Kaddish was substantially more religiously perilous at the dawn of the nineteenth century, when it was the universal Ashkenazic custom to select a single mourner to recite the congregation's Kaddish, while the other mourners stood in silent assent. This one mourner usually was stationed at the front of the congregation. Today, virtually all synagogues follow the Sephardic custom that all mourners in the synagogue recite Kaddish simultaneously and do so while standing at their own seats, no matter in which section of the synagogue. Permitting a woman to say Kaddish in that earlier congregational environment was an exceptionally difficult task, but today it is infinitely easier to do. Today, reciting the Kaddish is open to all women who want to express their grief in this manner and speak to the Almighty on behalf of their beloved departed relatives.

What to do? The local rabbi should be the final arbiter of this question, not only on the matter of *halakhah*, but also on communal policy. This is his prerogative. Detailed halakhic disputation need not capture the day.

The leading rabbinic authority on the subject of women and Kaddish was Rabbi Yosef Eliyahu Henkin, a universally recognized scholar with impeccable halakhic credentials, who published his responsum in *Ha-Pardes*, a reputable halakhic journal. It was Rabbi Henkin who boldly contended that women should be *encouraged* to recite the mourner's Kaddish in the synagogue—when they can get to shul.

Remarkably, I believe, there is little chance that women saying Kaddish in the synagogue will lead to a breakdown of Jewish tradition. There is ubiquitous, inescapable *kol isha* in our media-driven culture. Consequently, there will be less concern with the distraction. In our wide-open society, the display of intimacy is so ever-present, the mere sound of a woman's voice in prayer will hardly lead to breathless fantasies.

On the contrary, my worry is that if women in traditional synagogues are not given the opportunity to express themselves through *halakhot* in sensitive areas such as mourning, the consequences will be destructive. There is a need to empower women religiously—not pander to political and cultural correctness—always staying within the framework of *halakhah*. There is a need to encourage women's participation in synagogue life; to allow women to express their innermost spiritual yearnings in a traditional mode; and to trust contemporary rabbinic leadership to be receptive to a woman's continuing religious needs. This was fundamentally Rabbi Henkin's contention. It is fifty years later. Should we not finally hear his voice?

If a woman sincerely desires to recite the Kaddish—out of religious reasons or out of sheer respect for a deceased parent—and if she determines that it generally will not interfere with other significant duties—she has a choice of three ways to memorialize the deceased:

1. She can listen closely to the Kaddish of the men in the congregation, while concentrating on her own bereavement.

2. She can follow the age-old rabbinic suggestion of responding fervently to every phrase of the mourner's Kaddish with an emphatic "Amen." The rabbis equated a woman's "Amen" with a man's full recitation of Kaddish. She thereby brings the same merit upon her beloved.

3. She can stand and recite the full Mourner's Kaddish whenever she attends the synagogue—at every Sabbath, festival, or weekday service of the year, on yahrzeit, and at every Yizkor service.

Kaddish by a woman should be performed at her discretion, and it should be done discreetly. She should recite those sacred words with a tremor of holiness; she should be spiritual and also soulful; and, above all, she should reflect the feminine value of *tzeni'ut* —being dignified, modest and undemonstrative. Men should recite Kaddish with identical reverence and dignity.

No woman should commit to reciting the Kaddish one

hundred percent of the time and under all conditions, lest she be forced to go back on her word. Vows are important to Jews, more so than reciting the Kaddish for a beloved parent. If a woman cannot recite Kaddish for some reason (for instance, if she is travelling) she should read a chapter of Psalms or Proverbs.

All Jewish people stand to benefit from a woman's holy resolve in saying Kaddish. May God bless them with *kedushah* (holiness) rather than Kaddish.

A Wife for her Husband

A wife desiring to say Kaddish for her husband during *sheloshim*—as some mourners for relatives other than parents do—falls into the same category as a daughter. Depending on the custom of the synagogue, she may rise with the other mourners to recite Kaddish. If she plans to do so, she will need to have permission from her parents, if they are both alive, as is the case of husbands who wish to recite Kaddish for their wives during *sheloshim*, which will be discussed later.

IS THE KADDISH OBLIGATION TRANSFERRABLE?

Relatives or friends cannot relieve the son of his obligation—whether or not an uncle happens to attend services regularly, or perhaps a brother was closer to the deceased than the son. It is the son who must recite the Kaddish, even though it will be irregularly, or even unconscientiously, performed. There is no doubt that the daily recitation of the Kaddish may become burdensome, but it is a burden that must be borne and, like other vital burdens in life, cannot be delegated.

No person may be hired to say Kaddish in the place of a living son, whether the designated person is very pious or moral or scholarly, or a rabbi or a cantor or sexton, whether or not he is a better person than the son. The Kaddish is not a magical incantation, some exalted abracadabra that opens the gates of Heaven and that needs saying, no matter by whom.

The son's *paying* for the Kaddish, rather than *praying* it, defeats every conceivable purpose of the sacred prayer. No value can be achieved by transferring this personal religious responsibility to a paid emissary. There is no possibility for a "merit of the children;" no respect given the deceased; no psychological healing; and no sanctification of the name of God. There is, in sum, nothing religious about the whole matter. It is another unfortunate consequence of the prevalent utilitarian idea that everything in this world can be bought. "Merit of the children" must be deserved; it cannot be bought. A bought Kaddish will only reflect adversely on the parent whose child has no time or patience for the reverence he should give.

If No Child Survives

Without a surviving child, the primary obligation to recite Kaddish is dissolved, and arrangements for its recitation by others should be made if at all possible. As to who must bear this secondary responsibility, there is much discussion in the responsa. Some maintain that this obligation should devolve first upon a younger brother of the deceased, as traditional religious mandate requires him to render respect to an elder sibling as to a parent.

Others maintain that this responsibility falls upon a grandson. In Genesis(48:5), Jacob likens his grandsons Ephraim and Manasseh—the sons of Joseph—to his own sons. Based on this, the talmud formulated the phrase *b'nai banim harei hem ke-banim*, "grandsons are the equivalent of sons." Nonetheless, the grandchild has no halakhic duty toward his grandparent.

Still others maintain that the obligation falls upon a son-in-law . There also is substantial opinion that would place the obligation upon the father, if he is alive, much as David prayed for his errant son, Absalom.

Fundamentally, according to Maimonides, and in our day to Rabbi Moshe Feinstein and Rabbi Ovadiah Yossef, if there is no son, Kaddish should be said by relatives.

Which relative? Clearly, in our day it would depend on which of these relatives feels closest to the deceased, finds it easier to accomplish the task of reciting Kaddish successfully, or feels religiously more impelled to do so. A friend may want to say Kaddish out of love or loyalty. In fact, a sharing of the responsibility may be easier and more effective. Whoever does undertake to say the Kaddish, however, should be one who is himself orphaned from one of his parents; otherwise he must obtain his parents' express consent to say Kaddish while they are alive.

If relatives or friends cannot, for one reason or another, accept the full obligation to recite Kaddish, should a stranger be employed to do so? In the absence of a son or relative, or a personal friend as a reliable substitute, Jewish families traditionally paid a sexton or another synagogue functionary to say Kaddish. They felt that it was better to pay for this service than to receive it for free. By paying the agent to act as their personal emissary, they felt assured of the recitation of Kaddish. The person who is engaged should not, by right, be saying the Kaddish for many others.

It should be noted that this custom, while it is practiced sincerely and conscientiously, has unfortunately brought a host of unintended consequences in its wake. It has caused people to think of respect for the dead in material terms. It has engendered the feeling that somehow the Kaddish is a sort of credit system that can be manipulated financially. It has encouraged people to "pay" for all religious services, like "hiring" a yahrzeit commemorator or Yizkor reciter, or an El Mal'e Rachamim prayer at the grave, a practice that is reprehensible to the religious spirit. Some people have come to believe that paying is more important than praying and to think of the synagogue as a celestial supermarket. They substitute the bank for the Bible and believe that they can erase all personal vices by contributions to charity. The harm this practice has caused far outweighs the good it has innocently sought to instill. As such, it should be minimized, if not totally abandoned.

There is, however, a wise recommendation made by some of our greatest scholars: to contribute to a religious institution—a yeshiva or day school, a home for elderly people, or a congregation—to enable a person to study Torah or Talmud every day and to recite the Rabbis' Kaddish in honor of the dead. This is a personal memorialization, a "merit of the children" that includes study and prayer, Torah and Kaddish, in a dignified and worthy manner. In fact, some leading rabbis made arrangements for this while they were still alive even though they had sons who would say Kaddish when they died.

FOR WHOM IS KADDISH RECITED?

Kaddish is said for a deceased father or mother, regardless of how strained the relationship between deceased and bereaved. While the primary obligation is only for a father and mother, there is a custom in major communities, though not all, that Kaddish also is said for other close relatives—brother, sister, son, daughter, and wife—for the thirty-day period, even if the deceased has children who already are saying Kaddish. The congregation's rabbi should decide this in conjunction with the mourners.

Kaddish also may be recited for Torah scholars, community leaders, and for Jews killed in war because of anti-Semitism, *al kiddush ha-Shem*, sanctifying God's name. It may be recited as well for a close friend and also at the graveside of a worthy Gentile, always providing a duly constituted minyan is present.

Age of the Deceased

Customs differ as to how old a deceased must be for Kaddish to be recited for him. Some communities set the minimum age at twenty, others at Bar Mitzvah, still others at approximately eight or nine years, depending on the maturity of the child and whether he can be considered *bar da'at*, knowledgeable and aware of basic religious requirements. Others maintain that a normal child who lived for more than thirty days should have Kaddish recited for him. While each case depends largely on community custom, it is generally held that Kaddish be said for a child who has reached a degree of maturity even though he is younger than Bar Mitzvah age. If the father insists, it may even be said after the death of an infant under thirty days.

Suicides

Suicides, especially when one is not sure of the motive, are honored with the recitation of Kaddish by their survivors. Mourners should be encouraged to recite it for the distinct spiritual benefit of the suicide (who, if the act was intentional, was guilty of a heinous crime). Indeed, it is recommended for this reason, that they recite it for the full year rather than for the customary eleven months. See the special section on suicides.

Transgressors

People who are considered sinners—out of spite or passion—and those who reject Judaism or who converted to other religions, are subjects of much scholarly controversy in regard to saying Kaddish. The majority opinion tends toward permitting Kaddish to be said for them. In fact, considering that even wicked parents, technically, deserve the child's respect; considering that Kaddish is designed to relieve the Divine punishment inflicted on perpetrators of sin; and also taking into account the religious good that accrues to the living through identification with God, the synagogue, and fellow Jews, Kaddish should be recited for the full twelve months. The denial of saying Kaddish by children of such individuals in the modern day is hardly acceptable.

Persons Missing and Assumed Dead

Such cases are quite exceptional and extremely difficult to judge. Expert rabbinic authority should be consulted. Generally, for all persons excepting married men, Kaddish may be recited when the missing person is assumed to be dead, even though the body has not been found. Married men who are assumed to be dead present a difficult problem. Recitation of the Mourner's Kaddish for them might lead others to consider the surviving widow to be of legally marriageable status, and this is religiously doubtful. In such cases, after due consultation with proper authorities, it might be advisable to have the son recite the Rabbis' Kaddish, not the Mourner's Kaddish, during services. If the body later is found, the Mourner's Kaddish merely need be continued for the balance of the eleven months for mourners of parents.

WHEN KADDISH IS RECITED AT SERVICES

The Burial Kaddish, the Mourner's Kaddish, and the Rabbis' Kaddish should each be recited at the appropriate place and time.

The Burial Kaddish

This Kaddish is not said at synagogue services but only at the cemetery, immediately after closing the grave. It contains a special paragraph inserted at the beginning, which includes reverence for the dead and consolation for the destruction of Jerusalem and the Temple, that is added only at this tragic moment. On this occasion it is recited on all days except those on which Tzidduk ha-Din and Tachanun are not recited.

The Mourner's Kaddish

This is recited primarily after Aleinu and also after the Psalm of the Day. It also is recited in the early morning service after the psalm Mizmor Shir Chanukat ha-Bayit le-David (Psalm 30). At the Minchah and Ma'ariv services, it should be recited after Aleinu, which concludes the service.

The Rabbis' Kaddish

The longer Rabbis' Kaddish is halakhically considered of greater importance than the others. This Kaddish is recited after Ein Keloheinu and the morning sacrifices section, both of which contain portions from the Torah and Talmud.

The mourner also should say the Half Kaddish following the public Torah reading. It is preferable for the mourner who cannot lead the full service to lead, at least, the concluding portion of the morning service (which is quite easy to learn), from Ashrei and U-va le-Tziyyon through the full Kaddish, Aleinu, and Mourner's Kaddish.

POSTURE OF KADDISH RECITATION

Mourners should rise for the Kaddish and say it standing, in unison with other mourners of the congregation. Although it was originally intended as an individual prayer, to be recited by one mourner in responsive style with congregants, since the nineteenth century Ashkenazic Jews have adopted the Sephardic custom of having all mourners recite it together. The Kaddish, being a prayer of holiness, must not be interrupted. The core response, "Let His great name be blessed forever and to all eternity," *Yehe shemeh rabba mevarakh le alam u-le-alemai alemayya*, is so important that the congregants should interrupt their own prayers in order to respond. The Kaddish concludes with a quotation from the book of Job asking God who makes peace in the heavens to bring peace to us all: *Oseh shalom bimromav hu ya'aseh shalom aleinu ve-al kal Yisra'el*. As the mourner recites this last line, he should take three short steps back, symbolizing the conclusion of his audience with God, and then three steps forward to his original stance.

IF A PARENT REQUESTS KADDISH *NOT* BE SAID

If a parent demands that his children *not* recite Kaddish for his deceased spouse, he is not to be obeyed. The Kaddish is expressive of a relationship between parent and child, and the surviving parent may not interfere with this lifelong relationship.

If the deceased left instructions that no Kaddish should be recited after his own death, one should examine the reason for the request. If it was to avoid inconvenience for his children, his request can be set aside by the children, and they can allow themselves to be inconvenienced. If the motive is a lack of belief in the purpose of the Kaddish itself, the children may use their own judgment in deciding whether or not it should be recited. Knowing the parent, if they feel the Kaddish recitation represents a principle he strongly rejected, he should be obeyed.

WHEN THE MOURNER CANNOT ATTEND SERVICES

Although we live in a fast-paced society in which transcontinental travel and global communications may cause sudden shifts of location, and the press of emergency transactions, business or personal circumstances, or illness may prevent one from attending synagogue, the Kaddish still should *not* be recited privately. It is a public prayer and simply must be recited in a quorum.

What should be done, in such cases, is what the Kaddish itself seeks to do: enhance the "merit of the children." The mourner should read a portion of the Bible—a chapter from the Five Books of Moses or the Prophets—or, if he is able, study a *mishna* or a page from the Talmud. This is a constructive and entirely valid substitute for the Kaddish when one finds it extremely difficult to attend one of the services.

Tradition recommends other ways to glorify a parent's teaching. Children should make it a practice to contribute to charity in their parents' memory. Even more spiritually effective and significant, mourners should strive to adopt one mitzvah, one special deed, that they will take to heart and practice regularly as a memorial tribute; for example, reading a book on Torah or Judaism for five minutes a day. This custom adds life to the influence of a parent who has passed on, and it enhances life for those who survive.

How magnificent is this tradition, which transforms a potential faith-shattering tragedy into a faith-building future, and which teaches, unwaveringly, that the only valid expression of grief is the ethical and religious betterment of oneself.

PRECEDENCE AMONG MOURNERS

In all the printings of *The Jewish Way in Death and Mourning* I assiduously have avoided the subject of who has priority in reciting Kaddish, leading services, and receiving *aliyyot* to the Torah. All of these can be subsumed under the title *chiyyuvim*, who is first in performing the obligatory public mitzvot. I have avoided this topic because it has always caused acrimony within the synagogue family, and I wanted this book to stand above that particular fray. I assume this will be the last grand revision of *The Jewish Way in Death and Mourning*, and I have chosen to include it only so as to make this book complete.

There are five categories of mourners who should receive priority, and they are, from top priority to lowest priority:

- a mourner during *shivah*
- a mourner during *sheloshim*
- a mourner for parents during the first twelve months
- a mourner on the last day of the year of Kaddish
- a mourner on his parent's yahrzeit.

There are several important points that congregations need to appreciate about their mourners:

1. Mourner's Kaddish. The difficulties of precedence in this regard have largely been solved. Today, and for the past 150 years or so, Kaddish is recited by all mourners in unison, or at least simultaneously.

2. Leading services. Usually the services can be divided so that everyone is honored with leading at least a part of the daily service on at least one day of the week.

3. An *aliyyah*, being called to the Torah, is a very sensitive

matter, as it should be. It is a treasured distinction, and when a congregant perceives an injustice as to who deserves an *aliyyah*, resentment can result. A mourner definitely should receive an *aliyyah*, in accordance with the above order, but surely when his yearlong bereavement and recitation of Kaddish come to an end.

These are only general guidelines. I leave the detailed questions to local rabbis, other authors, people's good will, and the reader's imagination. There remains only one truth we need to remember when dealing with this sensitive matter. That is, more consequential by far than the recitation of Kaddish, the leading of a synagogue service, or an *aliyyah* to the Torah is an altercation in the holy precincts of a synagogue. Kaddish serves to increase *kiddush ha-Shem*, the sanctification of God's Name; quarreling produces *chillul ha-Shem*, the desecration of God's Name. The Lord in Heaven did not issue a caring code of practice for Jews to survive their period of mourning so that they might be consumed in internecine warfare. That is a greater sin by far than all the observances are mitzvahs.

JOYOUS OCCASIONS

The observance that most affects the daily life of the mourner during the twelve-month period is the complete abstention from parties and festivities, both public and private. Participation in these gatherings simply is not consonant with the depression and contrition that the mourner should be experiencing. It borders on the absurd for a mourner to dance gleefully while his parent lies dead in a fresh grave. Thus, the Sages decreed that while complete physical withdrawal from the normal activities of society lasts only one week, withdrawal from joyous social occasions lasts a year (twelve Hebrew months) for one in mourning for one's parents and thirty days for other relatives. Joy, in terms of the mourning tradition, is associated largely with public, social events.

The Definition of Joy

The difficult problem in identifying a specific behavior with such complex and nebulous sentiments is which social occasion should be defined as joyous and thus prohibited the mourner. There are, on the one hand, social gatherings, such as friendly get-togethers, parties, community meetings, pleasure trips and cruises, business gatherings, synagogue-sponsored events, fraternal meetings, and so on. On the other hand, there are religious celebrations, such as a bris, Bar Mitzvah, or wedding. Which ones are to be considered "joyous" in terms of the mourning tradition? What guidelines are to be used in making the determination? Clearly, the law cannot be decided by the frequency of smiles or by some computerized meter of internal jollity.

The Sages, through the centuries, therefore have established general criteria that define the parameters of "joyous" occasions. The first consideration is whether the party is religious or social. On this point, the great teachers were divided. The majority, which largely prevailed, held that only "true joy" was prohibited. True joy is that which goes to the roots of the person, his in-depth relationship to God and his family. This is what the Talmud had in mind when it prohibited the mourner from entering a wedding hall to participate in the gala dinner. The occasion of celebrating the observance of a mitzvah, such as a wedding or Bar Mitzvah, struck genuine joy in the heart of the person, and this the mourner was not permitted to experience.

The establishment of this criterion is not arbitrary but a consequence of the Jewish spiritual worldview. Man, Judaism holds, finds authentic happiness and deep satisfaction in the fulfillment of his obligations to God, not in the distractions of entertainment media and the superficial frivolities of our times, the games and contests of society at play. It is true that gatherings of one's fellows give unmistakable and positive joy—the Sages offered eloquent encomia for the comradeship in such social occasions. Yet the genuine delight that is derived is not nearly so profound or touching as the true joy of the religious occasion.

Thus, these scholars maintained that the primary prohibition was the *simchah shel mitzvah*, a *religious* joyous celebration. The archetypal example of this true joy festivity is a wedding ceremony and attendant feast.

A minority view, held by some of the most esteemed Sages in Jewish life, maintained that tradition primarily prohibited the *simchat mere'im*, the purely *social* joys, and the fun of the hail-fellows and the round of parties that often mark life. Any occasion celebrating the observance of a commandment, they say, surely would not be prohibited the mourner who wants to observe the commandment! Would these joys mar the spirit of the bereaved? Would they bring shame to the deceased? Can it be said that participation in religious family festivities distracts one's mind from the dead?

Committed Jews, eager to keep the law, anxious to do full honor to parents, and relatively unconcerned with the number of affairs they must miss during the year, keep both views, and avoid both religious and social festivities; exceptions to this custom were enumerated in the tradition, and these are considered below. Others follow the generally accepted customs of their communities and wisely discuss them with their rabbi.

The Conflict of Music and Mourning

Certain characteristics of celebrations were used as criteria for the halakhic definition of joy. Music, primarily dance music, and especially that which is enjoyed in the company of others, is a clear mark of gaiety. That is why music is prohibited to the mourner for parents for the full twelve-month period. A mourner should not attend a musical performance, a concert or opera, or listen to bands in any location.

May a mourner listen to recorded music? In order to understand the *halakhah* involved, we need to consider two points made by my teacher, Rabbi Joseph B. Soloveichik:

The reason music is prohibited is because it tends to spur dance, *rikkud*, which essentially is what is prohibited during mourning. Rabbi Joseph B. Soloveichik told my mother, when she was mourning her father, that she could listen to classical music because that would not trigger *rikkud*. On the other hand, classical ballet music would not be permitted, because its purpose is precisely to stir the sensation of *rikkud*, the swaying of the body to the rhythms. One easily can appreciate the halakhic attitude that *rikkud* is antithetical to *avelut* by seeing that on Simchat Torah the mourner could perform *hakkafot* (processions), marching in a circle with the Torah, but not dancing with the Torah. On Simchat Beit ha-Sho'evah, during the days of Sukkot, one could join in singing Shir ha-Ma'alot, but not in dancing to the tune. One can understand, therefore, that under specific circumstances, it is permissible to attend a wedding ceremony but not to dance at that wedding. There are moments, however, at a wedding reception or on a pleasure outing, when simply being present in a hall where there is dancing and dining, even without participating, is not permitted the mourner. A spirit of public lightheartedness is to be avoided.

The music that is halakhically prohibited is music used for dance, or as accompaniment to singing or communal religious chanting. The idea of music as an art form was unknown to civilization until the classical composers of the late Middle Ages. When the *halakhah* referred to music, it was not to the art of music, such as would prevent one from going to an art museum, which is perfectly all right.

Therefore, attendance at sports programs and other such gatherings that have no musical aspects is permitted. Watching television or listening to a radio program that has no musical essence, but where the music is an interruption such as a commercial, or the "Star-Spangled Banner," or "Hatikvah," is permitted.

The joy prohibited the mourner depends on the period of mourning, his relationship to the deceased, and the kind of celebration. Thus:

1. During *shivah*, the mourner must refrain from doing those things that even possibly evoke joy, such as the recitation of certain joyous verses from the prayer book (i.e., before Havdalah), romping with children, or even indulging heatedly in discussions with visitors to the house of mourning. These latter were considered *sechok*, pleasantries, unbe-

coming the bereaved and prohibited during mourning. Ecclesiastes (3:4) says, "There is a time for wailing (*bekhi*), and a time for laughter (*sechok*)." As mourning is surely the time for wailing, excessive laughter is not condoned.

2. Before *sheloshim*, which ends the mourning observance for those bereaved of relatives other than parents, joyous religious and social occasions, under normal circumstances, are prohibited. After *sheloshim*, all festivities are permitted these bereaved.

3. For those who mourn parents, the *sheloshim* period requires more intense restraint from joy than the remaining months of the year. For example, the bereaved are permitted to attend a Bar Mitzvah party or *se'udah* during *sheloshim* (but after *shivah*) so long as they avoid listening to instrumental music and participating in the dinner together with the celebrants (and the dancing, of course). All obviously may attend the synagogue service. After *sheloshim*, and for the balance of the year, however, they may participate fully in the dinner if the Bar Mitzvah lad—or others— delivers a talk on a Torah subject, thereby transforming a party into a religious celebration.

Following are some of the details of the laws that derive from these concepts. In complex situations, one should discuss the particulars with a rabbi so that he may decide on questions of law and propriety.

RELIGIOUS CELEBRATIONS

Even though certain events are religious, they also are celebrations, and we must judge whether or not they contravene the spirit of sadness that prevails during mourning.

Bris

Generally, the rule is after *shivah*, but during *sheloshim*, all mourners are permitted to attend a bris, *pidyon ha-ben*, Bar

Mitzvah, and *tena'im* (engagement) but should not participate in the meal. The custom is to be strict within *sheloshim* and more lenient after *sheloshim*. Where there is definitive local custom that does not adhere to these rules, it, however, should be followed.

The mourner who has just become a father may attend the bris of his son even on the very first day, immediately before or after interment. In such a case, *shivah* begins after the bris. He may dress in Sabbath clothes. He may help prepare and eat the festive meal, even (preferably) in his own home. If it is not in his own home, he may travel to the location of the bris. However, immediately after the bris, he should return to continue the *shivah* at the house of mourning.

A mohel who is in mourning may perform a bris, even during his *shivah*, if there is no other competent one available. He should not participate in the festive meal during *sheloshim* if he is mourning a parent, but may do so (after *shivah*) if he is mourning other relatives.

The *sandak* who is a mourner may attend the bris even during *shivah*, but should not participate in the festive meal during *shivah* as previously noted for the *mohel*. After *shivah*, he may wear leather shoes and dress for the occasion as well. However, it is not always considered entirely proper to invite a mourner to be the *sandak* in the first place.

Pidyon Ha-ben

The laws of *pidyon ha-ben* are similar to those of bris. The *Kohen*, in this instance, is permitted those matters that the mohel may do in performing the bris.

Bar Mitzvah

A parent in mourning may prepare the Bar Mitzvah party even during *sheloshim*, so long as it is after *shivah*. He should not, however, eat the meal with the guests. He may eat in another room and socialize with the guests during the meal proper, without music.

Such a parent may also dress for the occasion. The Bar

Mitzvah lad himself, if he is in mourning for one of his parents, may dress in his full Sabbath best. The religious ceremony of Bar Mitzvah is not cancelled even if the boy is in mourning. All mourners, whether or not they are related to the Bar Mitzvah, may attend the celebration during *sheloshim* but should avoid eating at the dinner or listening to music. After *sheloshim*, the mourner for parents may attend and participate in the meal if the celebrant speaks on matters of Torah, thus indicating that it is a *simchah shel mitzvah*, a religious occasion.

WEDDING

A wedding is the defining event of joy—and therefore the litmus test of the joy that is prohibited in the first year of mourning. But a wedding also is the highlight of life. If so, how do we manage to celebrate when we are in the midst of the sadness of mourning?

The Ceremony

1. If the ceremony takes place in a catering hall or similar type of location where music is played, the general rule is that mourners for parents should not attend during the twelve-month period, and for other relatives, the thirty-day period.

2. In the catering hall proper, if the orchestra is not present, mourners for parents may attend, after *sheloshim*.

3. If the wedding takes place in a synagogue, where customarily there is only vocal but no instrumental music, even the mourner for parents may attend after *shivah*. After the *sheloshim*, in such a case, the mourner for parents may even participate in the recital of the blessings at the ceremony and dress up for the occasion. If there is instrumental music, generally he should not attend at all until the end of the year.

4. If the mourner (even for parents) makes the tenth for the minyan, and there are no other available men to consti-

tute a quorum, he may attend the wedding and eat the meal, even during the *sheloshim*.

5. If the absence of the mourner, a parent, for example, will very likely cause a delay in the wedding date (and there is always a possibility that a delay might cause one of the couple to withdraw from the marriage), the mourner may attend at any time and under any conditions.

6. If the rabbi is a mourner, he may perform a wedding after *shivah*, but should avoid listening to the music.

7. When mourners do attend at exceptional times that are not normally permissible, they must perform some useful function:

- Relatives who attend after *shivah* but during *sheloshim* should serve as ushers or helpers at the ceremony, even if they are not mourning parents. Such mourners, of course, may attend after *sheloshim* without this requirement.
- Close friends of the celebrant who are in mourning should not attend the wedding ceremony during *sheloshim*. However, if they feel that their absence might cause the bride or groom remorse or heartbreak, they may attend and assist before the ceremony. After *sheloshim*, if they are mourning parents, these friends may attend the affair if they assist before the ceremony.

The Dinner

Dining at a celebratory meal with friends and relatives falls directly under the category of *simchah*, joy, and should be avoided by the mourner until after twelve months when mourning for parents and thirty days when mourning for other relatives. In pressing circumstances, mourners should proceed as follows:

1. Parents may attend the wedding during *shivah* and even during the first three days after interment. Rabbi Mosheh Feinstein wisely draws the conclusion that if the mourner need not sustain an irretrievable financial loss because of *shivah*, he surely should not sustain the greater loss of not

attending a child's wedding. Siblings and children of a bride or groom may attend the ceremony and eat at the dinner after *shivah*, during *sheloshim*, but should not be present during the music and dancing. They should, however, be of some help in the preparation or service at the meal, or in the serving of drinks, and so on.

2. Other relatives of the couple may join the wedding reception after *sheloshim* if they mourn parents (other mourners after *shivah*) but should help in serving.

SOCIAL AND BUSINESS GATHERINGS

While joy and mourning are contradictory emotions, there must be consideration for the essentials of earning a livelihood. If a rabbi is consulted, he undoubtedly will weigh this along with other factors.

1. Community business meetings, such as synagogue or fraternal organization membership meetings, are permitted the mourner after *shivah*.

2. While a social dinner (*se'udat mere'ut*), for three or four couples halakhically is permitted, large social gatherings—even charity dinners or dinners at which no music will be played—that bring joy and fellowship are prohibited to mourners for parents for twelve months and to other mourners for thirty days. However, if the motivation is not social gathering, a *simchah*, or sheer fun, but for the purpose of helping to house many guests or attending a charity dinner without desiring fellowship, or for helping draw others closer to Judaism, there are no restrictions on the number of invitees.

3. Pleasure cruises and group tours are similar to social dinners in the eyes of Jewish law, even if meals are eaten privately. These are considered largely to be "joy rides" and should be discouraged during *sheloshim* at least.

4. Sizable house parties are discouraged the mourner for parents for twelve months, and other mourners for thirty days, even though no full meal is served. There is no stricture against

get-togethers, inviting a few friends or relatives at a time. The important consideration to be remembered is that these events must not develop into social occasions. Fellowship is fine, but festivities are not appropriate.

5. Business parties, where gaiety and shoulder rubbing is the method and business deals the goal, also should be avoided during the full mourning period. If absence at such events might cause severe financial loss, they are permitted. Business conventions are, similarly, to be avoided in normal situations. However, if attendance is mandatory, or economically beneficial, the mourner may attend but should not be present during the playing of music and dancing. He should take his meals privately, or with several friends, unless the purpose of the meal itself is predominantly business, in which case he is permitted to dine with the convention, after the *sheloshim* period.

6. Professional musicians who derive all, or part of, their livelihood from playing at joyous occasions, may do so after *shivah*, as they are not playing for joy. If they are financially capable of sustaining the loss, they should avoid playing during the *sheloshim*.

7. Attendance at operas and concerts, theaters and movies is to be discouraged. Listening to radio and television depends on the above-mentioned criteria of joy. Generally speaking, broadcasts over radio and television of news and sports events are permitted, and musical commercials are of no significance.

THE MOURNER AND HIS MARRIAGE

The quintessence of all joyous occasions, in the Jewish view of life, is one's own wedding. When the Sages wished to convey the idea that happiness may be found everywhere, they said, "all the world is a wedding." To relatives, friends, and well-wishers, joy at the wedding must be defined in material terms, such as dining and dancing. Thus, the mourner may attend the ceremony if there is no music and if he does not participate in the banquet. But to the couple being married, the food and music are ancillary, merely incidental accompaniment to the significant moment under the wedding canopy. For them the definition of joy is the spiritual, personal bond that unites them. Were the wedding shorn of the material goodies, the smiles and the tinsel, and only the couple, the two witnesses, the minyan, and the rabbi were present, the wedding ceremony would still be the memorable peak of joy. The thrilling sounds of *mazal tov*, the beauty of flowers and music would be gone, but the essence remains for a lifetime.

Thus, for the mourner himself, marriage should be prohibited. But this is not a light matter. One can refrain from celebrations and music for a year, but marriage is of the fabric of life itself, and life inevitably must go on. And so all mourners, for parents or other relatives, were prohibited from marrying during *shivah* and permitted to marry after *sheloshim*. The laws of marriage during *sheloshim* will be considered later. The wedding can be held in the presence of the full complement of friends and material abundance and beauty and music and gaiety. It is, after all, the festival of festivals, and, therefore, shaving, haircutting, washing, and dressing in the finest apparel are permitted.

The mourning laws relating to marriage affirmed the need for life to go on and to be lived to its fullest, but they also considered that a close relative had just been taken from life. The glorious union of marriage and the bitter severance of death are two contrasting threads that intertwine, and the tradition understood the needs of both and determined how to unravel them in behavioral terms.

Following are the laws that flow from this understanding of human need at the rare moment of the coincidence of such paroxysms in life.

When Marriages May Take Place

1. Mourners should not be married during *sheloshim* except after an intervening holiday, and certainly not during *shivah*, even without pomp and music and a sumptuous re-

ception. Engagements should not be contracted or announced during this period. After the *sheloshim*, the wedding may proceed with all the adornments, the music and the food, and the bride and the groom and their parents may dress for the occasion, without showing any evident signs of mourning.

2. During *sheloshim* (but after *shivah*) there are exceptional circumstances when marriages may be contracted.

- If the groom is the mourner and he is childless, and if preparations have already been made—the date set, the food bought, etc.—so that postponing the wedding would cause a severe financial loss or a large group of people to be absent, the wedding may take place.
- If the date had not been set, but for some cogent reason, such as military draft, the wedding must be held during *sheloshim*, the couple may marry but not live as husband and wife until after *sheloshim*.
- If the bride is the mourner, the marriage may take place during *sheloshim* if she had already been engaged, the preparations made, and the groom is childless.

When Remarriages May Take Place:

- If the wife died, the husband must wait for the passing of the three major festivals (Passover, Sukkot, and Shavuot) before he remarries. Rosh Hashanah and Yom Kippur do not count as festivals for this purpose. Shemini Atzeret may be counted as a festival in certain cases involving a family's urgent personal circumstances. The ostensible reason for this delay is the hope that the duration of three separate holidays and the cycle of seasons would temper his despair, and he would not enter a second marriage with the first love still fresh in mind. This time span may be as long as a year if the death occurred soon after Sukkot, or only a few months if death occurred immediately prior to Passover.

There are notable exceptions to this general rule that express the *halakhah*'s leniency in this matter: If the husband did not have children, marriage may be held after *shivah* and the couple may live as husband and wife; if the husband has small children who need to be cared for, marriage may be held after *shivah*, but marital relations must be postponed until after *sheloshim*; if he cannot bear to live alone, no matter the amount of help available for his care, or for whatever reason (this is not an infrequent occurrence), he may be married during *shivah* but should have no marital relations until after *sheloshim*.

- If the husband died, the wife may remarry after three months, a considerably shorter time than the three-festival duration for a man. Evidently, the wife was considered better able to compartmentalize her emotions, always having to be more concerned with the rearing of her children than with her own feelings. The reason for the three-month delay is that it must be evident that she is not pregnant with a child from a deceased mate. If she were to remarry immediately without determining her pregnancy status, and then gave birth after seven months, there would be concern as to paternity. With DNA and other sophisticated testing, this is of considerably less concern. Under exceptional circumstances—if she finds unusual hardship in supporting her orphaned children, if it is medically determined that she is not pregnant, or if her fiancé is childless—she may remarry immediately after *shivah*.

Becoming a Mourner after the Ceremony

There is a lesser yet still serious clash of joy and sadness: becoming a mourner after the marriage ceremony.

- If one of the seven close relatives of the bride or groom died after the ceremony, but before the marriage was consummated, the couple must live apart until after *shivah*.
- If the relative died after the consummation of the marriage, the mourning is postponed until after the full week of wedding celebration. During this time, the mourner may care for personal hygiene and grooming, and may experience all the joys of living. When the week is over,

however, the garment of the mourner is rent and *shivah* begins in full, as noted above.

Marriage During Sheloshim

If marriage is to take place during *sheloshim*, the bride or groom may launder clothes, bathe, and get a haircut in preparation for the wedding. Music and dancing are permitted. The wedding is followed by the seven days of rejoicing, which are counted as part of *sheloshim*, and then he or she resumes what is left of the thirty-day mourning period.

Matchmaking

This is permitted at all times, even on the day of death itself. The *shaddekhan* (matchmaker) should be sensitive at such crucial moments.

CELEBRATION OF THE TALMUD

At the conclusion of the study of a tractate of the Talmud, a celebration (*siyyum massekhet*) is usually held (such as that attended by first born sons who, otherwise, would be required to fast before Passover). Such celebrations may be attended by mourners only after *sheloshim*, and they may participate in the meal that follows the Talmudic discourse. The festive meals at Hanukkah and at a housewarming are in the same category, providing that they partake of the character of religious celebration through Torah discussion or with religious songs and praise of God.

FESTIVITIES ON THE SABBATH

🦢

The Sabbath is a day when public mourning is avoided (even though personal mourning prohibitions remain in force). May one attend a public, joyous occasion on the Sabbath?

The general rule is that the Sabbath only adds to the *simchah* that is coincident with the special occasion and hence should make it doubly prohibitive. At the same time, however, if the community would ordinarily expect the mourner to attend, his absence would constitute public mourning, which is not permitted on the Sabbath. The following procedures, therefore, should be followed.

> *Sheva berachot*, post-wedding festivities held every evening for seven days after the wedding, should not be attended even on the Sabbath until after *sheloshim* for mourners for parents and after *shivah* for other mourners. The same is true for a bris, *shalom zakhar* (celebrated on the first Friday night following the birth of a son), and for a mother returning to the synagogue for the first time after childbirth, if a party is customarily made in her honor.

However, the above is intended for friends and distant relatives of the celebrant. Close relatives of the immediate family and prominent individuals, ordinarily expected to attend, may attend these celebrations and join in the meal. Their absence clearly would be an indication of mourning in public, which is prohibited on the Sabbath.

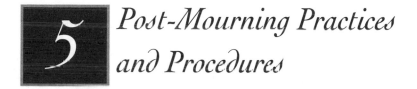

5 Post-Mourning Practices and Procedures

TIIE INITIAL SADNESS of the loss of a loved one evaporates in a world that demands our constant attention, but death does not easily slip out of our memory banks. The Jewish tradition insists that the dead not be forgotten, lost in the busyness of the here and now. Although the Sages also were insistent that the bereaved not mourn overly much, they provided guideposts to insure keeping that memory from departing completely.

THE MONUMENT

The epitaph was traditionally the distilled wisdom that described the deceased in a pithy phrase engraved in concrete. It was a material symbol of the deceased's life. Today, the monument remains important but it is rarely more informative than providing dates and names. The question is, why erect a monument at all?

"And Rachel died and was buried on the way to Ephrat, which is Bethlehem. And Jacob erected a tombstone on Rachel's grave" (Genesis 35:19–20). Erecting a monument actually is a very ancient tradition. Whether the stone is placed directly over the grave, as a footstone, or as a headstone, the monument serves three purposes:

1. To mark the place of burial, so that priests (*Kohanim*) may avoid defilement from the dead—a ritual impurity that the Bible prohibits. For this purpose alone a simple marker would be sufficient.

2. To designate the grave properly, so that friends and relatives may visit it. For this, only the name of the individual on a modest stone is required.

3. To serve as a symbol of honor to the deceased buried beneath it. For this purpose the heirs should erect as respectable a monument as they can afford but no more, avoiding ostentation.

Type of Monument

The cost of the monument usually depends on the type of monument. The expense for the monument is halakhically considered part of the burial costs. Thus, it is an obligation that the heirs assume, whether or not there are sufficient funds and whether or not these monies were left specifically for this purpose. Even if the decedent willed that no stone be erected, his behest is not heeded. The cost, the size, the shape, and the lettering of the monument should be determined by the monies available to the family, the decedent's desires, and the type of monument generally used on that particular cemetery. One should do honor to the deceased, but one should not use funds for a monument for the dead that are needed for the expenses of the living.

While the form of the marker is of little religious significance, what is important is that there be a clear, visible demarcation of the gravesite. For example, there are cemeteries that utilize small, flat stones that are flush with the earth, and it is difficult to determine whether they are footstones or headstones. These are not generally desirable, unless the whole outline of the grave is clearly evident. If the cemetery only permits footstones, they may be used, and their small size is not considered a belittling of the deceased. In the case of an infant, or of a public charity case, a small marker may be used. Even for stillbirths and infants not surviving thirty days, markers should be used. The purpose is so that the area will be recognizable, and priests will avoid contact with ritual impurity.

Husband and wife, two unmarried sisters, mother and daughter, father and son, or two brothers frequently use double monuments. Caution should be taken, however, before ordering them. Might the surviving spouse remarry? If she does, will she unquestionably desire to be buried next to the first mate? Will one of the unmarried sisters marry? Will the survivor desire to be buried in the Holy Land? Is the family contemplating a long-distance move? In the moment of grief, there are feelings of guilt and love that are not always sustained in the long future. Great care should be taken before finally ordering the double monument. (Which plot a remarried spouse should occupy is considered in Chapter 2, in the section "Plot and Grave.")

When to Erect the Monument

It is popularly assumed that the monument must be erected approximately twelve months after death. In reality, only a few scholars hold this view, and it is not strictly customary to follow their recommendation. There is every reason, based on major commentaries, numerous rabbinic sources, and long tradition, to arrange for the tombstone to be erected as soon after *shivah* as possible. For the reasons given, especially to honor the deceased, one should erect the tombstone as close to the end of *shivah* as possible. The Sages considered this so important that, in certain cases, they even permitted the mourner to leave the house of mourning during *shivah* to make the necessary arrangements. This was considered an integral part of burial arrangements.

The reason usually given for waiting twelve months is that the tombstone serves as a reminder, and that for the first twelve months the deceased is remembered in any case by the recitation of Kaddish and the avoidance of joyous occasions. Despite this rationale, however, honoring the dead should take priority over his being remembered, and arrangements for the stone should be made as soon as practicable. Indeed, it is not appropriate to recite a eulogy, even for the very righteous, after twelve months have passed.

Those who want to wait until the end of the year surely know that this is the custom generally held by American Jews, and following this, no matter the logic, will not keep them far from Jewish tradition.

If it is not possible to arrange for the monument soon after *shivah*, it may wait until *sheloshim* or soon thereafter. Naturally, the monument makers require time to cut the stone, but the honor to the deceased derives from the fact that the family orders it promptly. In addition, the days of *shivah* are probably an opportune time to discuss the tombstone, since the entire family is together and consultation among them is simple.

The family should take care in selecting a monument maker. Recommendations of friends and suggestions by the cemetery owners should be sought. Members of the family should inspect the monument after it is designed and engraved and before scheduling the unveiling, to check the proper location of the stone and to check the wording and spelling.

Inscription and Style

Good taste, quiet dignity, and the avoidance of ostentation are the primary guidelines for selecting a monument. The cost of the monument is usually determined by the lettering, carving, ornamentation, and finish, rather than by size alone.

Inscriptions in past years used to occupy the entire slate and often abounded in well-intentioned exaggerations, sometimes to the point of utter and barefaced falsehoods. Many phrases that were used could be applied only to the most righteous of people. This is no longer the type of inscription used. What is recommended is a short Hebrew descriptive phrase, such as *Eshet Chayil* (Woman of Valor), *Ishah Chashuvah* (Woman of Worth), or *Ish Tam ve-Yashar* (A Wholesome and Upright Man). A rabbi can provide many examples. In addition, the inscription should contain the Hebrew name of the deceased, the parents' Hebrew name, the deceased's full English name, and the Hebrew and English dates of birth and death. It is most appropriate to include the Hebrew dates whenever secular dates are inscribed. An additional name, given in times of illness, is used in the monument inscription only if it was in use for more than thirty days and if the deceased had recovered from that illness.

Styles of monuments vary. The particular shape is of no consequence to the tradition. However, sculptured animals, or the face of the deceased, if carved in relief, are out of place in Jewish cemeteries. Photographs mounted on monuments are in questionable taste. Some authorities even maintain that they are prohibited. It does seem that a person should be remembered without having his portrait to stare at. If already established, however, these tombstones are better left to stand as they are and should certainly cause no disputes. It is quite legitimate, however, to have "the hands of blessing" engraved for a deceased *Kohen* as a perpetual reminder of the family heritage. Symbols such as a Star of David, the Tablets of the Law, or an open Torah scroll also can be sculpted on a monument.

Following are facts one should have ready when preparing to purchase a monument:

- The name of the cemetery and the exact location of the plot.
- The deceased's full English name.
- The full Hebrew name of the deceased and his or her father.
- The birthdate (this may be omitted).
- The date of death (and the approximate hour of death if death occurred near twilight in order to determine the exact date).
- The relationship to family: mate, parent, grandparent, friend, etc.
- Jewish status: *Kohen* or *Levi*.

UNVEILING

The service of unveiling or commemoration is a formal dedication of the monument. It is customary to hold the unveiling within the first year after death. It can be held at anytime between the end of *shivah* and the first yahrzeit.

Unveilings are held on those days when grave visitations may be made, as outlined below. They are held in all weather and, in our day, precisely on time. With a shortage of rabbis for the large number of unveilings that are concentrated in the few Sundays of spring and fall, it clearly is advisable to call the rabbi many weeks in advance and to set the date after consulting with him.

The unveiling ceremony is the formal removal of a veil, cloth, or handkerchief draped over the stone. It symbolizes the completion of the tombstone. The unveiling may be performed during the service by anyone the family designates.

The service consists of the recitation of several Psalms: 1, 15, 23, 90, 91, 103, and 121, and, on certain days, when the Tachanun prayer is not recited, Psalm 16; a eulogy; the removal of the veil; and the El Mal'e Rachamim and Kaddish. For purposes of reciting the Kaddish, a minyan is required. In the minyan are included all Jewish male adults present. If no minyan is available, the unveiling may still be held, but without the Kaddish.

The rabbi may suggest placing a pebble on the monument upon leaving. This custom probably serves as a reminder of the family's presence. Also, it may hark back to Biblical days when the monument was a heap of stones. Often, the elements, or roving vandals, dispersed them, and so visitors placed additional stones to assure that the grave was marked.

Customarily, a rabbi will deliver the eulogy; if the family prefers, they may designate a family member or friend to do this. If the rabbi was not personally acquainted with the deceased, it is advisable to outline the deceased's life and goals before the service. If the family is enthusiastic in its admiration, rather than bored and indifferent, the eulogy will reflect this sincerity and devotion.

Unveiling cards often are sent to friends and family several weeks in advance of the date. One should be sent to the rabbi as well. Care should be taken to record the precise location of the grave and specific and clear instructions on how to reach the cemetery and the gravesite.

In earlier ages a snack may have been served at the cemetery because of the long trip involved. Or perhaps a drink was served, so that in raising the glass of wine, mourners could say, *le-chayyim*, "to life," implying "not to death." Today, however, drinking is associated primarily with socials and bars, and a spirit of levity usually prevails. Eating and drinking on the cemetery grounds are in questionable taste. This custom should be discouraged.

GRAVE VISITATIONS AND PRAYERS

The traditional attitude of Judaism did not encourage excessive grave visitation. The rabbis were apprehensive that frequent visitations to the cemetery might become a pattern of living rather than foster closure, thus preventing the bereaved from placing the death in proper perspective. They wanted to prevent making the grave a sort of totem at which the mourner would pray to the dead, rather than to God, and thereby violate one of the cardinal principles of Judaism: that God is One and that there are no intermediaries between a Jew and his God.

Proper Times for Visiting

Various customs have arisen regarding the proper times for visiting the graves of dear ones.

Propitious times to visit the grave include days of personal calamity or of decisive moments in life; on the *yahrzeit*; on the concluding day of *shivah* and *sheloshim*; on fast days, such as Tishah be-Av; before the High Holy Days; and on *erev* (the eve of) Rosh Chodesh, the day prior to the first days of the month, especially of Nisan and Elul. One or another of these days seems proper for families to visit their beloved dead. There is no rule of thumb as to the annual frequency of such visitation, excepting that people should avoid the extremes of constant visitation on the one hand, and of complete disregard on the other.

Visitation should not be made on *chol ha-mo'ed*—the middle days of Passover and Sukkot—nor on Purim, as these are days of joy.

There is some dispute regarding the propriety of visiting at certain other times, such as Rosh Chodesh, Hanukkah and *erev* Purim, Lag ba-Omer, the days in Nisan that precede Passover, and all days on which the Tachanun prayer is not recited. Consequently, these days should be avoided for unveiling and visitation, if at all possible. If there is some cogent reason—for instance, family members must leave town, or will be visiting from out-of-town at certain other times; or a mate wishes to remarry following the unveiling and insists upon waiting until that time; or some other legitimate reason (and not mere arbitrariness)—the visit may be held at those times. If the unveiling is held on these days, in order not to provoke unnecessary tears, the rabbi will not recite the El Mal'e Rachamim memorial prayer. He is asked to temper his eulogy so as not to bewail the dead but praise them. These days are days of national joy, and the spirit of tragedy should not prevail. However, selected Psalms and Kaddish may be recited.

Personal Prayers and Devotions

Formal and personal prayers certainly are appropriate upon visiting the graveside of the departed.

1. If one has not visited a cemetery in thirty days, he should recite the following blessing addressed to the deceased: *Barukh Atah Adonai Eloheinu Melech ha-Olam, asher yatzar etkhem badin, ve-zan ve-khilkel etkhem ba-din, ve-hemit etkhem ba-din, ve-*

yode'a mispar kullkhem ba-din, ve-hu atid le-ha-chayotkhem u-le-kayyem etkhem ba-din. Barukh Atah Adonai, mechayyeh ha-metim.

"Praised be the Eternal, our God, the Ruler of the Universe who created you in judgment, who maintained and sustained you in judgment, and brought death upon you in judgment; who knows the deeds of everyone of you in judgment, and who will hereafter restore you to life in judgment. Praised be the Eternal who will restore life to the dead."

2. It is entirely proper for learned Jews to study the Mishnah for several minutes at some distance from the graveside.

3. Several chapters from the Book of Psalms usually are recited. Also, Psalm 119, whose verses are grouped according to the alphabet, may be read, selecting those portions that begin with the letters of the name of the deceased. These Psalms may be recited as close to the grave as desired. Some people customarily place their hand on the tombstone during the recitation.

4. Much care must be taken to direct one's personal prayers at graveside to God. To pray to the deceased, or to speak directly to him in the form of prayer, borders on blasphemy. It is sheer necromancy, outlawed by the Bible (Deuteronomy 18:11) along with sorcerers, soothsayers, and enchanters. Not all the good intentions in the world can justify praying to the dead as intermediaries. That is an abomination to a people that has based its faith on the unity of God and has abhorred spiritualizing via ghosts and wizards. Better no visitation to the cemetery at all than one that induces "inquiries of the dead."

There is a tradition, however, that mourners ask the deceased to be a *melitz yosher*, an advocate or "friend of the court," in our prayer for God's help.

Memorial Prayer

The El Mal'e Rachamim is a memorial prayer of undetermined origin that has been taken to heart by all Jews. Its ubiquitous, universal appeal and profound emotional effect has caused it to be chanted at funerals and unveilings, at every visit to the cemetery, and by the service leader in the synagogue on Sabbaths before yahrzeit and at Yizkor services. This prayer may be recited in English without any loss of religious significance.

YIZKOR

☙

Recalling the deceased during a synagogue service is not merely a convenient form of emotional release, but an act of solemn piety and an expression of profound respect. The Yizkor memorial service was instituted so that the Jew might pay homage to his forbears and recall the life of goodness and traditional observances.

This memorial service is founded on a vital principle of Jewish life, one that motivates and animates the Kaddish recitation. It is based on the firm belief that the living, by acts of piety, decency, and generosity, can redeem the dead. A child can bring honor to a parent. The "merit of the children" reflects the value of parents. This merit is achieved, primarily, by living on a high ethical and moral plane, and by being responsive to the demands of God and sensitive to the needs of fellowman. Contributions to charity and prayer to God accomplish the formal expression of this merit.

It is understandable, therefore, that when Yizkor was first introduced into the service, probably during the massacres of the Crusaders and the early medieval pogroms, it was recited on Yom Kippur. On that holiest day of the year, when Jews seek redemption from their sins, they seek atonement as well for members of the family who have passed on. "Forgive Thy people, whom Thou hast redeemed" says the Bible in Deuteronomy 21:8. The Sages say that "Forgive Thy people" refers to the living; "whom Thou hast redeemed" refers to the dead. The living can redeem the dead. Atonement should be sought for both. One scholar even suggests that Yom ha-Kippurim, the technical name for the Day of Atonement, is written in the plural, "atonements," because on that day the Jew must seek atonement for both those who are present and for those who sleep in the dust.

But even prayer is not sufficient or a dignified and meaningful memorial. It must be accompanied by charity, as the personal, material demonstration of kindness. Thus, Yizkor came to be recited on major holidays when Deuteronomy 15-16 is read, which contains the phrase, "Every man shall give as he is able" (Deuteronomy 16:17). Those chapters direct people to be charitable, to support the poor, the orphan, the widow, and the Levites who depend on their graciousness. The Torah emphasizes that on the three major festivals of Passover, Shavuot, and Sukkot no person may appear at the Temple empty-handed. Each person must be generous according to his ability. Accordingly, the proper memorial service contains a phrase denoting a sum of charity that is being pledged. This declaration should not be taken lightly; it is not just another liturgical formula. If no charity will be given, the phrase should not be included. It is preferable not to promise than to renege on a promise. Thus, the Yizkor service recited on Yom Kippur, Passover, Shavuot, and Sukkot includes both prayer and charity.

The Rubric of the Memorial Service

There are two distinct prayers that are traditionally referred to as *hazkarat neshamot*, recalling the dead. First is the El Mal'e Rachamim, recited by the rabbi or cantor publicly at funeral and unveiling services, at holiday Yizkor services, after the Torah readings on Monday and Thursday mornings, and on Saturday afternoons for yahrzeit. The second *hazkarat neshamot* prayer refers to the synagogue Yizkor service. This is designed to be read by the individual congregant, silently, on Yom Kippur and the three major festivals.

One Yizkor prayer may be recited for all one's deceased, citing the individual names in the spaces indicated; one prayer may be recited for each deceased; or separate paragraphs may be recited for males and females. One should be sure that the Hebrew text is worded properly, in the plural or singular, male or female. Prayer books usually indicate for whom the Yizkor paragraph is intended. The Yizkor may be read in translation. (See Appendix One).

The name of the deceased should be recited in Hebrew, giving both the name of the deceased and the name of the deceased's father; for example, Shemu'el ben Yitzchak. The Sephardic tradition replaces the father's name with the mother's name; for example, Shemu'el ben Channah. The bereaved should learn and remember these names. If they are absolutely not ascertainable at the time, the English names may be used.

For Whom Is Yizkor Recited?

Yizkor may be said for all Jewish dead: parents, grandparents, mates, children, family, and friends. It may be recited for suicides and for sinners. A question of propriety usually arises regarding Yizkor for a deceased first mate after remarriage. The only reason it would not be said is to spare the present mate's feelings. Because Yizkor is recited silently, this should not be a concern, and the prayer may be recited if the surviving spouse desires it.

When Is Yizkor Recited?

Many believe Yizkor should not be recited during the first year.

1. Despite this common practice, there is every indication that Yizkor should be recited beginning with the first holiday after death. Yizkor is a redemptive prayer for the dead; precisely for this reason it should be recited during the first year, when the soul is said to be judged. There is no legitimate religious reason to delay it.

2. Some say that Yizkor is recited only for fifty years after death. This is totally without foundation. Yizkor is recited through all of one's lifetime. The memory of the departed does not end in a particular year; it is retained forever.

3. Yizkor is recited after the morning Torah reading on Yom Kippur, on the last day of Pesach and Shavuot, and on the seventh day of Sukkot, called Shemini Atzeret. It is recited on these days even if they fall on the Sabbath, at which time

memorials are, otherwise, inappropriate to the festive nature of the day. In most synagogues, Yizkor is recited after the rabbi's sermon, immediately before the Musaf (Additional) service.

Requirement of a Minyan

Yizkor should be recited at synagogue services. If one cannot attend these services because of illness, or because there is no minyan available, one should recite Yizkor privately at home, although it is distinctly and unquestionably preferable to recite it at a public synagogue service. In this respect, it is unlike the Kaddish, which may not be recited privately under any circumstances.

Candle Lighting for Yizkor

It is an ancient custom, on the four holidays when Yizkor is recited, as on the yahrzeit itself, to light a candle for all the departed. It is best that the lights be flaming wicks, as the flame and candle mystically symbolize the relation of body and soul. However, if this is not available, electric bulbs or gaslight may be used. For Yizkor memorial purposes, one light will serve adequately to recall all the departed.

YAHRZEIT

Despite the Germanic origin of the word *yahrzeit*, the designation of a special day and special observances to commemorate the anniversary of the death of parents already was discussed in the Talmud. This religious commemoration is recorded not as fiat but as a description of an instinctive sentiment of sadness, an annual rehearsing of tragedy that impels one to avoid drinking wine and eating meat—symbols of festivity and joy, the very stuff of the good life—in the face of the image of death.

Tradition regards this day as commemorative of both the

enormous tragedy of death and the abiding glory of the parental heritage. It is a day set aside to contemplate the quality and lifestyle of the deceased, and to dwell earnestly upon its lessons. It is a day when one relives the moment of doom, perhaps even fasts to symbolize the unforgettable despair. It is a day conditioned by the need to honor one's parent in death as in life, through study and charity and other deeds of kindness. It also is conditioned by the irrational but all-too-human feeling that it is the day itself that is tragic, a day that just might bring some misfortune with every annual cycle. For that reason one slows one's activities and spends a good part of the day safely in contemplation at home or the synagogue.

Yahrzeit may be observed for a spouse, sibling, or for any relative or friend, but it is meant primarily for parents. Its observance could take place in three locations: the home, the synagogue, and the cemetery.

Home Yahrzeit Observances

Mourning is not confined to a place, and its observance is not confined to synagogue or cemetery but to the hearth and the heart of the home.

1. Fasting. It was customary for some mourners to fast for parents on the yahrzeit from the time of the Minchah service of the previous day until dark at the end of the day of yahrzeit. If one has committed to this custom of fasting on the yahrzeit, it becomes a sacred obligation to continue the practice at every yahrzeit in the future. If one cannot fast, either because of weakness, or for any other cogent reason, he should at least try to avoid eating meat and wine and participating in festivities. Because of this strict emphasis on keeping one's word, it may be wise not to begin a tradition of fasting unless one is very sure he will be able to continue. To end this custom, he might have to seek release from his vow before a *beit din*, a Jewish rabbinical court. If yahrzeit occurs on a holiday, or on other days of public joy on which the Tachanun prayers are not recited, one should not fast, as it conflicts with the joyous spirit of the day.

2. Yahrzeit candles. The lighting of a yahrzeit candle is a custom dating back to very early times and is observed by almost all Jews. The lighting takes place at dark on the evening before the anniversary and, on Sabbaths and holy days, *before* the regular candle lighting. It is customary to allow the lights to extinguish themselves, rather than to put them out after dark at the end of yahrzeit. If there is any real danger of fire, one should extinguish them directly. If one forgets to light candles on the evening before, he should do so in the morning. He may light the candle by taking a light from another flame. On the Sabbath this may, of course, not be done, as it is Biblically imperative that one may not make a fire (put on the lights) on the Sabbath. If one forgets to light candles altogether and yahrzeit has passed, it is advisable to make a contribution to charity.

The lights should be candles of wick and paraffin. If these are not available at all, gas or electric lights are permitted. As the flame and wick symbolize soul and body, it does appear significant to use the candle for the symbol of life rather than a bulb. Yahrzeit candles generally are available in stores in most cities with Jewish populations.

If all the children are in one house during yahrzeit, one candle suffices. However, it is preferable, in terms of respect for the deceased parent, for each child to light his own candle. If they are in different homes, separate candles are, of course, required. In commemorating the yahrzeit of several close relatives at once, there could be a candle lit for each deceased. Do remember: the candle is not a fetish but a symbol; overindulging by lighting numerous candles for every deceased one remembers is not necessarily desirable.

3. Torah study and charity. One should make donations to religious schools or synagogues, to medical institutions or to the poor, on behalf of the deceased on yahrzeit. One should also make every effort to study some religious text on this day. It may be a *mishnah*, which is the traditional yahrzeit study, or, if one is not able to do so, a chapter of the Bible, in any language.

Synagogue Yahrzeit Observances

On the Sabbath prior to yahrzeit, the El Mal'e Rachamim memorial prayer is recited after the Torah reading at Minchah. If possible, the mourner should chant the *maftir* portion and lead the Saturday night Ma'ariv service. In any case, he should receive an *aliyyah*, a Torah honor. This *aliyyah* is considered a "required" honor. The synagogue usher or rabbi should be made aware of the yahrzeit.

On the day of yahrzeit one should lead, if at all possible, all synagogue services. Those who cannot would do well to learn at least the Minchah service, which is brief and simple. The rabbi will be delighted to teach the mourner or direct him to the cantor, sexton, or any knowledgeable Jew. He should recite the Kaddish at every service of the day. In addition, there is usually a psalm added to the morning service so that the yahrzeit observer may recite at least one Kaddish without the accompaniment of other mourners as occurs in many synagogues.

It is customary, though by no means mandatory, to bring light refreshments—liquor or soda and cake—to the synagogue for all to partake after early morning services and to toast *le-chayyim*, "to life." This light repast should not, of course, be allowed to develop into a full-fledged party.

Cemetery Yahrzeit Observances

The annual visit to the grave at yahrzeit is a popular custom. At graveside, one can recite Psalms, selections of which are indicated in the section on unveilings, and then the El Mal'e Rachamim prayer in Hebrew or any language. It is far better to recite the prayer oneself rather than to hire an intermediary or proxy. Intent is important, not the specific language of the prayer. Mishnah should be studied at the graveside, if at all possible. The Hebrew or English text may be used.

The Date of Yahrzeit

Kaddish is recited for eleven months; other mourning observances are kept for twelve months. Yahrzeits, however, are commemorated in terms of years, not months. Below are guidelines for determining the yahrzeit.

1. The yahrzeit is commemorated each year on the date of death: if a parent died on the fourth day of Elul 5760, the first yahrzeit is observed on the fourth day of Elul 5761, the second on the fourth day of Elul 5762, and so on.

Many authorities, and this may include your rabbi, maintain that in the case of a long delay between death and burial—especially if the burial took place several days after death (perhaps the deceased was buried overseas), or if the remains were missing and then found and buried many months later—the first yahrzeit only is commemorated on the anniversary of burial. For the sake of clarity and consistency, I suggest that the date of death always be used. This has had the approval of significant rabbis through the ages.

2. The Hebrew lunar calendar has twelve months: Tishrei, Cheshvan, Kislev, Tevet, Shevat, Adar, Nisan, Iyyar, Sivan, Tammuz, Av, and Elul. The first day of the month is called Rosh Chodesh or the New Moon. Each Hebrew month has either twenty-nine or thirty days. In those months that have thirty days (Tishrei, Shevat, Nisan, Sivan, Av, and, in a leap year [see below], Adar I), two consecutive days of Rosh Chodesh are celebrated—the first falls on the thirtieth day of that month, the second on the first day of the new month. The months of Kislev and Tevet sometimes have one and sometimes two days of Rosh Chodesh.

If death occurred on Rosh Chodesh Kislev or Tevet in a year when Rosh Chodesh is celebrated for one day, then in years when Rosh Chodesh Kislev or Tevet is celebrated for two days, yahrzeit is observed on the second day of Rosh Chodesh, which is really the first day of the month.

However, if death occurred on the first or second day of a two-day Rosh Chodesh Kislev or Tevet, yahrzeit is observed on the day of death every year that has a two-day Rosh Chodesh. In years when Rosh Chodesh is only one day, yahrzeit is observed on the twenty-ninth day of the previous month, the month in which death occurred.

3. In leap years in the Jewish calendar, an extra month,

Adar I, is inserted prior to the regular Adar (which then becomes Adar II).

- If death occurred in Adar I of a leap year, yahrzeit is observed in Adar in regular years and in Adar I in leap years.
- If death occurred in Adar II of a leap year, yahrzeit is observed in Adar II in a leap year and in the regular Adar in non-leap years.
- If death occurred in Adar of a regular year, the yahrzeit in leap years is customarily observed in Adar I. (Some rabbis say yahrzeit should be observed on both Adar I and Adar II, and this should be followed, if possible.)
- In a leap year, Adar I always has thirty days and Adar II twenty-nine days. If death occurred in a leap year on the first of the two days of Rosh Chodesh Adar I (the thirtieth day of Shevat), the yahrzeit in regular years remains the first day of Rosh Chodesh Adar.

4. If it is not possible to determine the date of death accurately, for example, in the case of those who died in the Holocaust or in the case of war casualties, the mourner should choose a probable date. Out of respect to the deceased, the date should be observed distinctly for that parent and should not be the same date as the yahrzeit for the other parent.

When one is unsure of the day of death, whether it was the fifth or sixth day of the month, for instance, the mourner should choose the earlier date. If the earlier date is the true date, fine; if not, the mourner merely has anticipated the day, indicating a degree of respect for the deceased.

5. If death occurred at a great distance from the mourners and the time difference establishes different dates of death, yahrzeit generally is observed according to the date in the city in which the deceased died.

6. If death occurred at dusk, yahrzeit should be observed on the date of the following day.

7. When yahrzeit falls on the Sabbath or holidays, candles must be lit before the onset of evening. The cemetery may be visited either one day before or one day after the Sabbath or holiday. The yahrzeit fast, if this is observed, should be de-

layed until the day after the Sabbath or holiday. All other synagogue ceremonies should be observed on the Sabbath or holiday.

8. One who has forgotten to observe yahrzeit on the proper date should observe it as soon as he remembers. If he cannot find a minyan on that day, he can recite Kaddish at the next Ma'ariv service.

9. In an emergency, if the mourner is sick, disabled, or otherwise prevented from observing any of the yahrzeit customs, he may deputize a friend or a synagogue official to observe yahrzeit for him. "A person's messenger is as himself." What was written above with regard to paying somebody to recite the Mourner's Kaddish on a daily basis for the first eleven months after death, however, applies equally to the one-day-a-year yahrzeit observance.

MEMORIAL BY PROXY

In the weeks leading up to the High Holidays, relatives and friends throng Jewish cemeteries in an annual display of respect for the dead. Often visitors are greeted by so-called rabbis who, for a fee, will recite the beautiful Hebrew memorial prayer to the compassionate God, the El Mal'c Rachamim. A memorial by proxy cannot buy "the shelter of God's wings" for either the deceased or the mourner. The El Mal'c Rachamim may be recited in English without any loss of religious significance—and must be recited by the mourner him- or herself.

Many mourners request the services of the "Mal'e-makers" because they sincerely desire to pay additional religious tribute to their beloved by recitation of the prayer in the language of the siddur, the Jewish prayer book, or to contribute charity to such a person, many of whom are observant, learned, and dignified Jews, certainly qualified to receive compensation for the service they perform. This is different matter.

Cemetery visitors should beware of those less scrupulous peddlers of prayer. Visitors should, at all times, be mindful of the respect that is to be shown the departed. Graves must not be trampled; a trip to the cemetery is not a social call. A visit at the approach of the holiday season affords an opportunity to prepare for the coming High Holy Days, to reflect on the meaning of our Judaism, the brilliant faith that was our ancestors'—and that is ours.

Special Situations

🦅

THE GENERAL PRINCIPLES and *halakhah* cover the standard, unexceptional, cases that occur in the majority of instances. Special situations, however, require specific solutions, and they reveal the profound depths of the halakhic minds of the Sages. These situations include the special limitations of the *Kohen*; news of death that is inordinately delayed; infant death; and the mourning procedures to be followed in the cases of intermarriage, suicide, and Torah violators. A special section has been added in this revision for discretionary mourners—those who are not mandated to observe the rituals of *avelut* but who wish to do so in order to express their grief in a traditional framework.

KOHEN
🦅

To be able to accept the fact of death is a blessing; to respect the dead is an act of devotion. But to love death is wicked; to worship the dead a monstrous blasphemy. There is a balance, a delicate, sensitive balance, between accepting death and loving it, between honoring the dead and worshiping at their graves. The consequence of this difference is a wide conceptual chasm between the faith that affirms life and also expects immortality beyond the grave, and the faith that denies the value of life as it seeks and strives for the beyond with all its power.

Judaism teaches through the laws and traditions of mourning the proper respect and honor for those who have passed on. Man must accept the inevitable and undeniable end of life. But the end of life must not be his conscious goal. "Choose life" (Deuteronomy 30:19). "The dead do not praise the Lord" (Psalms 115:17). In fact, the Levitical regulations make clear, the dead defile the living. The dead must be buried for their own honor; but they may not be handled excessively, dressed lavishly, held up for view, mummified and masked, or primped and painted.

Judaism emphasizes life and demonstrates this emphasis in the beautiful, though complicated, fabric of the laws of ritual impurity. Leviticus (21:1) commands the Tabernacle priests: "None shall defile himself for the dead among his people." Those whose lives are dedicated to maintaining the holiness of the Temple are profaned by contact with the dead. The sanctity of the priesthood is easily blemished.

Further, the greater the level of sanctity during life, the greater the intensity of defilement in death. Animals that die, defile in a relatively minor way. Pagans who die defile—but only on direct contact with the corpse. Jews who die defile the entire domain in which they rest. The *Kohen*, with certain exceptions, may not enter a building that contains the dead. "Behold," declares the Talmud, "the bones of a donkey render purity. The bones of Johanan, the High Priest, render impurity. For in accordance with the degree of their belovedness is their defilement" (*Yadayim* 4:6).

The laws of defilement prevented the all too common worship of the dead and affirmed the holiness and sacred value of life.

The laws of defilement of the *Kohen* had been given to a people only recently liberated from Egypt, where the primary concern of the priesthood was death, embalming, burial. The

Egyptian priest was a sort of undertaker, and the priesthood a cadaverous profession. In vivid contrast, the *Kohen*'s concern was exclusively life, his service exclusively for the living. The Bible had to expressly permit the *Kohen* to attend to the corpses of his seven close relatives. Following is a sketch of the laws of priestly purity.

Degrees of Defilement

The *Kohen* may be disqualified from performing the formal priestly benediction service, in our day as in ancient times, if he is defiled by a body that has been dead for more than forty days, or even by a limb separated from a human body. The defilement may be contracted in one of two ways.

1. Defilement by direct contact is contracted either by touching, carrying, or moving the corpse, which the *Kohen* is prohibited from doing.

2. Defilement of domain refers to the *Kohen*'s being present in the same enclosure with the corpse while it rests there. While the deceased is present, the entire house—all its rooms and floors—is considered Levitically impure. Hence, the *Kohen* may not enter the house of the deceased. If the corpse already is there, he must leave at once. Even if the common cover the *Kohen* and the corpse share is only a roof extension or beam, latticework, a bridge, or even a tree, it is considered a common domain and it defiles.

When Must the Kohen Defile Himself?

While the *Kohen* may not compromise the sanctity of his priesthood by contact with the dead, the Bible specifically commands him to prepare, handle, and concern himself with the bodies of his seven nearest relatives: wife, father, mother, son, daughter, brother (but not if he is a brother only from his mother's side), and unmarried sister. The Bible does not give mere permission to defile in these cases, it commands him to do so—even if others are available to make arrangements. The *Kohen* should stay in the domain of the deceased. This command of defilement prevails until the closing of the grave but not one moment longer. Immediately after the filling of the grave, he may not wait even for the Burial Kaddish but must depart quickly.

Met Mitzvah, *the Abandoned Deceased*

For a corpse left unattended even the High Priest had to defile himself and provide for its proper burial. Such a corpse is termed *met mitzvah* and requires singular devotion and care.

In our days, the rule of *met mitzvah* would apply to the deceased who does not have a sufficient number of Jews to serve as pallbearers or care for other burial arrangements. In such a case, the *Kohen* may not move from the corpse's side even to find another Jew to serve in his stead. He is under biblical obligation to remain with the corpse and honor him.

The Kohen *at the Funeral Chapel*

The *Kohen* may not enter the funeral chapel or any one of its rooms if the deceased (not one of the seven relatives) is housed there. However, the *Kohen* may stand outside the chapel, close to the wall, to hear the funeral service. Families of the deceased will usually understand the absence of the *Kohen* if they are given even the simplest explanation. One need not consider himself overly pious or very religious in order to preserve the privileged heritage that his father and faith have conferred upon him.

The Kohen *at the Cemetery*

There are two rules of thumb the *Kohen* must follow when accompanying any corpse out-of-doors:

1. The *Kohen* may not come within six feet of any grave at the cemetery. In difficult circumstances, some contend that he may come within four and a half feet, since the casket is buried deep in the earth. The *Kohen* certainly should not touch any tombstone.

2. If the casket is not yet interred—it is being carried to the gravesite or is at the gravesite before burial—the *Kohen* may come as close as one and a half feet from it. He should take care not to touch it, carry it, or be pushed against it.

The Kohen *at Unveilings*

The *Kohen* may not attend an unveiling even for the seven close relatives for whose burial he is commanded to defile himself, unless he can be assured that he will not need to walk within six feet of *any* grave. If this is possible, if the grave is at the edge of the cemetery, or if he stands at the edge of the cemetery even if the grave is further inside, he may attend. Of course, in such instances, he may not personally unveil the monument, even for his parents. The sister, wife, or mother of the *Kohen* may do this for him.

The Family of the Kohen

Wives and daughters of the *Kohanim* are not bound by these laws of defilement and are permitted to practice all regular procedures applicable to all Jews.

Sons of a *Kohen* are themselves *Kohanim*. A child, as soon as he is capable of being educated in these matters, should be taught the laws of the *Kohen*. This education should not wait until Bar Mitzvah, when he is obligated to fulfill the laws.

DELAYED NEWS

In our new world of instant global communications, extended delay in receiving news is relatively rare. Even without the benefit of advanced electronic engineering, evil tidings seem to have an unfailing homing device and always find their mark. Yet, bad news often is withheld to protect the ill and the weak; delayed because families are in "disconnect," dispersed to distant corners of the globe; or kept back simply because people have lost touch—even if they live close by, the extended family of aunts, uncles, and cousins no longer is close-knit. What are the mourning laws in cases of delayed news? The tradition divides delayed news into two categories: news that arrives within thirty days of the date of death and news that arrives after the thirtieth day.

Brief Delay

A "brief delay" refers to news that arrives within thirty days of the day of death but after *shivah* has begun. In such instances, the mourner immediately begins the mourning practices from the time of hearing the news through all the laws as though he had just returned from the cemetery. The mourner must rend his garment and recite the Tzidduk ha-Din blessing; he does not don *tefillin* on that day. Neighbors are obligated to provide him with the customary meal of consolation.

If the news comes during *shivah*, he must observe *shivah* from that moment. Under the following four conditions, he need not observe the full *shivah* but may join other mourners and rise from *shivah* when they do, even if it means observing *shivah* for only one hour on the last day.

1. He must not have begun to observe mourning before meeting the other mourners.
2. The "primary mourner" must be present. A primary mourner is one who was responsible for the funeral arrangements or for disposal of the deceased's belongings; he is considered to be an authoritative family member, not necessarily the head of the family, whether a spouse, child, or sibling of the deceased. He should be older than thirteen years of age. If responsibility is shared equally among the mourners, then any one of them or all of them may be considered primary mourners.
3. The other mourners must be sitting *shivah* in the city where either death or burial occurred.
4. He is not too distant from the other mourners (more than one day's travel time by any means of transportation).

If news came late on the thirtieth day but before dark, it is considered a brief delay even though other relatives completed the *sheloshim* that morning. The thirtieth day must have passed completely for the news to be considered an extended delay.

The unusual circumstance of news coming precisely on the thirtieth day from the day of burial and the thirty-first from the day of death is a subject of dispute in Jewish law. Therefore, if *shivah* can be observed, it should be done. If there are difficulties attendant upon doing this, it may be considered an extended delay and the procedure outlined in the next section should be followed.

If news arrived on the Sabbath or holiday, which happens to be the thirtieth day, it is considered an extended delay.

If a holiday occurred between the time of death and the arrival of the news, this does not have the effect of suspending *shivah* or *sheloshim*, as the mourners had not yet acknowledged the mourning.

If news arrived during a holiday, mourning begins on the night immediately following the end of the holiday. The days of the holiday are counted toward *sheloshim*, but only the last day of the holiday is counted toward *shivah* as well.

If news arrived on the Sabbath, only personal mourning observances should be followed, as outlined above, and the Sabbath is counted as the first day of *shivah*. After the Sabbath, the mourner rends the garment and accepts full mourning. If a holiday occurs immediately after the Sabbath, the *shivah* is suspended.

The question arises in religious literature as to whether one may intentionally withhold the news of death from the mourner until after the thirtieth day. The mourner, for example, may be troubled by family or business setbacks, may be in the hospital, or may be preparing for his wedding. A delayed communication would require fewer mourning observances and the tragedy would confront the mourner at a better time. While this may be necessary in instances of those who are sick or weak, or mentally ill, these cases should be decided by competent doctors and by the considered and informed judgment of the family. In ordinary, uncomplicated situations, the rule generally to be followed is that news may be withheld from all relatives other than a son or daughter.

In our day of hospices and of medical candor, however, the truth generally is revealed, and it has been determined to be helpful in almost every circumstance.

Extended Delay

"Extended delay" is defined as news that arrives after the end of the thirtieth day counted from the day of death. Thus, if death occurred on a Wednesday, *sheloshim* is completed on Thursday, four weeks later. Thursday night would be the beginning of an extended delay.

The length of time that has elapsed since the death is seen as mitigating the severity of grief. The mourner, therefore, practices only a token observance. It is sufficient for him to remove his shoes, sit on a low stool, and stop all work and study for approximately one hour. He need not desist from washing and working after that time. For relatives other than parents, the mourner need not stop working at all if it is difficult for him to do so.

Mourners for parents, at any time, whether after thirty days or even after the full year, must rend their clothes and recite the Tzidduk ha-Din.

As for other relatives, the mourner need not rend the garment after thirty days but should recite the Tzidduk ha-Din upon hearing the news. If it is not recited on the day of the arrival of the news, it is not recited at all.

For parents, while the laws of *shivah* and *sheloshim* are suspended, the mourning practices for the full year obtain until twelve months from the day of death. If news arrives after the year, all mourning is suspended. However, if the mourner desires to recite Kaddish he should not be denied the privilege.

INFANTS

☙

Today, infant mortality among American Jews has diminished considerably; therefore, the trauma of death in such cases has grown exponentially. Our senses have sharpened and our awareness has been heightened.

According to Jewish law, a life that endures for more than thirty calendar days (including the thirtieth day) establishes the person as a viable human being. An infant who does not live for thirty days is called a *nefel*. This thirty-day viability ruling applies only to an abbreviated pregnancy; for example, to an infant born prematurely or stillborn, or even a miscarriage. An infant carried to full term, even if he does not survive for thirty days—even if he died immediately after a live birth or lived his life only in an incubator—should be mourned fully. Concerning a child who was not expected to live, the circumstances are complex, and a rabbi should be consulted.

Parents of an infant who dies prematurely do not need to observe the stringent set of Jewish mourning laws.

The laws of *aninut* are not obligatory for the family. However, the infant should be given the Jewish last purification rites of *taharah*, in accordance with the specific procedures of the *chevrah kaddisha*.

Adult-type shrouds are not necessary; a plain white blanket is equally appropriate. Burial should not take place on holidays except for unusual circumstances; a local rabbi should make the determination. There also is no categorical need for a cortege of family members to accompany the deceased. It is preferable that three persons be present at interment, but none of the burial ceremonies, such as the recital of the Tzidduk ha-Din or Kaddish prayers, or the formal consolation service, need be performed.

The infant, male or female, should be given a name that should be announced before burial. If this was omitted, it may be given after burial. Rending the clothing need not be done; if it is, the blessing usually recited at the *keri'ah* should not be said. The custom is to circumcise male infants who

215

have not undergone circumcision until then, usually during *taharah*. The procedural requirements of the Jewish law of circumcisions need not be applied, but it should be performed by a Jew, preferably a mohel. If no mohel is available, it should be performed by a member of the *chevrah kaddisha*.

There are parents, however, who deeply desire to express the profound pain of their souls and to articulate their grief in Jewish terms. Should we simply disregard the sentiments of these parents and ignore bereavement practices for them? Of course not. In addition to following *taharah* procedures, they certainly may avail themselves of the rituals for discretionary mourners. (Please see the section on "Discretionary Mourners" below.)

Rabbis and therapists often advise taking advantage of the halakhic leniency to have the infant interred quickly and inconspicuously. That is, in fact, the practice that has obtained for centuries in world Jewry. Whatever parents decide is best for themselves and their families, they deserve our respect and understanding.

One of the great contemporary rabbis, Rabbi Ezekiel Bennet, willed that he be buried among the infant dead.

DISCRETIONARY MOURNERS

There are people who are under no halakhic obligation to practice prescribed mourning mitzvot but who feel unfulfilled in their bereavement, experiencing frustration or guilt because they have not given bereavement its fullest religious expression.

Among them are:

- Parents mourning for infants. The parents may have hoped for this child and planned for the child for many years.
- Parents who wish to mourn their adult children for longer than the required thirty days and who may feel stifled if their legitimate expression is taken away.

- Adopted children grieving for those who have taken them in and cared for them, when their natural parents did not.
- Adoptive parents for their children, whom they loved enough to sacrifice the stuff of their lives.
- Converts for natural relatives who are Gentiles, although they are not "related" according to Jewish law, converts being considered as "newborns."
- A spouse who wishes to mourn his or her mate longer than the thirty-day period required by *halakkah*.
- The divorced, not ritually obligated one another, yet harboring fondness that may not dissolve.
- The engaged, but not yet married, who are not legally related but amorously and morally committed.
- The married couple that is separated, for whom there possibly may be no formal mourning obligations. Often, one cannot ignore years of shared experiences and hopes, even though they are marked by sadness.
- Those living in communities that do not require relatives other than children to say Kaddish but who dearly wish to do so.
- Those who suffered a death immediately before a major holiday, when *shivah* is not fully observed, and feel unfulfilled, with their obligations to the deceased strangely disconnected.
- Those who heard belated news of a death, so that halakhically they are exempt from observing the full mourning practices.
- In-law children or parents, who love each other, often as deeply as natural-born parents and children or siblings, and who deeply desire to express their heartfelt feelings. In fact, Maimonides (*Avel* 2:5) recommends that spouses mourn for their mate's parents out of respect for their spouse.
- Grandchildren for a beloved grandparent. The tradition equates grandchildren with children, especially when a son or daughter does not keep the laws of mourning. The reverse situation, a grandparent mourning a grandchild, is heart-rending and cries out for religious expression. May he or she not be a discretionary mourner?

- Siblings, who may feel their heart rent because they may have been more than brother and sister—close personal friends. Is it not true that siblings have the longest-lasting relationships of all relatives? Usually they know one another long after parents have died.
- And there are others whom the *halakhah* does not obligate us to mourn ritually, but for whom we wish to express a structured, authentic grief.

It is natural that many spiritual-minded people should want to express the pain of the loss that gnaws inside them. While the standard obligations of *avelut* are not binding upon them for specific halakhic reasons, they often can find solace, satisfaction, and closure by articulating their feelings in traditional religious expressions that tie them and their loss to Jewish ancestors, Jewish history, and the contemporary Jewish community. All such people are discretionary mourners.

Does the halakha, in fact, recognize the needs of these stricken Jews? Definitely. The law is elastic enough to embrace those technically not obligated to mourn and allow them to fulfill themselves by paying respect to the deceased and satisfying their religious and personal desires.

The mourning practices that discretionary mourners elect are certainly permitted to them, and in cases where they demonstrate a need for them, they should be encouraged to mourn. There are instances of discretionary mourning in the Bible, for example, when David mourned Abner and shared in the meal of condolence (2 Samuel 3:35). The rabbis in the Talmud phrased it pithily: "Whom we mourn *for*, we mourn *with*" (*Mo'ed Katan* 20b)—that is to say, close relatives of a mourner, out of respect for him, should mourn along with him in his presence.

In the middle ages, Rabbi Asher ben Yechi'el (known as Rosh) said: "Whoever wishes to take upon himself the burden of mourning for one he does not legally need to mourn should in no way be deterred" (*K'lal* 20:27). Similarly, Rabbi Moses Isserles, one of the greatest halakhic authorities in Jewish history, who lived in the sixteenth century, strongly cautioned Jews not to stand in the way of other Jews who wished to ritually mourn someone, despite the fact that it was not legally required of them.

The halakhic respondent Israel ben Petachyah Isserlein declares: "The custom indeed is that all relatives [not just children] participate in certain mourning practices, such as changing their seats in the synagogue out of respect for the deceased. The great scholars of Austria have instituted that these relatives should observe as true *avelim* do for thirty days" (*Terumat ha Deshen*, vol. 1,291).

Maimonides astutely notes the effect of feeling grief beyond what the law prescribes. He said: "It is natural and understandable that a person should mourn a mate longer than he does other relatives, above the halakha's mandate" (*Avel* 6:5).

Indeed, the Jewish community often mourns the passing of a great scholar or communal leader who is not one of the seven relatives; all Jews are encouraged to mourn individuals who leave no living relatives obligated to mourn them; mourners are given the choice of staying away from joyous celebrations long beyond the halakhic end of *avelut*. Of course, it should be clearly noted, the Sages admonish mourners not to mourn overly much, not to make too frequent grave visitations, not to pray directly to the dead, and not to adopt extreme measures that make a fetish out of an observance.

There are several caveats to discretionary mourners.

The Sages caution discretionary mourners not to violate any other mitzvot in the process of performing nonmandated practices, such as purposely not studying Torah because it is joyful, or making an unnecessary blessing over the *keri'ah* garment, which is not required to be torn. They also exhort the mourner-by-choice not to practice *all* the mourning laws, because outsiders may come to the mistaken conclusion that the *halakhah* obligates them. These meta-halakhic practices are voluntary, though deeply spiritual, expressions of choice demonstrating personal feelings of grief.

There may be traditional Jews who are made uneasy by the fact that people can undertake observances that the *halakhah* did not enjoin. They fear that a "creative" keeping of our customs might subjectivize our ancient tradition of law. Their concerns should not be taken lightly. For example, the *halakhah* always has prized those who were "commanded and obeyed" above those who were not commanded but who voluntarily obeyed. On the surface, one might have expected such a person to be considered on a higher spiritual plane. Not so. Judaism is not a skein of charming folkways, but a world of laws, not unlike the Constitution of the United States, which cannot simply and arbitrarily be amended, no matter how valuable the purpose. In Judaism, obedience to God's law, as He gave it, is the highest good.

But Judaism does have a long history of dealing with man at the heights of his exaltation and victory and at the nadir of his failures and depressions. As we have a *masorah* of *halakhah*, a tradition of law, so we have a *masorah* of *regesh*, a tradition of feeling, customs that are precisely configured to deal with moments of quaking fear and also with astounding joy. This is true especially as it relates to the traditions of mourning. The rabbis indulged the world-shattering sentiments of people who had lost those dearest to them for all time. This was no light matter. They recognized the wild thoughts that trans-fixed the *onen* while the deceased was not yet buried. They called it "*aninut she-ba-lev*," the "*aninut* of the heart"—not the formal practice but the profound sentiment—and they did not require the *onen* to perform fundamental commandments. As a matter of halakhic principle, the rabbis decided all religious questions of *avelut* according to the more lenient interpretation of the law.

The practices suggested for those who are not required to mourn according to the Torah and the rabbis are practices that enable the profoundly distressed to express grief in a time-honored fashion. It cannot be emphasized too strongly, however, that no bereaved person should ever be imposed upon or cajoled into observing rituals that the wise and age-old *halakhah* did not require of him. We do not know what is inside anyone else's heart and mind, and ultimately we cannot possibly know what is truly best for them. It is unwise to recommend that they mourn electively in certain unprescribed ways. If there is any doubt whatever as to whether or not to do something "additional," surely the *halakhah* is the very best fallback position. It has made no requirement in certain cases, and we should abide by its decision, unless it is otherwise deeply needed. It is unseemly to cause anyone who has suffered a severe loss a sense that they are doing less than is proper, when surely they are not.

Given these parameters, the grief-stricken should elect to observe faithfully those practices that are in accord with their sensibilities. Because the subject is delicate, tailored to people's needs, and is a "new" category in Jewish mourning laws, I want to speak to mourners directly.

Which observances may discretionary mourners adopt?

1. *Shivah*. Sit *shivah*, in a way that accommodates both mourners and visitors. The *shivah* procedures should not be observed as in full mourning for a Jewish parent. Full observance, in the case of a convert, for example, might indicate to friends not intimately acquainted with the family that the parent was Jewish. This might give rise to difficulties— like encouraging the marriage of a convert to an unsuspecting *Kohen*, a union that is not permitted in Jewish law.

2. Graveside service. Hold a religious service and speak words of consolation and eulogy. Choose readings from the Psalms and chapters from the Prophets that express your inner feelings. Such a religious service is preferably held at graveside, directly before the interment, rather than in a full funeral setting in the chapel. That will keep the service understated yet expressive, less ceremonial but more moving. Also, please note that there is still a requirement for a minyan to say Kaddish, and the Burial Kaddish should be said, including as it does a prayer for a peaceful future.

3. Accompaniment to the final resting place. In the case of an infant, accompany the body to the cemetery. Close friends and relatives will do this if requested. This demonstrates not only respect for the deceased child, but comfort for the family, as few other practices can do. (See the section on infant death above.)

4. Kaddish. Recite Kaddish for *sheloshim*, or more if you like, on yahrzeits, and at Yizkor four times a year. If you want to

continue the Kaddish beyond thirty days, no one has the authority to deny you that. While it is not customary in some communities to recite Kaddish for *sheloshim* for relatives other than parents (although in some halakhic sources—the writings of Rabbi Moses Isserles and the *Kitzur Shulchan Aruch*—it as an established and acceptable custom), brothers, sisters, mothers, fathers, and spouses may say Kaddish even beyond thirty days. In the case of a convert mourning a non-Jew, it is preferable, however, for him to recite a psalm instead, as is customary on yahrzeits. In that way, a distinction is made between mourning a Jew and a non-Jew. The decision to do either rests with the bereaved, based on his sensibility, his unique style of Jewish expression, and his relationship to the deceased.

5. Joyous occasions. The most obvious ritual mourning practice in such instances is a negative one: do not participate in manifestly joyous occasions, which are hardly in the spirit of bereavement. This is the most conspicuous of the practices that discretionary mourners should adopt.

6. Yahrzeit. Observe the yahrzeit and light a candle for the soul of the deceased. Keep in mind that this is not a vow to observe every yahrzeit for the rest of your life or you will be halakhically bound to do so every year.

7. Study and charity. The two hallmarks of the Jewish Weltanschauung should be remembered: studying Torah—or Mishnah or any other significant Judaic text—and giving charity to a worthy cause, whether a contribution of effort or funds, in memory of the deceased. This bespeaks bereavement in the ancient tradition, even if not halakhically prescribed.

8. Moderation. Great care needs to be taken, hopefully in accord with a spiritual leader, to keep these by-choice practices modest and moderate, while of course being expressive and consoling. The child or parent that you mourn has lived and loved and enriched your life considerably. Keeping him or her in memory may well bring you the comfort you seek.

Done in the right measure, these practices may provide a significant step toward closure of this chapter in the family's history. I believe strongly in the power of hope. That is my prayer in writing this chapter.

SUICIDES

Man is the magnificent creation of an all-wise and all-merciful God. The awesome determination of life and death is not given to man. As it is God's prerogative to grant life, so it is His sole decision to take life: "Perforce were you born," say the rabbis of the Talmud, "and perforce must you die" (*Ethics of the Fathers*, 4:29). One who takes his own life is a murderer, just as one who takes another's life. "I will seek your blood for your souls," is applied by the Midrash to one who destroys his own soul. A deliberate suicide, in effect, denies the Lordship, the supreme mastery of God, when he decides that he is the lord of his own soul. He commits not only an act of violence but of sacrilege.

In halakhic practice, it is quite rare that a suicide is thought to be deliberate. We seldom have objective proof, such as a suicide note or a tape in which the suicide claims that he has committed this act out of spite. Even such statements cannot fully be trusted. Deliberate suicide, when it does happen, is considered an even more heinous crime than murder. The murderer has the possibility of repenting his vicious deed. Not so the suicide. Death is considered a punishment that atones for all the evil that was committed in life. But the suicide has used this very act of atonement to commit his terrible crime.

The horror of this act in the eyes of people, however, is not primarily theological—the blasphemy of God—but moral, a betrayal of family and friends. It is the end of responsibility—abandoning children, leaving a spouse or parents staring vacantly at the end of a swinging, broken chain, betrayed and bewildered, a *Götterdämmerung*, with a vision of doom enough to haunt them all the days of their life.

What leaves one incredulous is not only the betrayal, but the ultimate uselessness of this irretrievable decision. In the fourth chapter of *Ethics of the Fathers* (verse 29), the Sages say: "Do not allow your natural impulse to convince you that the grave is a refuge, for perforce were you formed; perforce were you born; perforce you live; perforce you die; and perforce are you destined to give an account and reckoning before the supreme King of Kings, the Holy One, blessed be He." There is no refuge in death. Death brings surcease from anxieties and despair and conflict, but not oblivion. The dead shall rise to be judged.

It is the enormity of this crime that gave rise to the oft-quoted condemnation: "Suicides do not receive a share in the world to come." Ostensibly, this is because they have refused the rightful share of their duties in this world. They cannot receive Divine reward as they have denied the very rule of the Divinity.

One who was a deliberate suicide is neither eulogized nor mourned, although certain laws are observed. To classify a suicide deliberate, the death must meet numerous qualifications. Only a rabbinical authority can make the decision.

Definition of a Suicide

What is a true suicide? Can a person who coolly and deliberately plans and commits an act of suicide be considered a normal individual? And who is able, with any reliable degree of accuracy, to determine the nature, motivation, and purposeful quality of such an act? What mysterious force has impelled this person to perform an act so contrary to human nature?

Because of these difficult problems, the rabbis have dealt leniently with suicide. Suicide has a strict, legal, religious definition in Judaism that does not always accord with the off-hand conclusions of relatives and neighbors. It cannot be emphasized too strongly that police reports, court records, or legal analyses alone should not decide such a matter. Only a qualified rabbi, using halakhic criteria, can make the determination of suicide. There must be taken into consideration the possibility of insanity, intoxication or drug use, clinical depression, the motivation of the act, the possibility of a last-minute change of heart, the complex problem of whether or how the act was planned. The determination cannot be made easily, least of all by those not acquainted with the letter and the spirit of Jewish law.

The rabbi, in cooperation with psychiatrists and law enforcement officials, will have to determine answers to the following questions before rendering his decision:

1. Is there even a remote possibility that this was a murder and not suicide? Is the determination of suicide a probability or a certainty?

2. Might the deceased have been insane, even temporarily? Might he have been under the influence of liquor or narcotics or barbiturates?

3. Was the deceased motivated by extreme suffering, by enormous fear of punishment—either at the hands of God or of society—or by terrible anxiety? Might he have been in a depression, which would ameliorate the transgression?

4. Was the act of suicide planned in advance, to make an ideological statement, such as an existential thinker, believing that on balance life is not worth living and prescribing self-destruction? Was that plan expressed verbally or committed to writing? How long before the suicide was it made? Could it have been merely an exercise in emotional exaggeration as exasperated people are sometimes wont to do? Did death come as the suicide planned it?

5. Did death come instantly or did the deceased linger, during which time he might have tried to alter the course of events or repent of the crime?

6. Was the final act the result of some cruel, fashionable game or fancy, or in the spirit of reckless abandon?

7. Was it a consequence of uncontrolled anger or was he literally consumed with hatred?

With these facts available, the rabbi will be able to decide the mode of burial and the procedures for mourning. It again should be emphasized that this decision is not a police matter and, certainly, the layman should not make it, no matter how well-versed he is in Judaism.

Mourning Traditions for the Suicide

The principle followed in these laws is that no honor is given the suicide for a crime that deserves only rebuke. However, respect for the bereaved family must be scrupulously considered as they are the real victims. Therefore, all aspects of the mourning traditions that affect the honor of the living are to be observed, while those laws designed solely for the honor of the dead are suspended.

Aninut

The period between death and burial, *aninut*, in which the mourner is exempt from performing the positive commands, is based upon two needs. One need is the time-consuming concern for the details of the burial arrangements, and the mental anguish attendant upon it, and the other is the desire to honor the deceased that preoccupies the mind of the bereaved. While the second principle does not apply to the deliberate suicide (there is no honor in self-destruction), the first obviously does, since burial is required. The period of *aninut*, therefore, extends from death only to the time when all arrangements have been completed with the undertaker and cemetery, and not, as is customary, until the interment.

Burial

The procedure for *taharah* and requirements for shrouds, casket, and grave are the same as for other Jewish dead. The only difference is the location of the grave. If the suicide is definitely an intentional suicide, he is to be buried at least six feet from surrounding graves. Sometimes cemeteries reserve a special section for suicides. It usually is located near the fence or border of the cemetery.

Keri'ah

While commentators dispute this matter in halakhic literature, the opinion generally followed is that mourners do rend their clothing, even for deliberate suicides.

Eulogy

No eulogy should be made for a deliberate suicide, despite

the good qualities he has demonstrated in life, as it is in his very act of dying that he committed sacrilege. Eulogizing these dead would constitute an act of hypocrisy. The unveiling of the monument should be performed with the recitation of Psalms but without benefit of eulogy.

Mourning Observances

If there is even a remote possibility that the family's honor would be compromised if no mourning laws were to be observed, the mourning laws should be followed down to every last detail. This applies even in the rare case where the deceased is halakhically considered a deliberate suicide.

Kaddish

While the Burial Kaddish at graveside is really a prayer and not recited, the Mourner's Kaddish is recited regularly, morning and night. Although the Mourner's Kaddish normally is recited for eleven months, if the deceased is beyond doubt a deliberate suicide, the Mourner's Kaddish should be recited for the full year, as he certainly requires and will receive the full redemptive effect of the Kaddish.

Comforting the Bereaved

While the deceased may not be specially honored and should receive no public recognition, the family of the deceased must be given every courtesy. The mourners should be accompanied to the cemetery and should be visited at home. These mourners, surely more than others, require the healing comfort of understanding friends and neighbors. Great care should be taken during the hours of consolation. The rabbinic dictum that the bereaved should be allowed to open the conversation while visitors listen attentively seems to be the best advice for this tragic moment. Visitors who come to console should beware: do not speak without thinking.

Yizkor and Yahrzeit

Yizkor should be recited at the regular time even for deliberate suicides, and no variations are to be made in the prayers. Yahrzeit is observed as for other relatives.

THOSE WHO DO NOT WISH TO BE MOURNED

If the deceased explicitly requested that he not be mourned by the observance of *shivah*, his will should be honored. Much depends on the reason for the request. If the purpose was to alleviate the burdens of the survivors, to enable them to go to work, or to spare the family the trouble of observance, the request should be dismissed and the deceased honored.

If, however, the deceased intentionally wished to violate the tradition, the mourners in consultation with a rabbi must judge whether the request was issued out of ignorance of Jewish values and their true significance. If out of ignorance, the laws of mourning should be observed. If it was a willful denial of Jewish values, however, Jewish tradition would dictate following his request and not honoring him by the observance of *shivah*

THE INTERMARRIED

The child of a Jewish mother is legally Jewish, even if the father is a Gentile. Hence, the child is to be mourned as any full Jew, and he, in turn, is obligated to mourn other relatives. Understandably, he is not legally required to observe mourning practices for his Gentile mother or father, unless the father converted to Judaism before he was born. This does not address the personal feelings of bereavement one experiences upon the death of a natural parent. For further information on this delicate matter, turn to "Discretionary Mourners."

If the mother is not Jewish but the child was formally converted to Judaism, he is mourned as a Jew. If the Gentile mother converted to Judaism after the conception but before the birth of the child, the child is considered Jewish. The child is mourned and is obligated to mourn under the same laws as other Jews.

In the case of a child born out of wedlock, if the mother is Jewish, the child is considered Jewish. All laws of mourning must be observed.

VIOLATORS OF TORAH

The *halakhah* considers five categories of sinners. These do not exhaust all the varieties of historical defectors from the faith, but they do provide us with general guidelines for dealing with violators of Torah in bereavement circumstances.

1. The apostate. An apostate is a defector from the faith, who denounces Judaism openly and adopts another religion without compulsion. He is not permitted burial in a Jewish cemetery and is not to be mourned at all. For all intents and purposes, his defection is accepted as de facto severance from the faith community, and he is, therefore, not honored by the faithful. Permitting burial or any other religious observance for an apostate would leave the door open for the defection of others. The realization that the native privileges and rights of the Jewish people will not be accorded the apostate historically has served as a deterrent to those considering such a step.

2. Spiteful sinners. Those who publicly, purposefully, and arrogantly disown the ways of Israel, her faith and practices, her laws and traditions, but do not formally defect from Judaism by embracing another faith, are granted the rights of *taharah* and the wearing of shrouds. They also are interred in a Jewish cemetery, albeit in a peripheral part. However, there is no mourning, such as the rending of clothing, *aninut*, or

shivah. The Jewish community must be forgiving to a certain point; beyond that, it must safeguard its own existence. By such treatment of the deceased sinner does it hope to prevent others from following his example.

3. Mindless sinners. Those who violate the laws and traditions of Israel as a result of ignorance or a misguided sense of social necessity are not considered spiteful sinners. Mindless sinners receive the full measure of dignity afforded all Jewish dead. They must be mourned in the manner prescribed for all other deceased.

4. Executed criminals. Those who are executed by the government for reasons that, under Jewish law, would have brought upon them a sentence of capital punishment (such as murderers) are not to be mourned. If the crime would not have warranted capital punishment under Jewish law, the criminal must be mourned and full burial rights accorded him. This is an unusual problem; each individual case requires rabbinic interpretation and application of *halakhah.*

5. Cremated Dead. Those who choose not to be buried in the ancient Jewish manner have shown a final defiance of the tradition of the faithful and are not to be mourned. Their ashen remains are not to be interred in a Jewish cemetery. If the cremation was a consequence of misinformation or ignorance, a rabbi should be consulted. Of course this in no way refers to those who succumbed in a fire, were torched by enemies, or died *al kiddush ha-Shem.* Such people are to be accorded full Jewish honors.

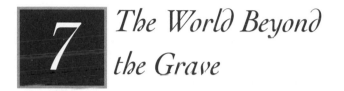

7 The World Beyond the Grave

MAN HAS HAD AN ABIDING faith in a world beyond the grave. The conviction in a life after death, unprovable but unshakable, has been cherished since the beginning of thinking man's life on earth. It makes its appearance in religious literature not as fiat, commanded irrevocably by an absolute God, but rather appears plantlike, growing and developing naturally in the human soul. It then sprouts forth through sublime prayer and sacred hymn. Only later is it extrapolated in complicated metaphysical speculation.

The afterlife has not been "thought up"; it is not a rational construct of a religious philosophy imposed on believing man. It has sprung from within the hearts of masses of men, a sort of *consensus gentium,* inside out, a hope beyond and above the rational, a longing for the warm sun of eternity. The afterlife is not a theory to be proven logically or demonstrated by rational analysis. It is axiomatic. It is to the soul what oxygen is to the lungs. There is little meaning to life, to God, to man's constant strivings, to all of his achievements, unless there is a world beyond the grave.

The Bible, so vitally concerned with the actions of man in this world, and agonizing over his day-to-day morals, is relatively silent about the world to come. This very silence is a tribute to the awesome concept, taken for granted like the biosphere in which we live. No elaborate apologia, no complex abstractions are necessary. The Bible, which records the sacred dialogue between God and man, surely must be founded on the soul's eternal existence. It was not a matter of debate, as it became later in history when whole movements interpreted Scripture with slavish literalism and could not find the afterlife crystallized in letters and words; or later yet, when philosophers began to apply the yardstick of rationalism to man's every hope and idea and sought empirical proof for this conviction of the soul. It was a fundamental creed, always present, though rarely articulated.

If the soul is immortal then death cannot be considered a final act. If the life of the soul is to be continued, then death, however bitter, is deprived of its treacherous power of casting mourners into a lifetime of agonizing hopelessness over an irretrievable loss. Terrible though it is, death is a threshold to a new world—the world to come.

A PARABLE

Conveying hope and confidence in the afterlife, even though this hope must be refracted through the prism of death, is the parable of twins awaiting birth in the mother's womb. Inspired by the inventive analogy of a contemporary Israeli rabbi, the late Y. M. Tuckachinsky, contained in a few Hebrew sentences, I adapted it thirty years ago for the first edition of *The Jewish Way in Death and Mourning*. It has been reprinted many times. It continues to speak to readers to this day.

Imagine twins growing peacefully in the warmth of the womb. Their mouths are closed, and they are being fed via the umbilical cord. Their lives are serene. The whole world, to these brothers, is the interior of the womb. Who could conceive anything larger, better, more comfortable? They begin to wonder: "We are getting lower and lower. Surely if it continues, we will exit one day. What will happen after we exit?"

Now the first infant is a believer. He is heir to a religious tradition that tells him there will be a new life after this wet and warm existence of the womb. A strange belief, seemingly without foundation, but one to which he holds fast. The second infant is a thoroughgoing skeptic. Legends do not deceive him. He believes only in that which can be demonstrated. He is enlightened and tolerates no idle conjecture. What is not within one's experience can have no basis in one's imagination.

Says the faithful brother: "After our 'death' here, there will be a new great world. We will eat through the mouth. We will see great distances, and we will hear through the ears on the sides of our heads. Why, our feet will be straightened! And our heads—up and free, rather than down, and boxed in."

Replies the skeptic: "Nonsense. You're straining your imagination again. There is no foundation for this belief. It is only your survival instinct, an elaborate defense mechanism, a historically-conditioned subterfuge. You are looking for something to calm your fear of 'death.' There is only this world. There is no world to come!"

"Well then," asks the first, "what do you say it will be like?"

The second brother snappily replies with all the assurance of the slightly knowledgeable: "We will go with a bang. Our world will collapse and we will sink into oblivion. No more. Nothing. Black void. An end to consciousness. Forgotten. This may not be a comforting thought, but it is a logical one."

Suddenly the water inside the womb bursts. The womb convulses. Upheaval. Turmoil. Writhing. Everything lets loose. Then a mysterious pounding—a crushing, staccato pounding. Faster, faster, lower, lower.

The believing brother exits. Tearing himself from the womb, he falls outward. The second brother shrieks, startled by the "accident" that has befallen his brother. He bewails and bemoans the tragedy, the death of a perfectly fine fellow. Why? Why? Why didn't he take better care? Why did he fall into that terrible abyss?

As he thus laments, he hears a head-splitting cry and a great tumult from the black abyss, and he trembles: "Oh my! What a horrible end! As I predicted!"

Meanwhile as the skeptic brother mourns, his "dead" brother has been born into the "new" world. The head-splitting cry is a sign of health and vigor, and the tumult is really a chorus of *mazal tovs* sounded by the waiting family thanking God for the birth of a healthy son.

Indeed, in the words of a contemporary thinker, man comes from the darkness of the "not yet" and proceeds to the darkness of the "no more." While it is difficult to imagine the "not yet," it is more difficult to picture the "no more."

As we separate and "die" from the womb, only to be born to life, so we separate and die from our world, only to be reborn to life eternal. The exit from the womb is the birth of the body. The exit from the body is the birth of the soul. As the womb requires a gestation period of nine months, the world requires a residence of seventy or eighty years. As the womb is *prozdor*, an anteroom preparatory to life, so our present existence is a *prozdor* to the world beyond.

WHAT IS IMMORTALITY?

The conception of an afterlife is fundamental to the Jewish religion; it is an article of faith in the Jews' creed. The denial of the afterlife constitutes a denial of a cornerstone of the faith. This concept is not merely an added detail that may lose its significance in some advanced age. It is an essential and enduring principle. Indeed, the Mishnah (*Sanhedrin* 10:1) expressly excludes from the reward of the "world beyond" he who holds that the resurrection of the dead is without biblical warrant. Maimonides considers this belief one of the thirteen basic truths that every Jew is commanded to hold.

The concept of afterlife entered the prayer book in the philosophic hymns of Yigdal and Ani Ma'amin. Centuries later, hundreds of thousands of Jews, packed in cattle cars, en route to the crematoria, sang the Ani Ma'amin, the affirmation of the coming of the Messiah.

Philosophers such as Hasdai Crescas in the fourteenth century changed the formulation and counting of Maimonides' thirteen fundamental truths, but still kept immortality as a fundamental principle without which the Jewish religion is inconceivable. Simeon ben Zemah Duran, in the early fifteenth century, reduced the fundamentals to three, but resurrection was included. Joseph Albo, in the same era, revised the structure of dogmas, and still immortality remained a universally binding belief. No matter how the basic principles were reduced or revised, immortality remained a major tenet of Judaism. Indeed, we may say of immortality what Hermann Cohen said of the Messiah: "If the Jewish religion had done nothing more for mankind than proclaim the Messianic idea of the Old Testament prophets, it could have claimed to be the bedrock of all the world's ethical culture."

Strange as it may appear, despite the historic near-unanimity of scholarly opinion on the fundamental belief, the practical details of immortality are ambiguous and vague. There is no formal eschatology in Judaism, only a traditional consensus that illuminates the way. The veil has never been pierced, and only shadowy structures can be discerned. But, as a renowned artist remarked, the true genius of a painting can be determined at dusk when the light fades, when one can see only the outline, the broad strokes of the brush, while the details are submerged in darkness. The beauty of the concept of immortality and its colossal religious significance does not lie in its details.

Maimonides denies that man can have a clear picture of the afterlife, and he compares earthbound creatures with a blind man who cannot learn to appreciate colors merely by being given a verbal description. Flesh-and-blood man cannot have any precise conception of the pure, spiritual bliss of the world beyond. Thus, says Maimonides, the precise sequence in which the afterlife will finally unravel is not a cardinal article of the faith, and the faithful should not concern themselves with the details. So it is often in Judaism that abstract principles must be held in the larger, conceptual sense, while the formal philosophic details are blurred. Precisely the reverse is true about the pragmatic religious behaviors—the observances of the faith—that are worked out to their most minute detail, although the basic concept behind them may remain unknown forever.

For all that, there is a consensus of belief based on Talmudic derivations from the Torah and philosophic analysis of statements uttered by the Sages. The concept is usually discussed under the headings of "Messiah" and "Resurrection of the Dead." (Concepts such as "Gehenna" and the "Garden of Eden" are too complicated for discussion in this work.) The term *olam ha-ba*, the "world beyond," while relatively unclear, seems to have encompassed the two basic concepts of Messiah and resurrection. Maimonides lists these two as cardinal principles of the Jewish creed.

THE MESSIAH

The generic term "Messiah" means "anointed one." Kings and priests were anointed in ancient times to set them apart as specially designated leaders of society. The Messiah will bring redemption to this world. It will be a time of true bliss, unparalleled in our own existence. It will not be a new world, a qualitatively different world, rather it will be this world brought to perfection. Universal peace, tranquility, lawfulness, and goodness will prevail, and all will acknowledge the unity and lordship of God.

Will the Messiah be a specific person, or will he only represent an era of perfection—the "days of Messiah"? Traditional Judaism believes, without equivocation, in the coming of an inconceivably great hero, anointed for leadership—a descendant of the House of David, who will lead the world out of chaos. He will be of flesh and blood, a mortal sent expressly by God to fulfill the glory of His people. The traditional belief is that man must work to better the world and help bring the Messiah. It is unfoundedly optimistic to believe that mankind by itself will inevitably progress to such an era. A supernatural gift to mankind, in the person of the Messiah, will be required to bring the world to this pinnacle of glory. God will directly intervene to prevent the world from rushing head-long into darkness and will bring the redemption through a human personality. The personal Messiah, supernaturally introduced to mankind, will not, however, be a Divine personality. He will only bring about the redemption that is granted by God. The Messiah will have no ability to bring that redemption himself. He will have no miraculous powers. He, himself, will not be able to atone for the sins of others. He will have no superhuman relationship to God. He will be an exalted personality, of incomparable ability, who will usher in the rehabilitation of the Jewish people and the subsequent regeneration of all mankind.

How the Messiah will come and how we will be able to identify him has aroused the magnificent, imaginative inventiveness and poetic conceit of masses of Jews in every age. Many of these ruminations are contradictory. Some are founded in biblical interpretation, some on traditional beliefs handed down from father to son, while others are flights of folkloristic fancy.

The time of the coming of the Messiah has aroused such fantastic conjecture by so many who confidently predicted specific dates and signs, causing so much anxiety and unreasonable anticipation, and culminating in such heart-breaking and spiritually shattering frustration, that the Sages have had to chastise severely those who "count the days" to "bring near the end" of redemption.

While some theologians have sought to dispute the supernatural introduction of the Messiah or to denigrate the idea of a personal Messiah, there is no a priori reason to deny either. On the other hand, however, there does stand a millennium of unwavering conviction on the part of our most profound scholars and the great masses of Jews to affirm it. The authority of hundreds of generations will withstand superficial rational analysis, let alone the metaphysical misgivings and begrudging consent of contemporary, sophisticated theologians.

RESURRECTION OF THE DEAD

The body returns to the earth, dust to dust, but the soul returns to God who gave it. This doctrine of the immortality of the soul is affirmed not only by Judaism and other religions, but by many secular philosophers as well. Judaism, however, also believes in the eventual resurrection of the body, which will be reunited with the soul at a later time on a "great and awesome day of the Lord" (Joel 3:4). The human form of the righteous men of all ages, buried and long since decomposed, will be resurrected at God's will.

The most dramatic portrayal of this bodily resurrection is to be found in the "Valley of Dry Bones" prophecy in Ezekiel 37, read as the *haftarah* on the intermediate Sabbath of Passover. It recalls past deliverances and envisions the future redemption of Israel and the eventual quickening of the dead.

> The hand of the Lord was upon me, and the Lord carried me out in a spirit, and set me down in the midst of the valley, and it was full of bones; and He caused me to pass by them round about, and, behold, there were very many in the open valley; and, lo, they were very dry. And He said unto me: "Son of man, can these bones live?" And I answered: "O Lord, God, Thou knowest." Then He said unto me: "Prophesy over these bones, and say unto them: 'O ye dry bones, hear the word of the Lord: Thus saith the Lord God unto these bones: Behold, I will cause breath to enter into you, and ye shall live. And I will lay sinews upon you, and will bring up flesh upon you, and cover you with skin, and put breath in you, and ye shall live; and ye shall know that I am the Lord.'" So I prophesied as I was commanded; and as I prophesied, there was a noise, and behold a commotion, and the bones came together, bone to its bone. And I beheld, and, lo, there were sinews upon them, and flesh came up, and skin covered them above; but there was no breath in them. Then said He unto me: "Prophesy unto the breath, prophesy, son of man, and say to the breath: 'Thus saith the Lord God: Come from the four winds, O breath, and breathe upon these slain, that they may live.'" So I prophesied as He commanded me, and the breath came

into them, and they lived, and stood upon their feet, an exceeding great host. Then He said unto me: "Son of man, these bones are the whole house of Israel; behold, they say: 'Our bones are dried up, and our hope is lost; we are clean cut off.' Therefore, prophesy, and say unto them: 'Thus saith the Lord God: Behold, I will open your graves, and cause you to come up out of your graves, O my people; and I will bring you into the land of Israel. And ye shall know that I am the Lord, when I have opened your graves, and caused you to come up out of your graves, O My people. And I will put My spirit in you, and ye shall live, and I will place you in your own land; and ye shall know that I the Lord have spoken, and performed it, saith the Lord.'"

The power of this conviction can be gauged not only by the quality of the lives of the Jews, their tenacity and gallantry in the face of death, but in the very real fear instilled in their enemies. After destroying Jerusalem and callously decimating its Jewish population, Titus, the Roman general, returned home with only a portion of his Tenth Legion. When asked whether he had lost all of his other men on the battlefield, Titus gave assurance that his men were alive but that they were still on combat duty. He had left them to stand guard over Jewish corpses in the fields of Jerusalem because he sincerely was afraid that their bodies would be resurrected and they would reconquer the Holy Land as they had promised.

The belief in a bodily resurrection appears, at first sight, to be incredible to the contemporary mind. But when approached from the God's-eye view, why is rebirth more miraculous than birth? The adhesion of sperm and egg, the subsequent fertilization and development in the womb culminating in the birth of the astoundingly complex network of tubes and glands, bones and organs, their incredibly precise functioning and the unbelievably intricate human brain that guides them, is surely a miracle of the first magnitude. Curiously, the miraculous object, man himself, takes this for granted. In his preoccupation with daily trivia, he ignores the miracle of his own existence. The idea of rebirth may appear strange because we have never experienced a similar occurrence, for which reason we cannot put together the stuff of imagination. Perhaps it is because we can be active in creating life but cannot participate with God in the re-creation of life, taking a cadaver and making it live. Perhaps it is because, scientifically, re-creation flies against biological theory, even while we are slowly coming to know how life is developed, and our researchers are about to clone human life in the laboratory test tube. But who has created the researching biologist? And can we not postulate an omnipotent Divine Biologist who created all men? Surely resurrection is not beyond the capacity of an omnipotent God.

The Sages simplified the concept of bodily resurrection by posing an analogy that brings it within the experience of man. A tree, once alive with blossoms and fruit, full of the sap of life, stands cold and still in the winter. Its leaves have browned and fallen; its fruit rots on the ground. But the warm rains come and the sun shines. Buds sprout. Green leaves appear. Colorful fruits burst from their seed. With the coming of spring, God resurrects nature. For this reason the blessing of God for reviving the dead, which is recited in every daily Amidah prayer, incorporates also the seasonal requests for rain. When praying for the redemption of man, the prayer book uses the phrase *matzmi'ach yeshu'ah*, "planting salvation." Indeed, the Talmud compares the day of resurrection with the rainy season and notes that the latter is even more significant—for resurrection serves only the righteous while the rain falls indiscriminately on all men.

This is one supplementary reason why the body and all its limbs are required to be interred in the earth and not cremated, for it expresses our faith in the future resurrection. Naturally, the All-Powerful God can re-create the body whether it is buried, drowned, or burned. Yet, willful cremation signifies an arrogant denial of the possibility of resurrection, and those who deny this cardinal principle should not share in the reward for its observance. The body and its limbs—whether amputated before death, or during a permissible postmortem examination—have to be allowed to decompose as one complete organism by the processes of nature, not by man's mechanical act.

REVIVAL OF THE DEAD: A SYMBOLIC IDEA

Some contemporary thinkers have noted that the physical revival of the dead is symbolic of a cluster of basic Jewish ideas.

First, man does not achieve the ultimate redemption by virtue of his own inherent nature. It is not because he, uniquely, possesses an immortal soul that he, inevitably, will be resurrected. The concept of resurrection underscores man's reliance on God who, in the words of the Amidah, "Wakes the dead in great mercy." It is His grace and His mercy that reward the deserving and revive those who sleep in the dust.

Second, resurrection is not only a private matter, a bonus for the righteous individual. It is a corporate reward. All of the righteous of all ages, those who stood at Sinai and those of our generation, will be revived. The community of the righteous has a corporate and historic character. It will live again as a whole people. The individual, even in death, is not separated from the society in which he lived.

Third, physical resurrection affirms unequivocally that man's soul and his body are the creations of a holy God. There is a tendency to assume that the affirmation of a spiritual dimension in man must bring with it the corollary that his physical being is depreciated. Indeed, such has been the development of the body-soul duality in both the Christian tradition and in Oriental religions, and accounts for their glorification of asceticism. Further, even the Greek philosophers who were enamoured of the beauty of the body came to denigrate the physical side of man. They crowned reason as man's noblest virtue. For them, the spiritual-intellectual endeavor to perceive the unchanging truth was the highest function of man. Man's material existence, on the other hand, was always in flux, subject to change and, therefore, inferior. They accepted the immortality of the soul—which to the Greeks was what we call mind—which survives the extinction of his physical being. But they could not understand physical resurrection because they did not, by any means, consider the body worthy of being reborn.

To the contrary, Judaism has always stressed that the body,

as the soul, is a gift of God—indeed, that it belongs to God. *Ha-neshamah lach ve-ha-guf pa'alach*, the Jew declared, "The soul is yours, and the body is your handiwork" (recited on Rosh Hashanah). To care for the body is a religious command of the Bible. The practice of asceticism for religious purposes was tolerated, but the ascetic had to bring a sacrifice of atonement for his action. Resurrection affirms that the body is of value because it came from God and it will be revived by God. Resurrection affirms that man's empirical existence is valuable in God's eyes. His activities in this world are significant in the scheme of eternity. His strivings are not to be deprecated as vain and useless but are to be brought to fulfillment at the end of days.

The concept of resurrection thus serves to keep God ever in man's consciousness, to unify contemporary and historic Jewry, to affirm the value of God's world, and to heighten, rather than to depress, the value of man's worthy strivings in this world.

Which specific virtues might guarantee a person's resurrection is a subject of much debate. The method of resurrection, too, is an open question that invites conjecture.

While the details of the afterlife are thus very much a matter of speculation, the traditional consensus must serve to illuminate the dark path. In the words of Rabbi Joshua ben Chananiah (*Niddah* 70b): "When they come to life again, we will consult about the matter."

LIFE AFTER DEATH:
A COROLLARY OF JEWISH BELIEF

The existence of a life after death is a necessary corollary of the Jewish belief in a just and merciful and ethical God.

God Is Just

The Jew is caught in a dilemma: He believes that God is righteous and just, that God rewards the good and punishes the wicked. Yet, for all the strength of the Jew's belief, he lives in a world where he sees that life is unfair. He sees all too often the spiritual anomaly of *tzaddik ve-ra lo, rasha ve-tov lo*, "the righteous who suffer and the wicked who prosper." The Sages answer by saying that there is *spiritual* reward and *spiritual* punishment. The answer that religion gives is that the good, just, and eternal God revives the righteous dead, while the wicked remain the dust. It is in life after death at which time the just God balances the scales and rewards or punishes those who truly deserve it. This doctrine of resurrection is, thus, a necessary corollary of our belief in a just God.

God Is Merciful

But if we ask of God only that He be just, can we expect that we ourselves will be resurrected? Who is so righteous as to be assured of that glorious reward? Hence, we call upon God's mercy that He revive us. The concept of resurrection is an affirmation of His mercy. Thus, the fifteenth century philosopher Joseph Albo notes that in the prayer book the concept of resurrection is associated with *rachamim rabbim*, "great mercy," whereas God's gift of life and sustenance are considered only *chen, chesed,* and *rachamim*, "grace, kindness, and mercy."

Says Rabbi Albo: "The life of man is divided into three portions: The years of rise and growth, the middle years or the plateau, and the years of decline." These are described by the three adjectives—grace, kindness, and mercy. While one is young and vigorous one does not require an extra measure of assistance from God in being nourished. All that he needs is *chen*, Divine grace. In the second portion of life, man grows older, but he is still able and strong. He needs more than just Divine grace; he needs God's kindness, *chesed*. In the declining years, he is weak, dependent on others, and in desperate need of more than grace and kindness. He now needs *rachamim*, God's mercy.

But there is also a fourth portion of life: life after death. For this man requires more than grace, kindness, and mercy. He needs *rachamim rabbim*, "great mercy"! Thus, in Albo's scheme, resurrection is only a natural, further development of God's providence. In the words of the Amidah in the prayer book: *Mekhalkel chayyim be-chesed, mechayyeh metim be-rachamim rabbim.* "He sustains the living with kindness and revives the dead with great mercy."

God as an Ethical Personality

The concept of life after death also follows from a belief in God as the God of goodness. Rav Kook, the first Ashkenazic Chief Rabbi of Israel, cited the daily Amidah, "You support the falling, and heal the sick, and free those who are bound up, and keep Your faith with those who sleep in the dust." The prayer book lists a series of evils that befall man and asserts that God will save man from them.

Those who "fall" suffer financial failure, a defect in the structure of society. We believe that God who is good will overcome that defect. He will "support the falling." Worse than that is sickness, which is a flaw in the physical nature of man. We believe that God is good and will not tolerate such an evil forever. He will heal the sick. Worse yet is the disease of slavery, the sickness that man wishes on his fellowman. God will overcome this, too, for He not only supports the falling and heals the sick, He is the great emancipator of man. The worst evil of all, however, the meanest scandal, the vilest disgrace to that being created in the image of God is death, the end to all hope and all striving. But we believe in an ethical and good God. As He prevailed over the evils of a lifetime, so will He prevail over the final evil, that of death. Thus, we conclude by asking God who supports, heals, and frees also to keep faith with those who are dead.

THE MEANING OF DEATH

What is death? Is it merely the cessation of the biological function of living? Is it but the tragedy to end all other tragedies? Is it the disappearance of the soul, the end of consciousness, the evaporation of personality, the disintegration of the body into its elemental components? Is it an end beyond which there is only black void? Or, is there a significance, some deep and abiding meaning to death, one that transcends our puny ability to understand?

With all of modern man's sophistication, his brilliant technological achievements, the immense progress of his science, his discovery of new worlds of thought, he has not come one iota closer to grasping the meaning of death than did his ancient ancestors. Philosophers and poets have probed the idea of immortality, but stubbornly death remains, as always, the greatest paradox of life.

In practice, however, we must realize that what death means to the individual depends very much on what life means to him.

If life is a stage, and we the poor players who strut and fret our hour upon the stage and then are heard no more; if life is a tale told by an idiot, full of sound and fury, signifying nothing; if life is an inconsequential drama, a purposeless amusement—then death is only the heavy curtain that falls on the final act. It sounds its hollow thud: *La commedia è finita*, "the comedy is finished," and we are no more. Death has no significance, because life itself has no lasting meaning.

If life is only the arithmetic of coincidence, man a chance composite of molecules, the world a haphazard conglomeration without design or purpose, where everything is temporal and nothing eternal—with values dictated only by consensus—then death is merely the checkmate to an interesting, thoughtful, but useless game of chance. Death has no transcendent significance, since nothing in life has had transcendent significance. If such is the philosophy of life, death is meaningless, and the deceased need merely be disposed of unceremoniously and as efficiently as possible.

If life is only nature mindlessly and compulsively spinning its complicated web, and man only a high-level beast, and the world—in Schopenhauer's phrase—*"eine grosse Schlachtfeld,"* a great battlefield; if values are only those of the jungle, aimed only at the satisfaction of animal appetites, then death is simply a further reduction to the basic elements, progress an adventure into nothingness, and our existence on this earth only a cosmic trap. In this scheme, life is surrounded by parentheses, dropped, or substituted without loss of meaning to nature. Death, in this sense, is the end of a cruel match that pits man against beast and man against man. It is the last slaughter. Furtively, irrevocably, despairingly, man sinks into the soil of a cold and impersonal nature, his life without purpose, his death without significance. His grave need not be marked. As his days were a passing shadow, without substance and shape, so his final repose.

If life is altogether absurd, with man bound and chained by impersonal fate or ironbound circumstances, where he never is able to achieve real freedom and only dread and anguish prevail—then death is the welcome release from the chains of despair. The puppet is returned to the box, the string is severed, the strain is no more.

But if life is the creation of a benevolent God, the infusion of the Divine breath; if man is not only higher than the animals, but also "a little lower than the angels"; if he has a soul, as well as a body; if his relationship is not only the "I-it" of man and nature, but the "I-Thou" of creature with Creator; and if he tempers his passions with the moral commands of an eternal, transcendent God—then death is a return to the Creator at the time of death set by the Creator, and life after death the only way of a just and merciful and ethical God. If life has any significance, if it is not mere happenstance, then man knows that some day his body will be replaced, even as his soul unites with Eternal God.

In immortality, man finds fulfillment of all his dreams. In this religious framework, the Sages equated this world with an anteroom to a great palace, the glorious realm of the future. For a truly religious personality, death has profound meaning, because for him life is a tale told by a saint, not an idiot. It is, indeed, full of sound and fury that sometimes signifies nothing, but often bears eloquent testimony to the Divine power that created and sustained him.

The rabbis say *hai alma ke-bei hilula damya*, this world may be compared to a wedding. At a wedding two souls are united. In that relationship they bear the seed of the future. Ultimately, the partners to the wedding die—but the seed of life grows on and death is conquered: the seed of the future carries the germ of the past. This world is like a wedding.

Death has meaning if life had meaning. If one is not able to live, will he be able to die?

APPENDIX ONE

Prayers, Readings, and Psalms

PSALM 23

Eshet Chayil

"What Is Man?"

El Mal'e Rachamim

PSALM 91

Tzidduk ha-din

Burial Kaddish

Mourner's Kaddish

Rabbis' Kaddish

Yizkor

249

PSALM 23

כג מִזְמוֹר לְדָוִד, יהוה רֹעִי, לֹא
אֶחְסָר. בִּנְאוֹת דֶּשֶׁא יַרְבִּיצֵנִי, עַל
מֵי מְנֻחוֹת יְנַהֲלֵנִי. נַפְשִׁי יְשׁוֹבֵב, יַנְחֵנִי
בְמַעְגְּלֵי צֶדֶק לְמַעַן שְׁמוֹ. גַּם כִּי אֵלֵךְ
בְּגֵיא צַלְמָוֶת, לֹא אִירָא רָע כִּי אַתָּה
עִמָּדִי, שִׁבְטְךָ וּמִשְׁעַנְתֶּךָ הֵמָּה יְנַחֲמֻנִי.
תַּעֲרֹךְ לְפָנַי שֻׁלְחָן נֶגֶד צֹרְרָי, דִּשַּׁנְתָּ
בַשֶּׁמֶן רֹאשִׁי, כּוֹסִי רְוָיָה. אַךְ טוֹב
וָחֶסֶד יִרְדְּפוּנִי כָּל יְמֵי חַיָּי, וְשַׁבְתִּי
בְּבֵית יהוה לְאֹרֶךְ יָמִים.

*Mizmor le-David: Adonai ro'i, lo echsar. Binot deshe
yarbitzeni, al mei menuchot yenahaleni. Nafshi yeshovev,
yancheni ve-maggelei tzeddek le-ma'an shemo. Gam ki-
elech be-gei tzalmavet, lo ira ra ki atah immadi, shivtecha
u-mi-she-antecha hemah yenachamuni. Ta'aroch le-fanai
shulchan neged tzore rai, di-shanta va-shemen roshi kosi
revayah. Ach tov va-chesed yirdefuni kal yimei chayyai,
ve-shaveti be-vet Adonai le-orech yamim.*

The Lord is my Sheperd; I shall not want.
He has me lie down in green pastures,
He leads me beside the still waters.
He revives my soul;
He guides me on paths of righteousness for His glory.
Though I walk through the valley of the shadow of death,
I fear no harm.
For You are with me.
Your rod and Your staff do comfort me.
You set a table in sight of my enemies;
You anoint my head with oil. My cup overflows.
Surely goodness and mercy shall follow me in all the days
    of my life,
And I shall abide in the house of the Lord for ever.

ESHET CHAYIL
(PROVERBS 31 10–31)

אשת חיל (משלי לא:י-לא)

אֵשֶׁת חַיִל* מִי יִמְצָא, וְרָחֹק מִפְּנִינִים מִכְרָהּ.
בָּטַח בָּהּ לֵב בַּעְלָהּ, וְשָׁלָל לֹא יֶחְסָר.
גְּמָלַתְהוּ טוֹב וְלֹא רָע, כֹּל יְמֵי חַיֶּיהָ.
דָּרְשָׁה צֶמֶר וּפִשְׁתִּים, וַתַּעַשׂ בְּחֵפֶץ כַּפֶּיהָ.
הָיְתָה כָּאֳנִיּוֹת סוֹחֵר, מִמֶּרְחָק תָּבִיא לַחְמָהּ.
וַתָּקָם בְּעוֹד לַיְלָה,* וַתִּתֵּן טֶרֶף לְבֵיתָהּ, וְחֹק לְנַעֲרֹתֶיהָ.
זָמְמָה שָׂדֶה וַתִּקָּחֵהוּ, מִפְּרִי כַפֶּיהָ נָטְעָה כָּרֶם.
חָגְרָה בְעוֹז מָתְנֶיהָ, וַתְּאַמֵּץ זְרוֹעֹתֶיהָ.*
טָעֲמָה כִּי טוֹב סַחְרָהּ, לֹא יִכְבֶּה בַלַּיְלָה נֵרָהּ.
יָדֶיהָ שִׁלְּחָה בַכִּישׁוֹר, וְכַפֶּיהָ תָּמְכוּ פָלֶךְ.*
כַּפָּהּ פָּרְשָׂה לֶעָנִי, וְיָדֶיהָ שִׁלְּחָה לָאֶבְיוֹן.*
לֹא תִירָא לְבֵיתָהּ מִשָּׁלֶג, כִּי כָל בֵּיתָהּ לָבֻשׁ שָׁנִים.
מַרְבַדִּים עָשְׂתָה לָּהּ, שֵׁשׁ וְאַרְגָּמָן לְבוּשָׁהּ.
נוֹדָע בַּשְּׁעָרִים בַּעְלָהּ,* בְּשִׁבְתּוֹ עִם זִקְנֵי אָרֶץ.
סָדִין עָשְׂתָה וַתִּמְכֹּר, וַחֲגוֹר נָתְנָה לַכְּנַעֲנִי.
עוֹז וְהָדָר לְבוּשָׁהּ, וַתִּשְׂחַק לְיוֹם אַחֲרוֹן.*
פִּיהָ פָּתְחָה בְחָכְמָה, וְתוֹרַת חֶסֶד עַל לְשׁוֹנָהּ.*
צוֹפִיָּה הֲלִיכוֹת בֵּיתָהּ, וְלֶחֶם עַצְלוּת לֹא תֹאכֵל.
קָמוּ בָנֶיהָ וַיְאַשְּׁרוּהָ,* בַּעְלָהּ וַיְהַלְלָהּ.
רַבּוֹת בָּנוֹת עָשׂוּ חָיִל, וְאַתְּ עָלִית עַל כֻּלָּנָה.
שֶׁקֶר הַחֵן וְהֶבֶל הַיֹּפִי,* אִשָּׁה יִרְאַת יהוה הִיא תִתְהַלָּל.
תְּנוּ לָהּ מִפְּרִי יָדֶיהָ,* וִיהַלְלוּהָ בַשְּׁעָרִים מַעֲשֶׂיהָ.

Eshet Chayil mi yimtzah, ve-rachok mi-peninim mikhrah.
Batach bah lev balah, ve-shalal lo yechsar.
Gemalat'hu tov ve-lo ra, kol yemei chayyehah.
Dareshah tzemer u-pishtim, va-ta'as be-chafetz ka-peyha.
Hayetah ka-aniyyot socher, mi-merchak tavi lachmah.
Va-takam be-od laylah, va-titen teref le-veitah, ve-chok le-na'aroteyha.
Zamemah sadeh va-tikkachehu, mi-peri khappeyha nate'ah karem.
Chagerah be-oz matneyha, va-te'ammetz zero'oteyha.

Ta'amah ki tov sachrah, lo yikhbeh ba-laylah nerah.
Yadeyha shilechah va-kishor, ve-khapeyha tamekhu falech.
Kappah paresah le-ani, ve-yadeyha shillechah la-evyon.
Lo tira le-veitah mi-shaleg, ki khal beitah lavush shanim.
Marvaddim asetah lah, shesh ve-arggaman levushah.
Noda ba-she'arim balah, be-shivto im ziknei aretz.
Sadin asetah va-timkor, va-chagor natenah la-kena'ani.
Oz ve-hadar levushah, va-tischak le-yom acharon.
Piha patechah ve-chakhmah, ve-torat chesed al le-shonah.
Tzofiyyah halikhot beitah, ve-lechem atzlut lo tokhel.
Kamu vaneyha va-ye'asheruha, balah ve-yehalelah.
Rabot banot asu chayil, ve-at alit al kullanah.
*Sheker ha-chen ve-hevel ha-yofi, ishah yirat Adonai hi
   tithallal.*
*Tenu lah mi-peri yadeyha, vi-haleluha va-she'arim
   ma'aseyha.*

An accomplished woman, who can find?—Far beyond pearls is her value.

Her husband's heart relies on her and he shall lack no fortune.

She repays his good, but never his harm, all the days of her life.

She seeks out wool and linen, and her hands work willingly.

She is like a merchant's ships, from afar she brings her sustenance.

She arises while it is yet nighttime, and gives food to her household and a ration to her maidens.

She envisions a field and buys it, from the fruit of her handiwork she plants a vineyard.

With strength she girds her loins, and invigorates her arms.

She discerns that her enterprise is good—so her lamp is not snuffed out by night.

Her hand she stretches out to the distaff, and her palms support the spindle.

She spreads out her palm to the poor, and extends her hands to the destitute.

She fears not snow for her household, for her entire household is clothed in scarlet wool.

Luxurious bedspreads she made herself, linen and purple wool are her clothing.

Distinctive in the councils is her husband, when he sits with the elders of the land.

She makes a cloak to sell, and delivers a belt to the peddler.

Strength and majesty are her raiment, she joyfully awaits the last days.

She opens her mouth with wisdom, and a lesson of kindness is on her tongue.

She anticipates the ways of her household, and partakes not of the bread of laziness.

Her children arise and praise her, her husband, and he lauds her: 'Many daughters have amassed achievements, but you surpassed them all.'

False is grace and vain is beauty, a God-fearing woman— she should be praised.

Give her the fruits of her hand and let her be praised in the gates by her very own deeds.

WHAT IS MAN?

A second selection recited at most funeral services is "What I Man," consisting of verses from various Psalms.

יְהֹוָה, מָה אָדָם וַתֵּדָעֵהוּ, בֶּן אֱנוֹשׁ וַתְּחַשְּׁבֵהוּ.
אָדָם לַהֶבֶל דָּמָה, יָמָיו כְּצֵל עוֹבֵר.
בַּבֹּקֶר יָצִיץ וְחָלָף, לָעֶרֶב יְמוֹלֵל וְיָבֵשׁ.
לִמְנוֹת יָמֵינוּ כֵּן הוֹדַע, וְנָבִא לְבַב חָכְמָה.
שְׁמָר תָּם וּרְאֵה יָשָׁר, כִּי אַחֲרִית לְאִישׁ שָׁלוֹם. |
אַךְ אֱלֹהִים יִפְדֶּה נַפְשִׁי מִיַּד שְׁאוֹל, כִּי יִקָּחֵנִי סֶלָה.
כָּלָה שְׁאֵרִי וּלְבָבִי, צוּר לְבָבִי וְחֶלְקִי אֱלֹהִים לְעוֹלָם.
וְיָשֹׁב הֶעָפָר עַל הָאָרֶץ כְּשֶׁהָיָה, וְהָרוּחַ תָּשׁוּב אֶל הָאֱלֹהִים אֲשֶׁר נְתָנָהּ.

O Lord, what is man that You regard him, or the son of man that You take account of him? Man is like a breath, his days are like a passing shadow. You sweep men away. They are like a dream; like grass which is renewed in the morning. In the morning it flourishes and grows, but in the evening it fades and withers. The years of our life are threescore and ten, or even by reason of special strength fourscore; yet their pride is but toil and trouble. They are soon gone, and we fly away. So teach us to treasure our days so that we may get a wise heart. Observe the good man, and behold the upright, for there is immortality for the man of peace. Surely God will ransom my soul from the grave; He will gladly accept me. The Lord redeems the soul of His servants; none of those who take refuge in Him will be condemned. The dust returns to the earth as it was, but the spirit to God who gave it.

EL MAL'E RACHAMIM

The Memorial Prayer is a beautiful one having been chanted in the same way for many years.

For a Man

אֵל מָלֵא רַחֲמִים, שׁוֹכֵן בַּמְּרוֹמִים, הַמְצֵא מְנוּחָה נְכוֹנָה* עַל כַּנְפֵי הַשְּׁכִינָה,* בְּמַעֲלוֹת קְדוֹשִׁים וּטְהוֹרִים* כְּזֹהַר הָרָקִיעַ מַזְהִירִים,

אֶת נִשְׁמַת (name of the deceased)
שֶׁהָלַךְ לְעוֹלָמוֹ, בַּעֲבוּר שֶׁבְּלִי נֶדֶר
אֶתֵּן צְדָקָה בְּעַד הַזְכָּרַת נִשְׁמָתוֹ,
בְּגַן עֵדֶן תְּהֵא מְנוּחָתוֹ, לָכֵן בְּעַל
הָרַחֲמִים יַסְתִּירֵהוּ בְּסֵתֶר כְּנָפָיו
לְעוֹלָמִים, וְיִצְרוֹר בִּצְרוֹר הַחַיִּים
אֶת נִשְׁמָתוֹ, יהוה הוּא נַחֲלָתוֹ,
וְיָנוּחַ בְּשָׁלוֹם עַל מִשְׁכָּבוֹ. וְנֹאמַר:
אָמֵן.

El mal'e rachamim, shokhen ba-meromim, ha-metze menuchah nekhonah al kanfei ha-Shekhinah, be-ma'alot kedoshim u-tehorim ke-zohar ha-raki'a mazhirim, et nishmat [insert name of deceased] she-halakh le-olamo, ba'avur she-beli neder eten tzedakah be-ad hazkarat nishmato, Be-gan Eden tehe menuchato, lachen Ba'al ha-Rachamim yastirehu be-seter kenafav le-olamim, ve-yitzror be-tzeror ha-chayyim et nishmato, Adonai hu nachalato, ve-yanu'ach be-shalom al mishkavo. Ve-nomar: Amen.

O God, full of compassion, Thou who dwells on high. Grant perfect rest beneath the sheltering wings of Your presence, among the holy and pure who shine as the brightness on the heavens, unto the soul of [insert name of deceased] who has gone to eternity, and in whose memory charity is offered. May his repose be in paradise. May the Lord of Mercy bring him under the cover of His wings forever, and may his soul be bound up in the bond of eternal life. May the Lord be his possession, and may he rest in peace. Amen.

For a Woman

אֵל מָלֵא רַחֲמִים, שׁוֹכֵן בַּמְּרוֹמִים, הַמְצֵא מְנוּחָה נְכוֹנָה־ עַל כַּנְפֵי הַשְּׁכִינָה,־ בְּמַעֲלוֹת קְדוֹשִׁים וּטְהוֹרִים־ כְּזֹהַר הָרָקִיעַ מַזְהִירִים,

אֶת נִשְׁמַת (name of the deceased)
שֶׁהָלְכָה לְעוֹלָמָהּ, בַּעֲבוּר שֶׁבְּלִי
נֶדֶר אֶתֵּן צְדָקָה בְּעַד הַזְכָּרַת
נִשְׁמָתָהּ, בְּגַן עֵדֶן תְּהֵא מְנוּחָתָהּ,
לָכֵן בַּעַל הָרַחֲמִים יַסְתִּירֶהָ בְּסֵתֶר
כְּנָפָיו לְעוֹלָמִים, וְיִצְרוֹר בִּצְרוֹר
הַחַיִּים אֶת נִשְׁמָתָהּ, יהוה הוּא
נַחֲלָתָהּ, וְתָנוּחַ בְּשָׁלוֹם עַל
מִשְׁכָּבָהּ. וְנֹאמַר: אָמֵן.

El Mal'e Rachamim, shokhen ba-meromim, ha-metze menuchah nekhonah al kanfei ha-Shekhinah, be-ma'alot kedoshim u-tehorim ke-zohar ha-raki'a mazhirim, et nishmat [insert name of deceased] she-halakhah le-olamah, ba'avur she-beli neder eten tzedakah be-ad hazkarat nishmatah, Be-gan Eden tehe menuchatah, lachen Ba'al ha-Rachamim yastirehah be-seter kenafav le-olamim, ve-yitzror be-tzeror ha-chayyim et nishmatah, Adonai hu nachalatah, ve-tanu'ach be-shalom al mishkavah. Ve-nomar: Amen.

O God, full of compassion, Thou who dwells on high. Grant perfect rest beneath the sheltering wings of Your presence, among the holy and pure who shine as the brightness on the heavens, unto the soul of [insert name of deceased] who has gone unto eternity, and in whose memory charity is offered. May her respose be in paradise, May the Lord of Mercy bring her under the cover of His wings forever, and may her soul be bound up in the bond of eternal life. May the Lord be her possession, and may she rest in peace. Amen.

PSALM 91

צדוק הדין

הַצּוּר תָּמִים פָּעֳלוֹ, כִּי כָל דְּרָכָיו מִשְׁפָּט, אֵל אֱמוּנָה וְאֵין עָוֶל, צַדִּיק וְיָשָׁר הוּא.[1]

הַצּוּר תָּמִים בְּכָל פְּעַל, מִי יֹאמַר לוֹ מַה תִּפְעָל, הַשַּׁלִּיט בְּמַטָּה וּבְמַעַל, מֵמִית וּמְחַיֶּה,* מוֹרִיד שְׁאוֹל וַיָּעַל.[2]

הַצּוּר תָּמִים בְּכָל מַעֲשֶׂה, מִי יֹאמַר אֵלָיו מַה תַּעֲשֶׂה, הָאוֹמֵר וְעֹשֶׂה, חֶסֶד חִנָּם לָנוּ תַעֲשֶׂה, וּבִזְכוּת הַנֶּעֱקַד כְּשֶׂה, הַקְשִׁיבָה וַעֲשֵׂה.

צַדִּיק בְּכָל דְּרָכָיו הַצּוּר תָּמִים, אֶרֶךְ אַפַּיִם וּמָלֵא רַחֲמִים, חֲמָל נָא וְחוּס נָא עַל אָבוֹת וּבָנִים, כִּי לְךָ אָדוֹן הַסְּלִיחוֹת וְהָרַחֲמִים.

צַדִּיק אַתָּה יהוה לְהָמִית וּלְהַחֲיוֹת, אֲשֶׁר בְּיָדְךָ פִּקְדוֹן כָּל רוּחוֹת, חָלִילָה לְךָ זִכְרוֹנֵנוּ לִמְחוֹת, וְיִהְיוּ נָא עֵינֶיךָ. בְּרַחֲמִים עָלֵינוּ פְּקוּחוֹת, כִּי לְךָ אָדוֹן הָרַחֲמִים וְהַסְּלִיחוֹת.

אָדָם אִם בֶּן שָׁנָה יִהְיֶה, אוֹ אֶלֶף שָׁנִים יִחְיֶה, מַה יִתְרוֹן לוֹ, כְּלֹא הָיָה יִהְיֶה, בָּרוּךְ דַּיַּן הָאֱמֶת, מֵמִית וּמְחַיֶּה.

בָּרוּךְ הוּא, כִּי אֱמֶת דִּינוֹ, וּמְשׁוֹטֵט הַכֹּל בְּעֵינוֹ, וּמְשַׁלֵּם לְאָדָם חֶשְׁבּוֹנוֹ וְדִינוֹ, וְהַכֹּל לִשְׁמוֹ הוֹדָיָה יִתֵּנוּ.

יָדַעְנוּ יהוה כִּי צֶדֶק מִשְׁפָּטֶךָ, תִּצְדַּק בְּדָבְרֶךָ וְתִזְכֶּה בְּשָׁפְטֶךָ, וְאֵין לְהַרְהֵר אַחַר מִדַּת שָׁפְטֶךָ, צַדִּיק אַתָּה יהוה, וְיָשָׁר מִשְׁפָּטֶיךָ.

דַּיַּן אֱמֶת, שׁוֹפֵט צֶדֶק וֶאֱמֶת, בָּרוּךְ דַּיַּן הָאֱמֶת, שֶׁכָּל מִשְׁפָּטָיו צֶדֶק וֶאֱמֶת.

נֶפֶשׁ כָּל חַי בְּיָדֶךָ, צֶדֶק מָלְאָה יְמִינְךָ וְיָדֶךָ, רַחֵם עַל פְּלֵיטַת צֹאן יָדֶךָ, וְתֹאמַר לַמַּלְאָךְ הֶרֶף יָדֶךָ.

גְּדֹל הָעֵצָה וְרַב הָעֲלִילִיָּה, אֲשֶׁר עֵינֶיךָ פְּקֻחוֹת עַל כָּל דַּרְכֵי בְּנֵי אָדָם, לָתֵת לְאִישׁ כִּדְרָכָיו וְכִפְרִי מַעֲלָלָיו.

לְהַגִּיד כִּי יָשָׁר יהוה, צוּרִי וְלֹא עַוְלָתָה בּוֹ.

יהוה נָתַן, וַיהוה לָקָח, יְהִי שֵׁם יהוה מְבֹרָךְ.

וְהוּא רַחוּם, יְכַפֵּר עָוֹן וְלֹא יַשְׁחִית, וְהִרְבָּה לְהָשִׁיב אַפּוֹ, וְלֹא יָעִיר כָּל חֲמָתוֹ.

Whoever sits in the refuge of the Most High, he shall dwell in the shadow of the Almighty. I will say of Hashem, 'He is my refuge and my fortress, my God, I will trust in Him.' That He will deliver you from the ensnaring trap and from devastating pestilence. With His pinion He will cover you, and beneath His wings you will be protected; shield and armor is His truth. You shall not be afraid of the terror of night, nor of the arrow that flies by day; nor the pestilence that walks in gloom, nor the destroyer who lays waste at noon. Let a thousand encamp at your side and a myriad at your right hand, but to you they shall not approach. You will merely peer with your eyes and you will see the retribution of the wicked. Because [you said], 'You, Hashem, are my refuge'; you have made the Most High your dwelling place. No evil will befall you, nor will any plague come near your tent. He will charge His angels for you, to protect you in all your ways. On your palms they will carry you, lest you strike your foot against a stone. Upon the lion and the viper you will tread; you will trample the young lion and the serpent. For he has yearned for Me and I will deliver him; I will elevate him because he knows My Name. He will call upon Me and I will answer him, I am with him in distress, I will release him and I will honor him I will satisfy him with long life and show him My salvation. I will satisfy him with long life and show him My salvation.

TZIDDUK HA-DIN

The Tzidduk ha-Din or Justification of the Divine Decrees, is a magnificent and moving prayer recited immediately before, or immediately after, the body is interred (depending on local Jewish custom), when the reality of the grave confronts the mourners.

צדוק הדין

הַצוּר תָּמִים פָּעֳלוֹ, כִּי כָל דְּרָכָיו מִשְׁפָּט, אֵל אֱמוּנָה וְאֵין עָוֶל, צַדִּיק וְיָשָׁר הוּא.[1]

הַצוּר תָּמִים בְּכָל פֹּעַל, מִי יֹאמַר לוֹ מַה תִּפְעָל, הַשַּׁלִּיט בְּמַטָּה וּבְמַעַל, מֵמִית וּמְחַיֶּה,* מוֹרִיד שְׁאוֹל וַיָּעַל.[2]

הַצוּר תָּמִים בְּכָל מַעֲשֶׂה, מִי יֹאמַר אֵלָיו מַה תַּעֲשֶׂה, הָאוֹמֵר וְעֹשֶׂה, חֶסֶד חִנָּם לָנוּ תַעֲשֶׂה, וּבִזְכוּת הַנֶּעֱקַר כְּשֶׂה, הַקְשִׁיבָה וַעֲשֵׂה.

צַדִּיק בְּכָל דְּרָכָיו הַצוּר תָּמִים, אֶרֶךְ אַפַּיִם וּמָלֵא רַחֲמִים, חֲמָל נָא וְחוּס נָא עַל אָבוֹת וּבָנִים, כִּי לְךָ אָדוֹן הַסְּלִיחוֹת וְהָרַחֲמִים.

צַדִּיק אַתָּה יהוה לְהָמִית וּלְהַחֲיוֹת, אֲשֶׁר בְּיָדְךָ פִּקְדוֹן כָּל רוּחוֹת, חָלִילָה לְּךָ זִכְרוֹנֵנוּ לִמְחוֹת, וְיִהְיוּ נָא עֵינֶיךָ בְּרַחֲמִים עָלֵינוּ פְקוּחוֹת, כִּי לְךָ אָדוֹן הָרַחֲמִים וְהַסְּלִיחוֹת.

אָדָם אִם בֶּן שָׁנָה יִהְיֶה, אוֹ אֶלֶף שָׁנִים יִחְיֶה, מַה יִּתְרוֹן לוֹ, כְּלֹא הָיָה יִהְיֶה, בָּרוּךְ דַּיַּן הָאֱמֶת, מֵמִית וּמְחַיֶּה.

בָּרוּךְ הוּא, כִּי אֱמֶת דִּינוֹ. וּמְשׁוֹטֵט הַכֹּל בְּעֵינוֹ, וּמְשַׁלֵּם* לְאָדָם חֶשְׁבּוֹנוֹ וְדִינוֹ, וְהַכֹּל לִשְׁמוֹ הוֹדָיָה יִתֵּנוּ.

יָדַעְנוּ יהוה כִּי צֶדֶק מִשְׁפָּטֶךָ, תִּצְדַּק בְּדָבְרֶךָ וְתִזְכֶּה בְשָׁפְטֶךָ, וְאֵין לְהַרְהֵר אַחַר מִדַּת שָׁפְטֶךָ, צַדִּיק אַתָּה יהוה, וְיָשָׁר מִשְׁפָּטֶיךָ.

דַּיַּן אֱמֶת, שׁוֹפֵט צֶדֶק וֶאֱמֶת, בָּרוּךְ דַּיַּן הָאֱמֶת, שֶׁכָּל מִשְׁפָּטָיו צֶדֶק וֶאֱמֶת.

נֶפֶשׁ כָּל חַי בְּיָדֶךָ, צֶדֶק מָלְאָה יְמִינְךָ* וְיָדֶךָ, רַחֵם עַל פְּלֵיטַת צֹאן יָדֶךָ, וְתֹאמַר לַמַּלְאָךְ הֶרֶף יָדֶךָ.

גְּדֹל הָעֵצָה וְרַב הָעֲלִילִיָּה, אֲשֶׁר עֵינֶיךָ פְקֻחוֹת עַל כָּל דַּרְכֵי בְּנֵי אָדָם, לָתֵת לְאִישׁ כִּדְרָכָיו וְכִפְרִי מַעֲלָלָיו.

לְהַגִּיד כִּי יָשָׁר יהוה, צוּרִי וְלֹא עַוְלָתָה בּוֹ.

יהוה נָתַן, וַיהוה לָקָח, יְהִי שֵׁם יהוה מְבֹרָךְ.

וְהוּא רַחוּם, יְכַפֵּר עָוֹן וְלֹא יַשְׁחִית, וְהִרְבָּה לְהָשִׁיב אַפּוֹ, וְלֹא יָעִיר כָּל חֲמָתוֹ.

The Rock!—perfect is His work, for all His paths are justice; a God of faith without iniquity, righteous and fair is He.

The Rock!—perfect in every work. Who can say to Him, 'What have You done?' He rules below and above, brings death and resuscitates, brings down to the grave and raises up.

The Rock!—perfect in every deed. Who can say to Him, 'What do You do?' O He Who says and does, do undeserved kindness with us. In the merit of him [Isaac] who was bound like a lamb, hearken and act.

O righteous One in all His ways, O Rock who is perfect—slow to anger and full of mercy—take pity and please spare parents and children, for Yours, O Master, are forgiveness and mercy.

Righteous are You, Hashem, to bring death and to resuscitate, for in Your hand is the safekeeping of all spirits. It would be sacrilegious for You to erase our memory. May Your eyes mercifully take cognizance of us, for Yours, O Master, are mercy and forgiveness.

A man, whether he be a year old, or whether he lives a thousand years, what does it profit him?—As if he has never been shall he be. Blessed is the true Judge, Who brings death and who resuscitates.

Blessed is He, for His judgment is true, He scans everything with His eye, and He recompenses man according to his account and his just sentence. All must give His Name ackowledgment.

We know, Hashem, that Your judgment is righteous, You are righteous when You speak and pure when You judge; and there is no complaining about the attribute of Your judgment. Righteous are You, Hashem, and Your judgments are fair.

O true Judge, Judge of righeousness and truth. Blessed is the true Judge, for all of His judgments are righteous and true.

The soul of all the living is in Your hand, righteousness fills Your right hand and Your power. Have mercy on the remnant of the sheep of Your hand, and say to the Angel [of Death], Hold back your hand!

Great in counsel and abundant in deed, Your eyes are open upon all the ways of the children of man, to give man according to his ways and according to the fruit of his deeds.

To declare that Hashem is just, my Rock, in Whom there is no wrong.

Hashem gave and Hashem took, Blessed be the Name of Hashem.

He, the Merciful One, is forgiving of iniquity and does not destroy, frequently withdrawing His anger, not arousing His entire rage.

BURIAL KADDISH

קדיש אחר הקבורה

יִתְגַּדַל וְיִתְקַדַּשׁ שְׁמֵהּ רַבָּא. (—Cong. אָמֵן.) בְּעָלְמָא דִּי הוּא עָתִיד
לְאִתְחַדָּתָא, וּלְאַחֲיָאָה מֵתַיָּא, וּלְאַסָּקָא יַתְהוֹן לְחַיֵּי עָלְמָא,
וּלְמִבְנֵא קַרְתָּא דִּי יְרוּשְׁלֵם, וּלְשַׁכְלָלָא הֵיכְלֵהּ בְּגַוַּהּ, וּלְמֶעְקַר פֻּלְחָנָא
נֻכְרָאָה מִן אַרְעָא, וְלַאֲתָבָא פֻּלְחָנָא דִּי שְׁמַיָּא לְאַתְרֵהּ, וְיַמְלִיךְ קֻדְשָׁא
בְּרִיךְ הוּא בְּמַלְכוּתֵהּ וִיקָרֵהּ, בְּחַיֵּיכוֹן וּבְיוֹמֵיכוֹן וּבְחַיֵּי דְכָל בֵּית יִשְׂרָאֵל,
בַּעֲגָלָא וּבִזְמַן קָרִיב. וְאִמְרוּ: אָמֵן.

(—Cong. אָמֵן. יְהֵא שְׁמֵהּ רַבָּא מְבָרַךְ לְעָלַם וּלְעָלְמֵי עָלְמַיָּא.)
יְהֵא שְׁמֵהּ רַבָּא מְבָרַךְ לְעָלַם וּלְעָלְמֵי עָלְמַיָּא.

יִתְבָּרַךְ וְיִשְׁתַּבַּח וְיִתְפָּאַר וְיִתְרוֹמַם וְיִתְנַשֵּׂא וְיִתְהַדָּר וְיִתְעַלֶּה
וְיִתְהַלָּל שְׁמֵהּ דְּקֻדְשָׁא בְּרִיךְ הוּא (—Cong. בְּרִיךְ הוּא.) °לְעֵלָּא מִן כָּל
(From Rosh Hashanah to Yom Kippur substitute— °לְעֵלָּא וּלְעֵלָּא מִכָּל) בִּרְכָתָא
וְשִׁירָתָא תֻּשְׁבְּחָתָא וְנֶחֱמָתָא, דַּאֲמִירָן בְּעָלְמָא. וְאִמְרוּ: אָמֵן. (—Cong.
אָמֵן.)

יְהֵא שְׁלָמָא רַבָּא מִן שְׁמַיָּא, וְחַיִּים עָלֵינוּ וְעַל כָּל יִשְׂרָאֵל. וְאִמְרוּ:
אָמֵן. (—Cong. אָמֵן.)

Take three steps back. Bow left and say ... עֹשֶׂה; bow right and say ... הוּא; bow forward and say
וְעַל כָּל ... אָמֵן. Remain standing in place for a few moments, then take three steps forward.

עֹשֶׂה שָׁלוֹם בִּמְרוֹמָיו, הוּא יַעֲשֶׂה שָׁלוֹם עָלֵינוּ, וְעַל כָּל יִשְׂרָאֵל.
וְאִמְרוּ: אָמֵן. (—Cong. אָמֵן.)

Mourner: *Yitgadal ve-yitkadash shemeh rabba.*
Congregation: *Amen*

Mourner: *Be-alema de hu atid le-itchaddata, u-le-achayu'a metayya, u-le-assaku yat'hon le-chayyei alma, u-le-mivne karta di Yerushlem, u-le-shakhlala hekhleh be-gavvah, u-le-mekar pulchana nukhra'ah min ara, u-la-atava pulchanah di shemayya le-atreh— ve-yamlikh kudsha berikh hu be-malkhute vikareh, be-chayyekhon u-ve-yomekhon u-ve-chayye de-khal beit Yisrael ba-agala u-vi-zeman kariv. Ve-imru amen.*

Congregation: *Amen. Yehe shemeh rabba mevarakh le-alam u-le-alemei alemayya.*

Mourner: *Yitbarakh ve-yishtabach, ve-yitpa'ar ve-yitromam ve-yitnase, ve-yithaddar ve-yitaleh ve-yithallal shemeh de-kudesha, berikh hu.*

Congregation: *Berikh hu.*

Mourner: *Le-ella* [between Rosh Hashanah and Yom Kippur add: *u-le-ella*] *min kal*
    Congregation: *Amen.*

Mourner: *Yehe shelama rabba min shemayya, ve-chayyim, aleinu ve-al kal Yisra'el, ve-imru Amen.*
    Congregation: *Amen.*

Mourner: *Oseh shalom bimromav, hu ya'aseh shalom aleinu ve-al kal Yisra'el, ve-imru Amen.*
    Congregation: *Amen. birkhata ve-shirata, tushbechata ve-nechemata da-amiran be-ulema, ve-imru amen.*

May His great name be magnified and sanctified in the world that He will renew, reviving the dead, and raising them to eternal life, rebuilding the city of Jerusalem, and establishing therein His sanctuary, uprooting idol worship from the earth, replacing it with Divine worship—May the Holy One, blessed be He, reign in His majestic glory . . .

APPENDIX ONE

MOURNER'S KADDISH

יִתְגַּדַּל וְיִתְקַדַּשׁ שְׁמֵהּ רַבָּא. (אָמֵן. —Cong.) בְּעָלְמָא דִּי בְרָא
כִרְעוּתֵהּ. וְיַמְלִיךְ מַלְכוּתֵהּ, בְּחַיֵּיכוֹן וּבְיוֹמֵיכוֹן וּבְחַיֵּי
דְכָל בֵּית יִשְׂרָאֵל, בַּעֲגָלָא וּבִזְמַן קָרִיב. וְאִמְרוּ: אָמֵן.
(אָמֵן. יְהֵא שְׁמֵהּ רַבָּא מְבָרַךְ לְעָלַם וּלְעָלְמֵי עָלְמַיָּא. —Cong.)
יְהֵא שְׁמֵהּ רַבָּא מְבָרַךְ לְעָלַם וּלְעָלְמֵי עָלְמַיָּא.
יִתְבָּרַךְ וְיִשְׁתַּבַּח וְיִתְפָּאַר וְיִתְרוֹמַם וְיִתְנַשֵּׂא וְיִתְהַדָּר
וְיִתְעַלֶּה וְיִתְהַלָּל שְׁמֵהּ דְּקֻדְשָׁא בְּרִיךְ הוּא. (בְּרִיךְ הוּא —Cong.)
— °לְעֵלָּא מִן כָּל (From Rosh Hashanah to Yom Kippur substitute— °לְעֵלָּא וּלְעֵלָּא
מִכָּל) בִּרְכָתָא וְשִׁירָתָא תֻּשְׁבְּחָתָא וְנֶחֱמָתָא, דַּאֲמִירָן בְּעָלְמָא.
וְאִמְרוּ: אָמֵן. (אָמֵן. —Cong.)
יְהֵא שְׁלָמָא רַבָּא מִן שְׁמַיָּא, וְחַיִּים עָלֵינוּ וְעַל כָּל יִשְׂרָאֵל.
וְאִמְרוּ: אָמֵן. (אָמֵן. —Cong.)

Take three steps back. Bow left and say ... עֹשֶׂה; bow right and say ... הוּא; bow forward and say
אָמֵן ... וְעַל כָּל. Remain standing in place for a few moments, then take three steps forward.

עֹשֶׂה שָׁלוֹם בִּמְרוֹמָיו, הוּא יַעֲשֶׂה שָׁלוֹם עָלֵינוּ, וְעַל כָּל
יִשְׂרָאֵל. וְאִמְרוּ: אָמֵן. (אָמֵן. —Cong.)

Mourner: *Yitgadal ve-yitkadash shemeh rabba.*
Congregation: *Amen.*

Mourner: *Be-alema di vera khiruteh. Ve-yamlich malkhuteh, be-chayyekhon u-ve-yomeikhon u-ve-chayyei de-khal beit Yisra'el, ba-agala u-vi-zemon kariv. Ve-imru: Amen.*
Congregation: *Amen. Yehe shemeh rabba mevarakh le-alam u-le-alemei alemayya.*

Mourner: *Yitbarakh ve-yishtabach, ve-yitpa'ar ve-yitromam, ve-yitnase ve-yithaddar, ve-yitaleh ve-yithallal shemeh de-kudsha, berikh hu.*
Congregation: *Berikh hu.*

263

Mourner: *Le-ella min kal* [between Rosh Hashana and Yom Kippur substitute *Le-ella u-le-ella mi-kal*] *birkhata ve-shirata, tushbechata ve-nechemata, da-amiran be-alema. Ve-imru: Amen.*
Congregation: *Amen.*

Mourner: *Yehe shelama rabba min shemayya, ve-chayyim aleinu ve-al Kal Yisra'el. Ve-imru: Amen.*
Congregation: *Amen.*

Mourner: *Oseh shalom bimromav, hu ya'aseh shalom aleinu ve-al kal Yisra'el. Ve-imru: Amen.*
Congregation: *Amen.*

May His great name be magnified and sactified. In this world that He has created in accordance with His will, may He establish His kingdom during your lifetime and in your days and during the life of all the House of Israel, speedily, and let us say, Amen. Let His great name be blessed forever and to all eternity. Blessed, praised, glorified and exalted, extolled, honored, magnified and lauded is the name of the Holy One, blessed be He. He is greater than all blessings, hymns, praises, and consolations that can be uttered in this world, and let us say, Amen. May abundant peace descend upon us from heaven and may life be renewed for us and for all Israel, and let us say, Amen. May He who makes peace in the heavans, make peace for us and for all Israel, and let us say Amen.

RABBIS' KADDISH

יִתְגַּדַּל וְיִתְקַדַּשׁ שְׁמֵהּ רַבָּא. (–Cong. אָמֵן.) בְּעָלְמָא דִּי בְרָא
כִרְעוּתֵהּ. וְיַמְלִיךְ מַלְכוּתֵהּ, בְּחַיֵּיכוֹן וּבְיוֹמֵיכוֹן
וּבְחַיֵּי דְכָל בֵּית יִשְׂרָאֵל, בַּעֲגָלָא וּבִזְמַן קָרִיב. וְאִמְרוּ: אָמֵן.

(–Cong. אָמֵן. יְהֵא שְׁמֵהּ רַבָּא מְבָרַךְ לְעָלַם וּלְעָלְמֵי עָלְמַיָּא.)

יְהֵא שְׁמֵהּ רַבָּא מְבָרַךְ לְעָלַם וּלְעָלְמֵי עָלְמַיָּא.

יִתְבָּרַךְ וְיִשְׁתַּבַּח וְיִתְפָּאַר וְיִתְרוֹמַם וְיִתְנַשֵּׂא וְיִתְהַדָּר
וְיִתְעַלֶּה וְיִתְהַלָּל שְׁמֵהּ דְּקֻדְשָׁא בְּרִיךְ הוּא. (–Cong. בְּרִיךְ הוּא)

°לְעֵלָּא °לְעֵלָּא מִן כָּל (From Rosh Hashanah to Yom Kippur substitute—
וּלְעֵלָּא* מִכָּל) בִּרְכָתָא וְשִׁירָתָא תֻּשְׁבְּחָתָא וְנֶחֱמָתָא, דַּאֲמִירָן
בְּעָלְמָא. וְאִמְרוּ: אָמֵן. (–Cong. אָמֵן.)

עַל יִשְׂרָאֵל וְעַל רַבָּנָן, וְעַל תַּלְמִידֵיהוֹן וְעַל כָּל תַּלְמִידֵי
תַלְמִידֵיהוֹן, וְעַל כָּל מָאן דְּעָסְקִין בְּאוֹרַיְתָא, דִּי בְאַתְרָא הָדֵין
וְדִי בְכָל אֲתַר וַאֲתַר. יְהֵא לְהוֹן וּלְכוֹן שְׁלָמָא רַבָּא, חִנָּא
וְחִסְדָּא וְרַחֲמִין, וְחַיִּין אֲרִיכִין, וּמְזוֹנֵי רְוִיחֵי, וּפֻרְקָנָא מִן קֳדָם
אֲבוּהוֹן דִּי בִשְׁמַיָּא (וְאַרְעָא). וְאִמְרוּ: אָמֵן. (–Cong. אָמֵן.)

יְהֵא שְׁלָמָא רַבָּא מִן שְׁמַיָּא, וְחַיִּים (טוֹבִים) עָלֵינוּ וְעַל כָּל
יִשְׂרָאֵל. וְאִמְרוּ: אָמֵן. (–Cong. אָמֵן.)

Take three steps back. Bow left and say ... עֹשֶׂה; bow right and say ... הוּא; bow forward and say
וְעַל כָּל ... אָמֵן. Remain standing in place for a few moments, then take three steps forward.

עֹשֶׂה שָׁלוֹם בִּמְרוֹמָיו, הוּא בְּרַחֲמָיו יַעֲשֶׂה שָׁלוֹם עָלֵינוּ,
וְעַל כָּל יִשְׂרָאֵל. וְאִמְרוּ: אָמֵן. (–Cong. אָמֵן.)

Mourner: *Yitgadal ve-yitkaddash shemeh rabba.*
Congregation: *Amen.*

Mourner: *Be-alema dive-ra khiruteh. Ve-yamlikh malhuteh, be-chayyekhon u-ve-yomeikhon u-ve-chayyei de-khal beit Yisrael, ba-agala u-vi-zeman kariv. Ve-imru: Amen.*
Congregation: *Amen. Yehe shemeh rabba mevarakh le-alam u-le-alemei alemayya.*

Mourner: *Yehe shemeh rabba mevarakh le-alam u-le-alemei alemayya. Yitbarakh ve-yishtabach, ve-yitpa'ar ve-yitromam ve-yitnase, ve-yithaddar ve-yitaleh ve-yithallal shemeh de-kudsha, berikh hu.*
Congregation: *Berikh hu.*

Mourner: *Le-ella min-kal* [between Rosh Hashanah and Yom Kippur substitute: *Le-ella u-le-ella mi-kal*] *birkhata ve-shirata, tushbechata ve-nechemata, da-amiran be-alema. Ve-imru: Amen.*
Congregation: *Amen.*

Mourner: *Al Yisra'el ve-al rabanan, ve-al talmideihon ve-al kal talmidei talmedeihon, ve-al kal man de-asekin be-oraita, di ve-atra ha-dein ve-di vekhal atar ve-atar. Yehe le-hon u-le-khon shelama raba, china ve-chisdda ve-rachamin, ve-chayyin arikhin, u-mezonei revichei, u-purkana min kadam avuhon di ve-shemayya (ve-ara). Ve-imru: Amen.*
Congregation: *Amen.*

Mourner: *Yehe shelama rabba min shemayya, ve-chayyim aleinu ve-al kal Yisra'el. Ve-imru: Amen.*
Congregation: *Amen. Oseh shalom bimromav, hu be-rachamav ya'aseh shalom aleinu ve-al kal Yisra'el. Ve-imru: Amen.*
Congregation: *Amen.*

THE RABBIS' KADDISH

May His great Name grow exalted and sanctified (Cong.—Amen.) in the world that He created as He willed. May He give reign to His kingship in your lifetimes and in your days, and in the lifetimes of the entire Family of Israel, swiftly and soon. Now respond: Amen.

(Cong—Amen. May His great Name be blessed forever and ever.)

May His great Name be blessed forever and ever. Blessed, praised, glorified, exalted, extolled, mighty, upraised, and lauded be the Name of the Holy One, Blessed is He (Cong.—Blessed is He) —(From Rosh Hashanah to Yom Kippur add: exceedingly) beyond any blessing and song, praise and consolation that are uttered in the world. Now respond: Amen. (Cong.—Amen).

Upon Israel, upon the teachers, their disciples and all of their disciples and upon all those who engage in the study of Torah, who are here or anywhere else; may they and you have abundant peace, grace, kindness, and mercy, long life, ample nourishment, and salvation from before their Father Who is in Heaven (and on earth). Now respond: Amen. (Cong.—Amen).

May there be abundant peace from Heaven, and (good) life, upon us and upon Israel. Now respond: Amen. (Cong.—Amen.)

He who makes peace in His heights, may He, in His compassion, make peace upon us, and upon all Israel. Now respond: Amen (Cong.—Amen.)

YIZKOR

For a Man

יִזְכֹּר אֱלֹהִים־ נִשְׁמַת

שֶׁהָלַךְ לְעוֹלָמוֹ, בַּעֲבוּר שֶׁבְּלִי נֶדֶר אֶתֵּן צְדָקָה (name of the deceased)

בַּעֲדוֹ. בִּשְׂכַר זֶה תְּהֵא נַפְשׁוֹ צְרוּרָה בִּצְרוֹר הַחַיִּים־ עִם נִשְׁמוֹת אַבְרָהָם

יִצְחָק וְיַעֲקֹב, שָׂרָה רִבְקָה רָחֵל וְלֵאָה, וְעִם שְׁאָר צַדִּיקִים וְצִדְקָנִיּוֹת שֶׁבְּגַן

עֵדֶן.־ וְנֹאמַר: אָמֵן.

Yizkor Elohim nishmat [insert name of deceased] *she-halakh
le-olamo, ba'avur she-beli neder eten tzedakah ba-ado. Bi-sekhar
zeh, tehe nafsho tzerurah bi-tzeror ha-chayyim im nishmot
Avraham, Yitzchak, ve-Ya'akov, Sarah, Rivkah, Rachel, ve-Le'ah,
ve-im she'ar tzaddikim ve-tzidkaniyyot she-Be-Gan Eden. Ve-
nomar: Amen.*

May God remember the soul of [insert name of deceased]
who has gone on to his world, because, without making a
vow, I shall give to charity on his behalf. As a reward for
this, may his soul be bound in the Bond of Life, together
with the souls of Abraham, Isaac, and Jacob; Sarah,
Rebecca, Rachel, and Leah; and together with the other
righteous men and women in the Garden of Eden. Now let
us respond: Amen.

For a Woman

יִזְכֹּר אֱלֹהִים* נִשְׁמַת

שֶׁהָלְכָה לְעוֹלָמָה, בַּעֲבוּר שֶׁבְּלִי נֶדֶר אֶתֵּן צְדָקָה (name of the deceased)

בַּעֲדָהּ. בִּשְׂכַר זֶה תְּהֵא נַפְשָׁהּ צְרוּרָה בִּצְרוֹר הַחַיִּים* עִם נִשְׁמוֹת אַבְרָהָם

יִצְחָק וְיַעֲקֹב, שָׂרָה רִבְקָה רָחֵל וְלֵאָה, וְעִם שְׁאָר צַדִּיקִים וְצִדְקָנִיּוֹת שֶׁבְּגַן

עֵדֶן.* וְנֹאמַר: אָמֵן.

Yizkor Elohim nishmat [insert name of deceased] she-halekhah
le-olamah, ba'avur she-beli neder eten tzedakah ba-adah. Bi-
sekhar zeh, tehe nafshah tzerurah bi-tzeror ha-chayyim im
nishmot Avraham, Yitzchak, ve-Ya'akov, Sarah, Rivkah, Rachel,
ve-Le'ah, ve im she'ar tzaddikim ve-tzidkaniyyot she-be-Gan
Eden. Ve-nomar: Amen.

May God remember [insert name of deceased] who has gone
on to her world, because, without making a vow, I shall give
to charity on her behalf. As reward for this, may her soul be
bound in the Bond of Life, together with the souls of Abraham,
Isaac, and Jacob; Sarah, Rebecca, Rachel, and Leah; and together with the other righteous men and women in the Garden of Eden. Now let us respond: Amen.

The Ethical Will
of My Grandfather,
Rabbi Yehoshua Baumol, z'l
1880–1948

MY GRANDFATHER, ZEIDE, wrote his last will against the advice of his physicians who thought it too strenuous an effort for him to undertake in his severely frail condition. Under wraps, literally, of a blanket and an oxygen tent, he penned these notes, his last and lasting will, the final paragraphs of an intensely intellectual and singularly creative life.

He penned it on the back of blank checks in his checkbook on the night table. Amazingly, he wrote with a firm hand, never wavering; and there were no erasures, no crossings out, that might have triggered doubt about these fiercely held convictions. The checks contained no dollar amount, but they were intended to have the immortal message on the back endorsed by every generation to follow. The symbol is too compelling for me to avoid interpreting it—he left us a heritage, not an inheritance.

I imagine his scintillating mind aching inside his exhausted frame, his profound need to bequeath to his family these last lines, written in his hospital bed over a period of five days. He survived this first heart attack but succumbed to the second one, and he surrendered his soul to his beloved God on 4 Elul 5708, 8 September 1948.

The striking ideas, written by a deeply orthodox rabbi steeped in Talmud and responsa, are new and refreshing fifty years later. It is that thought which has prompted me to enshrine his ethical will as the climax of my work.

My brother, Dr. Norman Lamm, and Professor Jerome Eckstien, another member of our family, have translated the Hebrew will into English. Both the literate Jewish world and I are profoundly grateful.

FRIDAY

Here I am lying in bed in Beth Israel Hospital [in New York City], and my mind is agitated by the question, "What is life?" Why do we fear death so much? In the final analysis, will we not all die? What good will it do me if I live a few more years? If to acquire more Torah and good deeds, why do I need any more—to obtain a greater portion in Paradise? This is folly. And if to do the will of my Creator, is not my death also His will? What difference does it make if it is this will or that will? If to enjoy this world more, what profit is there in this? Or if to spare family members grief, will they not ultimately grieve when I finally do depart from this world? What is the difference whether now or later?

Truly, I say, when I lay [sick] in my brother's house, a cold sweat covered my face; I feared how the members of my family would react on the day that I closed my eyes. Their screams will reach the very heavens, and some will faint—perhaps all will. But the truth is I never feared death for myself, even for a moment.

I would like to write more, but I am afraid they won't understand me. Saturday night: Come what may, I will write!

SATURDAY NIGHT

Seemingly, I should fear the Day of Judgment because of punishment in the world of souls. But, believe it or not, I do not for a moment fear punishment, because I do not believe in any way that the blessed Lord, the Source of good and mercy, would punish anyone, even an utter sinner. Should you say, "Therefore, you don't believe in reward and punishment," [I say] God forbid! I believe with all my heart and mind in reward and punishment. But listen carefully to a "daydream."

> I died, and an angel brings me for judgment to the Court on High. The Chief Justice opens up my ledger and reads: "Have you done such and such?" and I answer, "True."
>
> "Such and such have you thought?" and I answer, "Yes."
>
> "If so," says the Chief Justice, "I must sentence you severely and prescribe punishment."
>
> "Punishment? God forbid that I should get a punishment!"
>
> "Why?" asked the Judge. "Did you not sin and confess?"
>
> "Yes, Sir," I answer; "but, my dear Sir, if you were I, you would have sinned as I did."
>
> The Judge is outraged: "That is a lie! I would have been strong and not sinned."
>
> "Sir," I respond, "if you would have been strong and not done as I, then you would not have been I but you, and I said that if you were I you would not have overcome [the temptation of sin]. And this is the proof—I, since I am I, was not strong [enough to resist sinning]."
>
> "According to you," says the Judge, "man has no free will, no control over his deeds."
>
> "No, no," I reply. "Man can control his deeds! Proof of this is that innumerable times I was strong enough and chose the good when I could

have chosen to do evil. But on those occasions when I was not strong, it was because the condition and character of my soul at that time were such that I was not able to be strong."

"According to your [thesis], then, you deserve punishment?"

"Yes," I respond, "but besides my true and correct claims, I do not believe, Sir, that you can be cruel enough to punish me. For you are righteous and full of mercy; how, then, can you look on indifferently as I convulse in terrible suffering—and, moreover, say to the angel, 'Hit him unrelentingly!' No, no! In no way can I believe this!"

"According to you, then," says the Judge, "there is no judgment and no punishment at all!"

"No, God forbid that I would say that; I believe in reward and punishment, as do you, and as do all the pure, pious, and righteous. But I think that the reward and punishment are spiritual and natural. That is to say, a man whose character and whose environment strengthened his reason to overcome his animal instincts, 'who walks uprightly and acts justly' [Psalms 15:2], who is 'pleasant to God and pleasant to man' [Midrash Aggadah to "Noah"], and who accumulates mitzvot and good deeds, [such a person's] soul is each day increasingly purified until the last moment, when it returns to its Source and cleaves unimpeded to the Supernal Light of the Ein Sof [the infinite, unfathomable God] and once again becomes a part, as it were, of the essence of the Ein-Sof. Is there a greater reward than this? Is there a greater delight than this?

"But a man whose character or whose environment caused him to lose the power to choose the good, who went off waywardly, [such a one's] soul is filled with dark stains, as thorns and

thistles join and thicken about it, and hence upon
separation from the body it is unable to return
and cleave to the Supernal Light. Is there a punishment greater than this? It is a thousand times
more bitter than death!"

As one vanquished, the Judge arises and
declares, "You are right!"

And I awoke.

SUNDAY

You may ask: What, then, is the purpose of Heaven and Hell,
and why the Day of Judgment? These are difficult questions
that I am powerless to engage in at present and to offer answers; but they are *only* difficult questions, and every difficult
question has an answer—if not immediately, then you will
find it after a while. In general, I am not overawed by any
question in the world, even if it is as great as an oil press and
hard as iron. If I were to become intimidated by difficult questions—Oh! I would already have lost my mind during these
times of [our people's] trouble unprecedented since the world
was created. But fortunately and happily, I am not intimidated by tough and perplexing questions. After all the perplexities, I hear a mighty, strong, and awesome voice in the
depths of my soul: "The Lord is God, He is truth, and His
Torah is truth!" Enough.

And about the perplexities, I say: "Let the Redeemer come
and the perplexities will be settled!"

MONDAY

Still, long life has a benefit—to purify the soul so that it can
return at the last breath to its root and die the "death with a
kiss", and to cleave unimpeded to the light of the Ein-Sof.

However, what are the means for the proper purification?
First of all, serious study of Gemara, Rashi, and Tosafot,

and study of spiritual matters. This is a wonderful purification. And for one incapable of this, his soul may be purified by the performance of mitzvot and good deeds out of full love and desire, not as one who rids his neck of a yoke.

But surpassing them all is one who acquired good traits:

He loves all people, ever judges them leniently, thinking always: "if I were in their place I would possibly have done as they did, and therefore why should I be angry with them?" The main thing is to be good to all and compassionate to all; at the least, to be unable to tolerate their pain and to rejoice in their welfare and tranquility.

To be involved with people and be pleasant to every person, so that they will not feel that you consider yourself better and more exalted than they. If they show you respect, accept and do not decline it, for why should you deny yourself this spiritual pleasure? I find nowhere that respect is counted among the forbidden pleasures! But there is a proviso: should they withhold the respect that you think you deserve, do not become angry; put yourself in their position and mind-set, and you will see that in their opinion you do not deserve more than they are giving you. Perhaps they are wrong, but how can they be blamed if they do not understand it differently, and why should you get angry and soil your soul that yearns for purity?

I do not believe there is any sin in feeling pride in your heart. I admit and confess that I sometimes feel pride in my heart; for example, when I esteem myself above Rabbi . . . , and consider myself more learned than he. What fault is there in this? On the contrary, I thank and praise the blessed Lord that He made me as He willed and graced me with the talent to delve and to discover new insights into His holy Torah. But here, too, there is a proviso: Never should I give [another person] reason to think that I consider myself better and more exalted than he.

I see no decrease of one's worth in enjoying this world, in food and drink and the like, even if they are not intended for the body's health; for though they may not purify the soul, they surely do not soil it.

Prayer with full intent of the heart is a marvelous purification. How may that be attained? By meditating for a while on [the verse] "how great are Your actions and how very deep are Your thoughts," until the heart is filled with love and joy, and tears of gladness fall without any intention to cry.

I know that some members of my family would rather I did not publish this document. They believe my grandfather's last words were too daring, too risky for an uninformed public, too likely to be misconstrued, with the result that his image might be tarnished.

I do not agree. People today may have an unsophisticated understanding of things halakhic, but they have good minds and can handle daring ideas, and they have sufficient respect for such an awesome rabbinic authority that there is little chance of untoward consequences. I hope that I am right, and I pray that my readers will benefit from my grandfather's wisdom, as I have.

My parents, my brother and sisters, and I, have always thrown up our arms when we found ourselves confronted by an insoluble difficulty: "Where is Zeide now?"

At least part of him is here.

APPENDIX THREE

Preparation of the Remains: A Guide for the Chevrah Kaddisha*

This guide is *not* intended for the general reader. The layman may find the details of *taharah* too morbid for casual reading so soon after the death of a relative. It is solely for the use of the prospective member of the *chevrah kaddisha* who is required to study and review the laws of *taharah*.

Man is created in the image of God and thus possesses dignity and value. Because God has created him, he is endowed with sanctity. To destroy man is to commit not only an offense against man, but sacrilege—the desecration of the name of God. An indignity inflicted on man is a profanation of the name of God. The body that housed the soul is sanctified by Judaism. It is a gift of Almighty God, and the sanctity adheres to the body even after the soul has left.

The care and consideration and respect that are bestowed upon the living must be accorded the dead as they are attended, prepared, and escorted to their final abode on earth.

---

*Much of the text of this Appendix is based on the work of Rabbi Solomon Sharfman of Brooklyn, New York.

To assist in the preparation and burial of the dead is one of the greatest mitzvot in our faith.

The association that is organized to perform this service is appropriately named *chevrah kaddisha*, the "holy society." It was one of the first associations to be established in the traditional Jewish community of the past. Membership in the *chevrah kaddisha* has always been accounted a unique privilege. The members must be Sabbath observers, of high moral character, and conversant with the laws and customs that are the responsibility of the office they occupy.

Jewish communities in America developed in haphazard fashion, and few were fortunate to have an active and well-informed *chevrah kaddisha*. Thirty years ago, the terrible abuses that were perpetrated upon the dead were largely a result of a severe lack of dedicated volunteers who were willing to ignore the uncomeliness, bother, and time demands of such work in order to prepare and bury the dead with honor and dignity. Charity became more impersonal, kindness more aseptic, and self-sacrificial communal service as rare as genuine saintliness. As the traditional Jewish communities have become more religiously intensive and more comfortable with practicing the *halakhah* in the American milieu, they have revived this most vital component of Jewish life.

The rules and regulations that govern the activities of the *chevrah kaddisha* are widely scattered in the literature of Jewish law. Customs have been transmitted by word of mouth from generation to generation, and they frequently vary in detail from country to country and community to community. No single outline of procedures can possibly reconcile all the differences, most of which have some valid basis in Jewish law and tradition. The following general outline embraces the procedures that are followed in most Jewish communities. It may serve as a guide for the newly-organized *chevrah kaddisha* that has no traditional custom of its own.

The *chevrah kaddisha* should meet at regular intervals to review the requisite rituals and practices and the problems that are encountered when it officiates. No individual should be permitted to participate without its express consent, lest its discipline be compromised.

MOVING THE DECEASED

1. Before it proceeds, a commitment should be obtained from the deceased's next of kin that there will be no interference with the *chevrah kaddisha* and that family members will conduct themselves in accordance with its rules and regulations. Then, usually at the funeral home, the work of the *chevrah kaddisha* begins.
2. The deceased is disrobed and covered with a sheet. The *chevrah kaddisha*, as a preliminary to its work, speaks directly to the deceased—as though he were living—referring to him by his Hebrew name and that of his father, and asks to be forgiven for any indignity they may unwittingly cause him.
3. Some straw or excelsior is placed on the floor and covered with a sheet, and the body is gently lowered to the sheet, feet toward the door. The windows of the room are opened.
4. The deceased's eyes are closed, the limbs are straightened out, and a handkerchief may be tied about the jaw if it falls. A solid object is placed beneath the head so that it will be slightly elevated. Candles are lit and placed near the head, except on the Sabbath and religious holidays.
5. The body remains covered at all times, and viewing by anyone, except by the *chevrah kaddisha* in the course of its duties, or for the purpose of identification, is not permissible.
6. Men perform the duties for men; women perform similar duties for deceased women. Where no women are available at the moment, men may lower the body, while it is fully clothed, in the same manner as for men.
7. Each member of the *chevrah kaddisha* should come prepared with a copy of the *Ma'avar Yabbok*, a handbook of *halakhot* pertaining to *taharah*, including prayers that are recited during the *taharah*.

GUARDING THE BODY

1. The body must be watched at all times, day and night, including on the Sabbath. The body is *never* left alone. The individual who serves as the watcher, or *shomer*, is exempt from all prayers and other religious duties during that time—he is engaged in the performance of a mitzvah and therefore exempt from performing other mitzvot. Where two people watch over the body, one performs his religious duties in another room, while the other remains with the body. Psalms and prayers for the departed are recited near the body.

2. The *shomer* should remain in the room with the body, if possible. Where it is not possible, such as in a morgue, the *shomer* should be able to see into the room and observe the body.

3. Smoking, eating, and unnecessary conversation are forbidden in the room in which the body lies.

4. Women, like men, may serve as *shomrim* (plural) for any deceased person, man or woman. It is preferable, where possible, that children, grandchildren, or other relatives of the deceased serve as *shomrim*.

PREPARATIONS FOR THE *TAHARAH*

1. The *taharah* should take place as close to the time of the funeral service as possible. Ordinarily, no more than three hours should elapse between the *taharah* and the funeral service.

2. Where this is not possible, as in the case when people will not be available at the proper time to perform the *taharah*, or in the summertime, when putrefaction rapidly may set in, the *taharah* may be performed earlier. In that event, the utmost care must be taken that the body and the *takhrikhim* (shrouds) not become soiled again before the funeral.

3. Before the *taharah*, the casket, the *takhrikhim*, and all the other necessary items must be prepared and ready.

Those who will participate should be assigned their functions in advance. No conversation is permitted except that which is necessary for the washing and cleansing of the deceased.

4. During the washing and the *taharah*, no immediate members of the family are permitted—not even the father-in-law, mother's husband, or brother–in–law of the deceased should be present. At the *taharah* of a woman, the females in similar relation to her also should not be present.
5. It is desirable that five, or at least four, members of the *chevrah kaddisha* participate in the *taharah*.

WASHING

1. The members of the *chevrah kaddisha* must wash their hands in the same manner as the ritual washing each morning: each hand, beginning with the right, is alternately washed three times with a washing cup.
2. The body is placed on its back on the *taharah* board, with the feet toward the door. At no time should it be placed face downward—it is inclined first on one side and then on the other side during the washing.
3. Out of respect for the person and his integrity, care should be exercised to keep the body covered at all times, particularly the private parts, except when they must be exposed in order to be washed.
4. A large container is filled with lukewarm water, into which a smaller vessel is dipped and poured upon the parts of the body to be washed.
5. The order of the washing is as follows: first the entire head, then the neck, the right hand, the right upper half of the body, the right lower half of the body, the right foot, the left hand, the left upper half of the body, the left lower half of the body, and the left foot. The body is then inclined on its left side and the right side of the back is washed in the same order as above. The body is then inclined on its right side and the left side of the back is washed.

6. The fingernails and toenails are cleansed and the hair is combed. Care should be taken that the fingers or other joints of the body do not bend or close. The body is washed completely. Internal cleansing is not customarily performed.

7. The blood that flowed at the time of death may *not* be washed away. When there is other blood on the body that flowed during the deceased's lifetime, from wounds or as a result of an operation, the washing and *taharah* are performed in the usual manner.

8. If the deceased died instantaneously through violence or accident and his body and garments are completely spattered with blood, *no* washing or *taharah* is performed. The body is placed in the casket without the clothes being removed. Only a sheet is wrapped around it, over the clothes. The blood is part of the body and may not be separated from it in death.

9. Where only part of the body was injured and covered with blood, and it is possible to perform a *taharah* on the remainder, rabbinic authority should be consulted.

10. Where blood flows continually after death, the source of the flow is covered and not washed. The clothes that contain the blood that flowed after death are placed in the casket at the feet of the deceased.

TAHARAH

1. After the body has been thoroughly washed and cleansed, the *chevrah kaddisha* members again wash their own hands, as described above. A clean sheet and the *takhrikhim* are made ready.

2. Two or three of the participants raise the body until it stands vertically on the ground. Some straw or wood is placed underneath the deceased's feet.

3. While some members of the *chevrah kaddisha* hold the body up, twenty-four quarts of water (nine *kavin*, according to Hebrew measurement) are poured over the head, so that the water flows down over the entire body.

4. This is the principal *taharah*, and enough members of the *chevrah kaddisha* should participate so that it may be performed properly, with dignity and sensitivity.

5. Where this is not possible, the body is raised upright on several pieces of wood, and the nine *kavin* of water are poured over the entire body.

6. The nine *kavin* of water do not have to be contained in one vessel or poured at one time. The usual procedure is that two members of the *chevrah kaddisha* each take a pail of water containing a minimum of twelve quarts, or three members each take a pail containing a minimum of eight quarts. The water is then poured in a continuous stream over the head and body of the deceased, not simultaneously, but in succession. Before the first vessel is emptied, the second starts, and the pouring of the third begins before the second has been emptied. No more than three vessels may be used, and at no time may the flow cease until the water from all the vessels has been successively poured over the body.

7. While the *taharah* is being performed, the *taharah* board is thoroughly dried by other members of the *chevrah kaddisha*. After the *taharah*, the body is placed on the board and covered with a clean white sheet with which it is completely dried.

8. The white of a raw egg, according to some customs, is mixed with a little wine or vinegar, and the head of the deceased is cleansed with the mixture.

TAKHRIKHIM

1. The *takhrikhim*, shrouds, should be made of white linen, sewn by hand with white linen thread, by pious women of integrity.

2. Where these shrouds are not obtainable or they are too costly, cotton or other inexpensive material may be used. In any event, the *takhrikhim* should not be too costly.

3. They should have no binding, seams, knots, or pock-

ets. In dressing the body, only slipknots are made where the garments are tied around parts of the body.

4. The *takhrikhim* for men consist of the following seven garments:

- *mitznefet* (headdress)
- *mikhnasayim* (trousers)
- *ketonet* (chemise)
- *kitel* (upper garment)
- *avnet* (belt)
- *sovev* (linen sheet)
- *tallit* (prayer shawl)

Women are clothed in the following:

- A cap
- *mikhnasayim*
- *ketonet*
- *kitel*
- *avnet*
- a face cloth, or a *sovev.*

5. The *takhrikhim* must be spotless. If they become soiled, they must be washed before use.
6. The *chevrah kaddisha* should have several sets of *takhrikhim* on hand for emergencies.

Order of Dressing

This is the order of dressing for men; women follow a similar pattern.

1. The *mitznefet* is placed on the head and drawn down to cover the entire head, the neck, and the nape of the neck.
2. The *mikhnasayim* extend from the belly to the ankles. Two participants draw the trousers up to the belly. They are tied at the belly by making three forms that are shaped to resemble the letter *shin* which stands for *Shaddai,* God's name. The trousers are tied around the ankles with a band. No knots are made.

3. The *ketonet* should be large enough to cover the entire body. It has an opening at the top to be slipped over the head, and sleeves for the arms. Two of the participants carefully draw the sleeves over the hands and arms, and slip it over the head and down over the body. At the neck, the bands are knotted with bows and shaped to resemble a *shin*.

4. The *kitel* may be open like a shirt or closed like the *ketonet*. It has sleeves for the arms and is drawn over the body. If there is a *kitel* that the deceased wore during his life, it should be used, but the metal snaps or buttons must be removed. Care should be taken when the *kitel* is put on the body that the sleeves of the *ketonet* not be moved from their position and that they extend to the waist. The *kitel* is tied at the neck in the same manner as the *ketonet*.

5. The *avnet* is wound around the body three times, over the *kitel*. Both ends are knotted at the belly with three bows in the shape of a *shin*.

6. Before placing the body into the casket, some straw, and a handful of earth from the Holy Land, are first put into a linen bag and placed inside the casket. The *sovev* is spread in the casket and the tallit spread over the *sovev*. The tallit should be one that the deceased wore during prayer in his lifetime. If that is not available, another may be used. The *atarah*, collar ornament, of the tallit must be removed.

7. The body is placed in the coffin and the tallit is wrapped around the body. One of the *tzizit* is either torn or tied up and placed in a corner of the tallit. The *sovev* is wrapped first around the head. It is customary to place broken pieces of earthenware, called *sherblach* in Yiddish, in the casket.

8. The casket remains closed, except in those communities where it is customary to briefly open the casket at the cemetery and insert the *sherblach*.

At the end of their holy service, the *chevrah kaddisha* asks forgiveness of the deceased because it may not have performed to perfection, and also because handling a person's body under these circumstances requires exquisite sensitivity and a devotional talent that even the best of us do not always possess.

APPENDIX FOUR

Guidelines for Social Conduct

MOURNERS FOR A PARENT

Religious Celebrations

	Shivah	Sheloshim	Twelve Months
WEDDING			
Ceremony (Singing permitted; no instrumental music.)			
	Do not attend[1]	Differing Customs[2]	Permitted
Meal			
	Do not attend	Do not attend	Do not attend[3]
Rabbi and Cantor			
	May not officiate	May officiate	May officiate
SHEVA BERAKHOT[4]			
Weekday			
	Do not attend	Do not attend	Do not attend
Sabbath			
	Do not attend	Permitted	Permitted

	Shivah	*Sheloshim*	**Twelve Months**
BAR/BAT MITZVAH			
Service			
	Do not attend[5]	Permitted	Permitted
Meal (no Music)			
	Do not attend	Do not attend[6]	Permitted
BRIS			
PARENTS Ceremony			
	Permitted at Synagogue only	Permitted	Permitted
Meal			
	Permitted at home only	Permitted	Permitted
***SANDAK* Ceremony**			
	Permitted at home only[7]	Permitted	Permitted
Meal			
	Do not attend	Permitted	Permitted
MOHEL Ceremony			
	May officiate[8]	May officiate	May officiate
Meal			
	Do not attend	Permitted	Permitted
RELATIVES and FRIENDS:			
Ceremony			
	Do not attend	Permitted	Permitted
Meal			
	Do not attend	Do not attend	Do not attend
***SHALOM ZAKHAR / KIDDUSH* for GIRLS**			
	Do not Attend	Do not attend	Permitted

	Shivah	**Sheloshim**	**Twelve Months**
PIDYON HA-BEN			
PARENTS Ceremony			
	Permitted	Permitted	Permitted
Meal			
	Permitted[9]	Permitted	Permitted
PIDYON HA-BEN (continued)			
KOHEN Ceremony			
	May officiate[10]	May officiate	May officiate
Meal			
	Do not attend	Do not attend	Permitted
RELATIVES and FRIENDS:			
Ceremony			
	Do not attend	Permitted	Permitted
Meal			
	Do not attend	Do not attend	Do not attend
PURIM			
MEGILLAH READING			
	Attend Synagogue	Attend Synagogue	Attend Synagogue
Meal			
	Permitted at home only[11]	Permitted at home only	Permitted at home only
MISHLO'ACH MANOT GIFTS			
	Send, but not receive	Send, but not receive	Send, but not receive
CHANUKAH PARTY			
	Do not attend	Do not attend	Permitted
SABBATH *KIDDUSH*			
	Do not attend	Permitted briefly for greetings on special occasions[12]	Permitted[13]

MOURNERS FOR A PARENT

Social Occasions

Shivah	*Sheloshim*	Twelve Months
BIRTHDAYS, ANNIVERSARIES, HOUSE PARTIES, ETC.		
Do not attend	Do not attend	
CHARITY BANQUETS and GRADUATIONS		
Do not attend	Do not attend	Permitted only for honoree,[14] but without music
INVITING GUESTS TO ONE'S OWN HOME		
Weekdays		
Not permitted	Not permitted	Permitted
On Sabbath		
Not Permitted	Permitted [15]	Permitted
DINING OUT		
Not permitted	Permitted with family only	Permitted but limited to few guests
PLEASURE CRUISES and GROUP TOURS		
Not permitted	Not permitted	Not permitted
FAMILY VACATIONS		
Not permitted	Permitted	Permitted

Shivah	Sheloshim	Twelve Months
RADIO AND TELEVISION		
Only news and educational programs are permitted	News, education, drama, and sports programs are permitted. No music is permitted except as background or commercials.	News, education, drama, and sports programs are permitted. No music is permitted except as background or commercials.
THEATER, MOVIES, and SPORTS		
Not permitted	Avoid public events and organized entertainment[16]	Avoid public events and organized entertainment
LISTENING TO MUSIC		
DANCING and LISTENING TO DANCE MUSIC		
Not permitted	Not permitted	Not permitted
CLASSICAL MUSIC		
Not permitted	Permitted only in private[17]	Permitted only in private
CONCERTS		
Not permitted	Not permitted	Not permitted
CANTORIAL SINGING and CONCERTS		
Singing permitted only at Services	Permitted	Permitted
COMPUTER/ INTERNET		
Permitted[18]	Permitted	Permitted
BUSINESS		
TRAVEL		
Not permitted	Permitted	Permitted
ENTERTAINMENT		
Not permitted	Not permitted[19]	Not permitted[20]

MOURNERS FOR RELATIVES OTHER THAN PARENTS

Religious Celebrations

	Shivah	*Sheloshim*
WEDDING		
Ceremony (Singing permitted; no instrumental music.)		
	Do not attend	Differing customs
Meal		
	Do not attend[21]	Do not attend
SHEVA BERAKHOT[22]		
Weekday		
	Do not attend	Do not attend
Sabbath		
	Do not attend	Permitted
BAR/BAT MITZVAH		
Service		
	Do not attend[23]	Permitted
Meal (no music)		
	Do not attend[24]	Permitted
BRIS		
PARENTS: Ceremony		
	Permitted at Synagogue only	Permitted
Meal		
	Permitted at home only	Permitted
SANDAK: Ceremony		
	Permitted at home only[25]	Permitted
Meal		
	Do not attend	Permitted

		Shivah	Sheloshim
BRIS (continued)			
MOHEL:	Ceremony		
		May officiate[26]	May officiate
	Meal		
		Do not attend	Permitted
RELATIVES and FRIENDS:			
	Ceremony		
		Do not attend	Permitted
	Meal		
		Do not attend	Do not attend
SHALOM ZAKHAR/ KIDDUSH FOR GIRLS			
		Do not attend[27]	Permitted
PIDYON HA-BEN			
PARENTS: Ceremony			
		Permitted	Permitted
	Meal		
		Permitted[28]	Permitted
KOHEN:	Ceremony		
		May officiate[29]	May officiate
	Meal		
		Do not attend	Do not attend
RELATIVES and FRIENDS:			
	Ceremony		
		Do not attend	Permitted
	Meal		
		Do not attend	Do not attend

	Shivah	Sheloshim
PURIM		
MEGILLAH READING		
	Attend synagogue	Attend synagogue
Meal		
	Permitted at home only[30]	Permitted at home only
MISHLO'ACH MANOT — Gifts		
	Send but not receive	Send but not receive
CHANUKAH PARTY		
	Do not attend	Permitted
SABBATH KIDDUSH		
	Do not attend	Permitted briefly for greetings on special occasions [31]

MOURNERS FOR RELATIVES OTHER THAN PARENTS

Social Occasions

	Shivah	Sheloshim
BIRTHDAYS, ANNIVERSARIES, HOUSE PARTIES, ETC.		
	Do not attend	Do not attend
CHARITY BANQUETS and GRADUATIONS		
	Do not attend	Permitted only as honoree, but without music[32]
INVITING GUESTS TO ONE'S OWN HOME		
Weekdays		
	Not permitted	Not permitted
Sabbath		
	Not permitted	Permitted [33]

	Shivah	Sheloshim
DINING OUT		
	Not permitted	Permitted with family only
PLEASURE CRUISES and GROUP TOURS		
	Not permitted	Not permitted
FAMILY VACATIONS		
	Not permitted	Permitted
RADIO and TELEVISION		
	News, education, drama, and sports programs are permitted. No music is permitted except as background or commercials.	News, education, drama, and sports programs are permitted. No music is permitted except as background or commercials.
THEATER, MOVIES and SPORTS		
	Not permitted	Avoid public events and organized entertainment[34]
LISTENING TO MUSIC		
DANCING and LISTENING TO DANCE MUSIC		
	Not permitted	Not permitted
CLASSICAL MUSIC		
	Not permitted	Permitted only in private[35]
CONCERTS		
	Not permitted	Not permitted
CANTORIAL SINGING and CONCERTS		
	Permitted only at Services	Permitted

	Shivah	*Sheloshim*
COMPUTERS/ INTERNET		
	Permitted[36]	Permitted
BUSINESS		
TRAVEL		
	Not permitted	Permitted
ENTERTAINMENT		
	Not permitted	Not permitted[37]

1. A parent in mourning may attend his or her child's wedding ceremony and also the meal, even during *shivah*. The parent may be seated at the head table, but should take each course at a different table with different guests. The parent's absence would represent a significant, irretrievable human loss, which, according to Rabbi Moshe Feinstein, is equivalent to severe financial loss. The parent should leave, however, when the music begins.

2. There was a debate between towering scholars in the seventeenth century, and communities have sided with one or the other regarding attendance at the event. The custom of the local community always holds sway.

3. Rabbis express halakhic leniency by permitting a mourner to attend an event that otherwise would be prohibited, such as attending a wedding, when his absence would sadden the bride or groom. The Sages ruled that the mourner should help cook or serve in another capacity where he is needed. Some authorities hold that the mourner should not eat at the wedding at all; others permit eating, but not while sitting with the other guests. Some rabbis restrict this to relatives only.

4. During *shivah*, parents in mourning may not attend *sheva berakhot* for their children, even on the Sabbath. During *sheloshim*, parents and other close relatives, whose absence would cause the bride or groom sorrow or hurt, may attend *sheva berakhot*. If a mourner would make the tenth man for the minyan at the meal, or if he didn't attend the wedding itself and would provide a "new face" at *sheva berakhot* (as the *halakhah* requires), he is permitted to attend.

5. During *shiva*, relatives and friends should not travel to another community for the Bar Mitzvah service. If the event takes place in one's own synagogue, no person need avoid attending services because of the occasion. Parents may attend their child's Bar/Bat Mitzvah in any synagogue.

6. Parents may attend the meal during *sheloshim* and beyond, but not during *shivah*.

7. If the bris is not held at his home, the *sandak* may attend after the third day of *shivah*.

8. The mohel may perform the ceremony if there is no other mohel available. Some hold that he may perform the bris at any time, no matter who is available.

9. Parents may attend the meal during *shivah* if it takes place in their own home.

10. The *kohen* may officiate *after* the first three days of *shivah*. If there is no other *kohen* available, he may officiate at any time.

11. The mourner may attend a Purim *se'udah* (feast) only in his own home with close family and friends, but he should temper his rejoicing—what should motivate his attendance is principally religious observance. This is true during *shiva, sheloshim,* and the rest of the twelve-month mourning period.

12. If the *kiddush* is for a special occasion, in honor of a Bar Mitzvah, for example, the mourner may drop by, say "*mazal tov,*" and drink a toast *le-chayyim,* but may not tarry there. The mourner may not attend a general, anonymously sponsored *kiddush* event.

13. The mourner may attend, whether a general *kiddush* or one in honor of a special occasion.

14. Rabbi Moshe Feinstein offers a noteworthy observation: being that the twelve-month observances are in honor of one's parent, becoming a community honoree is surely considered honoring one's parent. But the banquet should not be primarily a social occasion, rather a charitable one. Graduations may be attended by mourning parents during the twelve months, but they should remain outside during the playing of music.

15. This is called, *se'udat me'reut,* a social dinner. Some authorities hold that meals should be limited to three or four couples—family and very close friends—who typically are invited to Sabbath meals. However, Noda bi-Yehudah—Rabbi Ezekiel Landau—writes that mourners for relatives other than parents may indeed hold a *se'udat me'reut.*

16. While it is permissible to watch theatrical performances, movies, and sporting events on television, it is not permissible to attend live performances or games. Rabbi Aaron Soloveichik notes that in large theaters or stadiums much of the enjoyment comes from the enthusiasm of the throng.

17. Classical music does not fall into the same category as rhythmic dance music, or ballet and modern dance, which also are not permitted. According to some rabbis, notably Rabbi Joseph B. Soloveichik, listening to classical music is akin to enjoying an art museum which is permitted. Classical music may be listened to in private. Mourners should not attend concerts because public, organized enjoyment is not permitted.

18. Music via the computer or internet is not permitted. Computer games should not be played during *shivah* but are permitted thereafter.

19. Business entertainment is not permitted unless financial loss otherwise would be sustained.

20. See note 19.

21. Parents may attend the ceremony and the meal, even during *shivah*; their absence would be a significant and irretrievable human loss. They may be seated at the head table but should eat different courses at different tables. They should step out when the music begins.

22. See note 4.

23. See note 5.

24. Because Bar and Bat Mitzvahs are celebrated today with more pomp than weddings of fifty years ago, it is not appropriate for mourners to attend the festival meal during the *shivah* period. If the celebration will not be accompanied by music but will feature only singing and Torah discourse, one should check with one's rabbi about the permissibility of attending.

25. They may attend the meal during *shivah* if it takes place in their own home.

26. See note 8.

27. Relatives and friends may attend during *shivah* if their absence would prove hurtful.

28. See note 9.

29. See note 10.

30. The mourner may attend a Purim *se'udah* (feast) only in his own home with close family and friends, but he should temper his rejoicing— what should motivate his attendance is principally religious observance.

31. See note 12.

32. See note 14.

33. See note 15.

34. See note 16.

35. See note 17.

36. See note 18.

37. See note 19.

Bibliography

Following is a partial listing of the sources upon which halakhic decisions appearing in the text have been based. Specific reference is not made in the text proper.

Hebrew Sources

Torat Ha-Adam, Nachmanides
Ma'avar Yabok, Aharon Berachia of Modena
S'dei Chemed, Chayim, Chizkiah Madini
Aruch Ha-Shulchan, Ycchiel Michel Epstein
Emek Halachah, Yehoshua Baumol
Kol Bo Al Avelut, Leopold Greenwald
She'arim Ha-Metzuyanim Be Halachah, Shlomo Braun
Gesher Ha-Chayyim, Y. M. Tukachinsky
Otzar Dinim U-Minhaggim, J. D. Eisenstein
Mishmeret Shalom, Vol. II, Shalom Shachna Tcherniak
Torah Temimah, B. H. Epstein
Sh'vut Yaakov, Yaakov Reischer
Sridei Esh, Yechiel Weinberg
Terumat ha Deshen, Israel ben Petachyah Isserlein

In addition to the Biblical portions cited in the text, the Talmud tractates *Semachot* and *Mo'ed Katan*, Maimonides' *Hilchot Avel* (14 chapters), and Joseph Karo's *Shulchan Arukh, Yoreh De'ha* (chapters 335 through 403) were constantly consulted.

English Sources

The Kadish, David De Sola Pool
The American Way of Death, Jessica Mitford
Death, Grief and Mourning, Geoffrey Gorer
Man's Search for Himself, Rollo May
The American Funeral, Leroy Bowman
The Meaning of Death, Ed. Herman Feifel
The Loved One, Evelyn Waugh
For the Living, Edgar N. Jackson
Once There Was a World, Yaffa Eliach
Peace of Mind, Joshua Loth Leibman
Symptomatology and Management of Acute Grief, Eric Lindemann

In addition, numerous psychological and religious periodicals have been consulted. In many cases direct reference is noted in the text proper.

Glossary

Adar—The twelfth (and last) month of the Hebrew calendar.

Adar Sheni—the thirteenth month, added in leap years immediately following Adar. Literal meaning: Adar the Second.

Alav ha-shalom—"May he rest in peace." A phrase used after mentioning the name of the deceased.

Aleinu—A prayer that concludes all religious services.

Aliyyah, aliyyot (pl.)—A Torah honor that denotes being called to the reading of the Torah.

Amidah—The silent devotion known as the *Shemonah Esreh* which is recited in a standing position. It is of the essence of Jewish prayer, and follows the benediction immediately after the *Shema Yisrael.*

Aninut—The state of mourning between death and interment.

Av—The fifth month of the Hebrew calendar.

Avel—A mourner.

Avelut—The period of mourning.

Bar Mitzvah—A boy at the age of thirteen years and one day, as he becomes obligated to observe all mitzvot (commandments).

Bat Mitzvah—A girl at the age of twelve years and one day, as she becomes obligated to observe all mitzvot (commandments).

Bechi—Bewailing, mournful crying.

Bein ha-shemashot—The brief duration of time between sunset and sundown, between day and night, as it were.

Birkhat Ha-Gomel—The benediction that thanks God for recovery from serious illness or escape from mortal danger.

Bris—The circumcision ceremony at which time the eight-day-old boy enters the Covenant of Abraham.

Chen—Grace, charm.

303

Chevrah Kaddisha—Literally, "Holy Society." The group of people that prepares the body for burial and performs the rite of purification.

Cheshvan—The eighth month of the Hebrew calendar, sometimes referred to a *Mar Cheshvan*.

Chillul ha-Shem—The desecration of the name of God.

Chodesh—Month.

Chol ha-mo'ed—The festive weekdays between the first and last days of Passover and Sukkot.

Dayan Ha-Emet—The blessing which the mourners recite after death. Literal meaning "True Judge."

El Mal'e Rachamim—Literally, "God, Full of Compassion." A memorial prayer, sometimes referred to as the *"Mal'e."*

Elul—The sixth month of the Hebrew calendar.

Erev—The eve of.

Gan Eden—Garden of Eden. Paradise.

Geihinnom—The valley of Hinnom, outside of Jerusalem, the location of pagan altars for child sacrifice. Later it was the place for burning the refuse of the city. It is the Jewish equivalent of hell.

Gemilut chasadim—Acts of kindness.

Haftarah—A passage from the Prophets read after the Sabbath Torah reading.

Halakhah—Literally "the way." The law, which encompasses both the written Torah and the oral tradition.

Hallel—Songs of praise from the Book of Psalms recited on holidays after the Amidah.

Hanukkah—The holiday that celebrates the Maccabean victory over the Syrian Greeks in the second century before the common era. The Festival of Lights. Sometimes spelled *Chanukah.*

Havdalah—Separation. The ceremony that concludes the Sabbath, "separating" it from the weekday that follows.

Hazkarat Neshamot—Memorial prayer for the deceased.

Hesped—Eulogy.

Iyyar—The second month of the Hebrew calendar.

Kabbalat Shabbat—The service welcoming the Sabbath, read on Friday eve, before sunset.

Kaddish—The prayer praising God, recited in a quorum, a special form of which is recited in memory of a deceased parent. It is recited for eleven months or one year from the date of burial.

Kallut rosh—Lightheadedness, frivolity.

Kav, kavin (pl.)—A Hebrew liquid measure, approximately 2.6 quarts. (Nine *kavin* equals twenty-four quarts, as used in the *Taharah* procedure.)

Kavod ha-met—Respect for the deceased.

Kefiyyat ha-mittah—The overturning of the bed. A ritual performed in past times to indicate the despair of mourning.

Keri'ah—The rending of the garment of the mourner after death occurs.

Kiddush ha-Shem—The sanctification of the name of God.

Kippah—A headcovering. Skullcap or *yarmulke*.

Kislev—The ninth month of the Hebrew calendar.

Kohen—A priest in the Jewish religion. A descendent of Aaron who served in the ancient Temple.

Kol Nidrei—The prayer recited at the beginning of the Yom Kippur eve service, asking God for release from the vows made to Him.

Lag ba-Omer—The thirty-third day of the Omer, which extends from the second day of Passover to Shavuot. It celebrates the surcease from the plague that killed Rabbi Akiba's students. A minor festival that releases the Jew from the period of semi-mourning.

Le-chayyim—A toast. Literally "To life."

Levi—In terms of religious status, the Levi is second to the Kohen. He is called to the Torah for the second *aliyyah*.

Ma'ariv—Daily evening prayer service.

Maftir—The last portion of the weekly Sabbath Torah reading. It is the honor accorded one who will recite the *Haftarah* immediately after the Torah scroll is bound.

Mal'e Rachamim—See *El Mal'e Rachamim*.

Matzevah—Monument.

Megillah—A scroll. Although, technically, there are five scrolls, or *Megillot*, only the Book of Esther is known as *Megillah*. It is read on Purim eve and Purim morning.

Met mitzvah—An unburied corpse that does not have a sufficient number of Jews in attendance to perform the burial and the interment.

Midrash—Literally "inquiry" or "investigation." A genre of literature that interprets the Bible, usually homiletically, to extract its full and hidden meanings.

Mikvah—A pool of water designed for the rite of purification, primarily used by women after the monthly completion of the menstrual period.

Minchah—Daily afternoon prayer service, usually recited shortly before *Ma'ariv*.

Mishlo'ach manot—Gifts sent to the poor and to friends on Purim.

Mitzvah, mitzvot (pl.)—Commandment. Sometimes used to connote a good deed.

Mo'ed Katan—The name of a book of the Talmud that records many of the laws of mourning.

Mohel—One who performs a circumcision.

Nechamah—Consolation.

Nisan—The first month of the Hebrew calendar.

Olam ha-ba—The world to come.

Omer—The seven week period that is counted from the second day of Passover to Shavuot.

Onen, onenim (pl.)—A mourner between the time of death and interment.

Passover—The eight-day holiday that celebrates the Exodus from Egypt.

Perozdor—Corridor, vestibule.

Pidyon ha-ben—The redemption of the firstborn son. This ceremony is held on the thirty-first day after birth.

Purim—The festival celebrating the deliverance of the Jews of Persia from Haman's plot to kill them.

Rachamim—Mercy.

Rosh Chodesh—The first day of the Hebrew month, or New Moon. It is celebrated as a minor holiday.

Rosh Hashana—The Jewish New Year. The first of the High Holidays.

Sandak—The one who receives the honor of holding the infant during the ceremony of circumcision.

Sefirah—Literally "counting." The forty-nine days of the Omer, from the second day of Passover to Shavuot, observed as days of semi-mourning.

Shabbat—The seventh day of the week. A day of rest.

Shabbat shalom—Sabbath peace. The customary Sabbath greeting.

Shacharit—Daily morning prayer service.

Shalom—Literally "peace." Hello or goodbye.

Shalom aleikhem—Literally "peace be unto you". Hello. Also the name of a prayer welcoming the Sabbath.

Shalom zakhar—A celebration held on the first Friday eve after the birth of a son.

Shavuot—Pentecost. Celebrated seven weeks after Passover. A major holiday.

Sheloshim—The thirty-day period following interment.

Shema Yisrael—"Hear O Israel." Prayer recited at all services.

Shemini Atzeret—Eighth day of assembly. Celebrated as the last days of the Sukkot holiday.

Sherblach—Pieces of pottery or earthenware.

Sheva berakhot—The seven blessings recited at a wedding and on each night for seven nights following the wedding.

Shevat—The eleventh month of the Hebrew calendar.

Shin—Next-to-the-last letter of the Hebrew alphabet. It is formed of a base with three "fingers" extending from it.

Shiva—The seven-day mourning period that begins immediately after burial. One is said to "sit shivah."

Shofar—The horn blown at Rosh Hashanah services as a rallying call to Jews to repent of their evil deeds.

Shochet—One who slaughters meat for kosher consumption.

Siddur—A prayer book.

Simchah—Joy, celebration.

Simchah shel mitzvah—A religious celebration such as held at a Bar Mitzvah, a bris, a wedding, or upon the conclusion of studying a book of the Talmud, etc.

Simchat Torah—The holiday of the rejoicing of the Torah. It is the second day of Shemini Atzeret, and the last day of the Sukkot festival period.

Sivan—The third month of the Hebrew calendar.

Siyyum massekhet—The celebration held upon the conclusion of study of a book of the Talmud.

Sukkot—Tabernacles. The holiday that celebrates the Jewish wandering in the desert following the Exodus from Egypt.

Tachanun—Prayers of petition, following the Amidah.

Takhrikhim—Shrouds.

Taharah—Purification or cleansing.

Tallit—Prayer shawl.

Talmud—The literature that contains the Mishnah and the *Gemara*, the discussion on the Mishnah. It was compiled and edited by Rav Ashi in the fourth century C.E.

Tammuz—The fourth month of the Hebrew calendar.

Tefillin—Commonly called "phylacteries." They are small black cases that contain passages from the Bible and are affixed, by means of black straps, to the head and arms. These are not amulets, as phylacteries might connote, but rich Jewish symbols. They are worn only during weekday morning services.

Tevet—The tenth month of the Hebrew calendar.

Tishah be-Av—The ninth day of Av, which commemorates the destruction of both ancient Temples. It is observed through fasting and semi-mourning.

Tishrei—The seventh month of the Hebrew calendar.

Torah—The first five books of the Bible or, more commonly and correctly, the whole body of Jewish teaching.

Tzidduk ha-Din—The "Justification of God" prayer recited at the interment or immediately thereafter.

Tzitzit—Fringes on the four corners of the tallit.

Yahrzeit—The memorial anniversary of the date of death.

Yekara de'hayye—"For the good of the living."

Yekara d'schichva—"For the honor of the deceased."

Yizkor—The memorial service recited on Yom Kippur and on the final days of Passover, Shavuot, and Sukkot.

Yom Kippur—The Day of Atonement. The second of the High Holidays.

Index